Something Bad Happened and I Can't Feel God Anymore

Something Bad Happened and I Can't Feel God Anymore

The Resurrection of Women

by Medicine Road

"Medicine" - the white buffalo bull
born to our care in April 2009.

Published by Sacred Way Publishing
803 Hermitage Drive, Suite 201
Florence, AL 35630

ISBN: 978-0-578-10711-0

Cover design by Goode Dethero
Back cover photograph by Goode Dethero
Photo Credit: Barry Norris Studio;
"Medicine Road" Portrait by JD Challenger © 2007.

Printed in the United States of America

Contents

"If the women are healed,
so returns this world to Heaven."

White Earth — Cheyenne Indian
Medicine Woman

Dedication

This book is dedicated to the Creator,
Mary Magdalene of Nazareth,
Pte Ska Win — The White Buffalo Calf Woman —
of the Lakota, Nakota, and Dakota people[1],
and the countless women whose love, faith, and prayers
helped to give me the courage to stand.
And of course, to my husband and my children —
thank you, forever.

My Sister

This book was written in prayer. The subject matter addressed within these pages is not easy to read, nor is it light. Within these pages I deal with things that I believed I had to learn how to live with, as this world does not understand how to help women to heal from them. According to this world, once such things happen to a woman she is changed, forever.

In my life, I coped with things such as incest, molestation, rape, violence, hunger, verbal abuse, drugging, emotional abuse, racial discrimination, and societal judgment by either blaming myself, pretending that they had not happened, or telling myself that they were something other than what they actually were.[2] I did this because I did not believe that I could live in a world where such things existed. I wanted to love, and I wanted to see love all around me. Therefore, my mind did what it was designed by the Creator to do — it helped me to package things up so that I could rise out of bed each morning, put a smile on my face, and function.

However, one day, the tortures became too great for even me to bury. One day, I could not pretend that something was not very, very wrong. On this blessed day, a heart-felt prayer was answered. It was not mine, as I was too ill to pray for help anymore. It was a selfless prayer offered to the Creator by a person who loved me greatly. This prayer changed everything, forever. On that day, Heaven was open to me. The Creator's Angels began to help me to make the journey home, from the depths of darkness into the joy that comes from knowing that you walk aligned with the Creator.

Part of what kept me moving forward in this process was

my love for you. I knew that if I could complete the process that Heaven outlined for me, I could one day take each of the things that I was taught by these compassionate beings and deliver it — with great love — to you. I did not want you to have one more day without being able to feel Heaven's love. I did not want you to have to feel isolated or responsible for things that were not your fault. So, this book is not written like a modern-day self-help book, nor is it filled with stories that simply touch the surface of issues. The wisdom in this book took me many years to learn and many years to compile.

The events I describe in this book are true. I welcome you to take your time to read through them, and I would suggest that you find a quiet place to do so. If I have done what I set out to do, you will be feeling many things as you read through these pages. Please do not be frightened by this. In order for a person to be truly healthy, the body, mind, and soul must be aligned in the truth. I am speaking to each of these parts of you in these pages. This book was written in such a way as to help you to open your heart and your mind to the Creator's love.

It is important for you to know that I am in no way profiting from the writing or publishing of this book. As Heaven taught me, the Creator's love is already here for every single one of His children. So, I cannot charge you for what is already yours. That was the "old way" that so many of our ancestors understood. It is the only way that brings Heaven here to this earth. Selfless love, faith, and prayer — that is the path home to Heaven.

"*Wóphila*" is a wonderful word in the Lakota Indian language. It means, "thank you," as in "thank you for a great blessing given." So, I say *wóphila* to you, my sister!

May the Creator bless you,
Medicine Road

It has been prophesied that it is the women who will carry the water back to the people and teach them, once again, how to drink.

To know you are of the Creator and worthy of your Father in Heaven's love is the water that sustains us.

Many are thirsty, yet the Creator is everywhere waiting to quench our thirst.

The Grandmothers and the Grandfathers are reaching out from Heaven to guide us to the water, which is the love of the Creator.

Thank you, my Grandmothers and Grandfathers, for bringing me the water and teaching me how to drink. The time of drought for the Creator's children has come to an end.[3]

(Translated into the English language, "The Grandmothers," "The Grandfathers," or "The Grandmothers and The Grandfathers" are the terms traditionally used by American Indians to describe what Christianity refers to as "The Holy Spirit." They are the Heavenly Host of God's Angels acting in unison to serve Him.)

Opening Prayer

I am sending a voice,
Great Spirit, my Grandfather,
forgetting nothing you have made,
the stars of the universe
and the grasses of the earth.
You have said to me,
when I was still young and could hope,
that in difficulty I should send
a voice four times,
once for each quarter of the earth,
and you would hear me.
Today I send a voice for the
(women of my) People in despair ...
Hear me, not for myself,
but for (them) my People ...

(Portion of a prayer from
Black Elk of the Lakota Indians)

Acknowledgments

I did not walk this road alone, and I had the help, prayers, and support of many as I worked to compile this book. The artwork displayed on this cover is a photograph of a portrait titled "The Medicine Road," which was painted of me by the artist JD Challenger. The original portrait now hangs in our home. This man helped me, and had a vision of me, at a time when I did not have eyes for myself. The best way for me to say "thank you" to him, would be for me to tell you the story of how this painting came to be, and of how it has helped me.

When I was sick and dying, it was almost impossible for me to fall to sleep. My nervous system was destroyed, and I was too terrified to rest. My husband and I had come to know JD, and we admired the portraits he painted of Native Americans. They were powerful, vibrant, and filled with "what could be again." After I became ill, JD and my husband spoke. JD asked how I was doing. My husband told him that I was working very hard to heal, but that I was still having great difficulty. He mentioned that I stayed awake in the living room staring at the wall most nights (as we did not have television, and it was too difficult for me to focus enough to enjoy reading books.) He also told him that I struggled so much at times, that I had trouble even looking at myself in the mirror.

JD asked my husband if he could paint my portrait. This kind man would later tell me that he knew something was very, very wrong, and something inside of him told him that he could help. He warned me, "I am very behind on my work. So, I may not get to your painting for a while. It could be as long as a year. Also, I have trouble painting women, because no matter what has happened to them in their lives, they have a purity that I have trouble capturing."

In less than two month's time, I received a call from JD telling me that my portrait was finished. He told me that the Ancestors had kept him up most nights painting, and that they had shown him things exactly as they were to be. When my husband and I walked into his studio and I saw this portrait, I burst into tears. For the first time since my attacks, I felt the Holy Spirit (the Grandmothers and the Grandfathers), enter me completely. I was so overwhelmed with hope and love when I saw this portrait, that I believed for a moment that I was worthy. For that moment, my self-judgment was gone, so I could feel Heaven's love completely. I did not "block" the Creator, as I understood, finally, that I was worthy of being connected to Him. JD explained that he had painted the portrait on the largest canvas he had, and suggested that this portrait be hung on the wall that I stared at each night. Since I could not look in the mirror, this was to be my "mirror."

As we were preparing to leave his studio, JD said to me, "Did you see that you have some grey hair in this portrait? Do you see the eyes?" I cried again, for I knew that he had painted me "in the future," healed and without fear. He painted me the way I look when the Holy Spirit enters me. At that moment for sure, I knew that this was only the beginning, and that there was a purpose to my life. So, this is my "thank you" to you JD, for your wonderful vision, for your compassion, and for your heart. Thank you for loving my People, and for painting us as we will be again.

I also would like to thank my good friend, Goode Dethero, for helping me to design the cover of this book, for taking the lovely photograph on the back, and for gifting me with her editing suggestions. I have known Goode for years, and I can tell you that I have always seen her conduct herself with grace and compassion. She understands how to be a true friend, she does not judge others, and she is a joy to be around. Thank you Goode, for being the wonderful woman that you are!

I would also like to thank each of the women who were brave enough to contribute their stories. These stories can be found toward the end of the book, and I would encourage everyone to take the time to read them. You can even START there, if you have the urge to do so. Each of these ladies has walked her own road and has cultivated her own relationship with the Creator/God. These women each have different religious, cultural, ethnic, and economic backgrounds — yet, they have all developed a strong, and very real, connection to the Creator. I am very thankful that Heaven brought each one of these women into our lives, and I am honored that we were given the opportunity to have played a small role in their beautiful journeys.

There were also women who "took action" and helped me so that I could actually get this book written and completed. Ute and Jane, thank you so very much for helping me with my children and with the animals so that I could pack up my drum, computer, and animal skins and head down to the pastures to pray and write. And I thank each of you for your editing suggestions, your willingness to read my very rough drafts, and for "keeping the space clean" so I could hear Heaven and write. Running Water, thank you for your faith and your determination to help. Life can be challenging still, at times, and when I am in the middle of a battle and you walk into the room, it is proof to me of God's great majesty all over again. Thank you for choosing faith and hope when there was no earthly reason for you to do so.

This manuscript was edited by dozens of women. Copies were mailed to women who live in various places across the country. I made many changes to the manuscript based upon their observations and suggestions. Thank you to each of you. I am sorry that I cannot make it a "perfectly smooth" and culturally comfortable read for every person, but please know that I have tried my best. Terminology and concepts are often not universal, but I have followed Heaven's suggestions in hopes of reaching the broadest audience possible. Also, because I came to the world the way I did (my cultural, religious, and ethnic backgrounds), the Creator sent His Messengers to help me in a way that I would understand. Our Creator is that personal.

So, my apologies to you if some of the terminology does not resonate ... know that if you were here, and we were sitting in my tipi, walking amongst our Native American horse herds, or praying near our buffalo herd, I would adjust the language to suit your cultural, religious, or ethnic experiences. Heaven has taught me that I am not here to judge (as only the Creator can judge), but to join with them, deliver a message, and help to answer your prayers. If you find that you are having trouble with some of the terminology or concepts I am using, please flip to the back of the book and read through the stories of the other women who have contributed. I assure you there will be one there that will touch your soul.

And last, but certainly not least, thank you to the thousands of people that we have prayed with over the years. These people live across this country, and throughout this world. Many of these people have helped to gather others, donated their homes, churches, lodges, temples, or facilities so that people in their community could come together safely and be immersed in prayer and love, and offered transportation and support to those in need. Some of these people have faced ridicule from organized religion, family, and "friends," yet they have followed their hearts and held strong to their faith. They have learned that our time in this world is about helping others, and their love for the Creator and for their fellow neighbors is greater than their need for "modern" societal approval or acceptance. As a result of this great self-less love, I have seen countless miracles. Each one causes me to weep with gratitude and joy. So, THANK YOU to each and every one of you. And may you always feel the Creator's love and find His blessings all around you.

Wisdom from Heaven

Daughter: "Mother, what do I tell my sisters who believe that they are broken beyond repair? They are frightened, for they cannot feel God, their children, their mates, or themselves anymore. They have long given up the hope that Heaven hears the prayers in their hearts. What words can I give them that will help restore their faith in themselves and in God?"

White Earth: "The Creator has blessed Us, the Grandmothers and the Grandfathers, with wisdom from Heaven. This fills me with great joy. We have been sent as an answer to prayer. We are here to answer the prayers of The People, and those in Heaven who love them. The Creator has willed that we bring His children understanding — truth from Heaven — that will help to set His daughters, and those who love them, free."

Daughter: "Mother, this world teaches women that if certain things are done to their body, mind, and soul they are unworthy of God's love, and that they are forever changed and cannot be healed. Yet, such things were done to me and Heaven has healed me completely. My prayer is that all of my sisters be given this opportunity. I would ask that they be able to feel God's Grace and see His presence in their lives. I would ask that Heaven heal them so they can understand that they are sacred — a part of Him."

White Earth: "May the Creator's will be done. The following words are an answer to prayer. They are to be shared with all of His daughters and with those who love them. It is time to recover that which was lost; it is time to bring back the Old Medicine."

> *"The Creator gave only you, a woman, the power to bring forth life. Whether you have done so or not does not change the honor and covenant that God gave to you as a woman. In this world it is very difficult to understand that being born a woman is very much proof of God's love. Our capacity as women to feel love for our children (those of our body and those of the world) is very close to that which God feels for us. Our capacity to be a home, both physically and spiritually, for our mates is also proof of such love.*
>
> *God loves everyone so much that He gave them the free will to grow toward Him or away from Him. Unfortunately, many of God's children do not always grow toward Him, and they are frightened by any proof of God's great power and proof of His great love. Women — because they necessarily can hold His life, His love, and, therefore, such power — are often hurt in order to make others feel more power and to deny that of God. Such tragedy is dispensed against women from both men and other women.*
>
> *Only God can judge. Anger takes you further away from God and yourself. Forgiveness from a safe place is that which can bring you back to all that you are. So, We [the Grandmothers and the Grandfathers/ the Holy Spirit] come here to heal your body, your mind, and your soul and to help you learn your true nature and true strength. Fill your hearts with love and hope. Kindness is not the opposite of strength. For when you know your true strength as love, and the love that God feels for you, fear will blow away like the nothing that it is."*

Preface

The Resurrection of a Soul

There was once a little girl named Sweet Flower. She had faith in Creator, and she knew in her heart that Creator loved and believed in her. No amount of cruelty could take this understanding away from her. When those who called themselves her family would do terrible things to her body and mind, Sweet Flower could see that there was a sickness inside of their souls that only Creator could heal. In response, she did what her ancestors knew to do. She would go outside — for her it was a small space between her house and a neighbor's where the soil smelled rich — and she would talk to Creator. She would forgive these people and ask for Him to heal their sickness. She understood that what was done to her by others did not change her in Creator's eyes.

As the years passed, Sweet Flower went out into the world to seek medicine that would mend those she loved who were broken. She met others in the world. These men and women saw her light, and many were frightened by it. Those who were far from Creator were determined to possess it or destroy it. In most cases, Sweet Flower did not even get a chance to say, "No." They tried to take her light away. They tried to take Creator away from her. When these people were finished doing terrible things to her body, mind, and soul, Sweet Flower did what her ancestors knew to do. In response, she would kneel in prayer and ask for Creator to heal the souls of those who had taken from her. She survived such encounters battered and confused. She began to take responsibility for things that were not her fault. She began to believe that she had done something to "deserve" such treatment. She blamed herself. Yet through faith she did not lose the understanding that Creator was there for her.

Years passed, and Creator sent Sweet Flower her husband. She could see this man's soul, and she knew that she was home. The world had been hard on him, too. He told her that through her eyes he saw Creator. In their hearts they wanted to help each other to heal. They would raise children together. One day, some people came. They took Sweet Flower away and did terrible things to her body, mind, and soul. For the first time in her life, Sweet Flower let go of what she knew to be true. The unquestioning faith that she had as a child was gone. She became confused. She believed that what others did to her body and mind changed her virtue in the eyes of Creator. She believed that if others could do whatever they wanted to do to her, then she must have no free will of her own. She believed that she was no longer worthy of Creator's love and that He had left her. She began to be afraid of Creator, and she believed that she no longer had the right to pray to Him for help.

Because of this, she decided that she must no longer be connected to Creator. She was lost to Him. But Creator had sent her a husband whose soul remembered the wisdom of his ancestors. Despite his grief, fear, and confusion, he turned toward Creator instead of pushing Him away. He climbed a mountain held sacred by the ancestors and, in prayer, he offered himself to Creator. He asked for Him to heal the woman he loved. He expected nothing for himself in return, not even her love. Her mind was lost and her body was dying. He offered his own life if Creator would heal her. He offered to undertake any task even if it would bring condemnation or his own death.

Creator answered this great prayer by sending His Angels to minister to Sweet Flower. They came before her bruised and battered body, and explained to her that Creator had spoken and that she was to be completely healed. They told her that her soul would be resurrected and that they would teach her the Old Medicine, sacred things that this world had long since forgotten. But Sweet Flower wanted to know something very important. It was a question that had been in her heart since she was very small. It was one that she had prayed about since those sad, lonely days of her childhood. "But what about the others who are suffering in this world? Will Creator also send His messengers for them? Will Heaven's tears also bathe their broken bodies, minds, and souls and wash them clean? Will He come for them too?"

The Angels taught Sweet Flower that long ago people in many parts of the world once understood and practiced the Old Medicine. It was for all of Creator's children, no matter their religion, the color of their skin, their country of origin, the language they spoke, or what the world had done to them. With this response, Sweet Flower began to believe again. For this was the Creator she knew as a child. This was the loving Father who "had the whole world in His hands." She decided to make a commitment that some who came before her had also chosen to do. She opened her heart once again to Creator, and allowed His Angels to prepare her to return this great medicine to her People, for they were all Creator's children, and He would have their suffering end as He had hers so end.

"A nation is not conquered until the hearts of its women are on the ground."

(Cheyenne Indian Belief)

Introduction

Heart on the Ground

I am Sweet Flower, and the parable outlined above is my story[4]. However, there are elements of this story that countless women across the world have also experienced. They know what it feels like to suffer. They know what it feels like to wonder whether or not their prayers are being heard. They know what it feels like to be confused. They know what it feels like to judge themselves for their perceived failures. They know what it feels like to have their dreams shattered. Sadly, they also know what it feels like to be abused "in the name of love."

Unfortunately, very few women have experienced the same "storybook ending" as described in this parable. For when the world delivers its blows and they are in need of help, there is often nobody beside them who has the faith and selfless love to reach up to Heaven on their behalf. This does not mean that these women are "bad" and that the Creator has forgotten them. It simply means that this world has worked very hard to remove the sacred. The Creator and His[i] unconditional love are no longer a "reality" for most societies, and so we do not turn to Him in times of great need as many of our ancestors once understood to do.

---

[i] Throughout these pages I refer to "the Creator" or "God" as "He." This is not because The Creator is literally "male," but because the Holy Spirit taught me that the relationship that most accurately describes the one that the Creator has with each of us is that of a "loving father." There is no gender, as we understand it, in Heaven.

Throughout the history of mankind's time here on this earth, elders have passed such stories down to younger generations. "Bad things" happened to "good girls" or "good women" and the Creator sends His Grace to heal them. In today's modern world such events are called "miracles." In the past they called them "signs of His great power." These stories were used as examples to teach The People about the power of the Creator, love, and faith. As we have opened our arms to "civilization," we have closed our hearts to the reality and wonder of Heaven. With this shift, such stories and practices have become lost or even shunned.

For tens of thousands of years cultures around the globe have used stories, or parables, to teach and to help people heal. Indeed, Jesus mastered this technique more than 2,000 years ago, and some of His stories have been preserved in the Bible and other Holy texts.[5] My American Indian ancestors preferred the art of storytelling so much that they chose to perfect it rather than to develop written languages.[6] They found that the spoken word gave the person or people at the receiving end of the message the best chance of accurately assessing the intent and character of the messenger, as well as the "truth" of the words spoken.

Thankfully, at a time when I needed it most, the Creator came for me. He sent His Heavenly messengers to teach me that what the world had convinced me to see as "truth" was nothing more than illusion. The truth is that nothing that this world has done to any of us here or that we have done to ourselves — no matter how violent, humiliating, degrading, embarrassing, painful, or frightening — is permanent. The Creator and His Angels are ready and willing to heal you completely. They are simply waiting for you to give them permission to intervene on your behalf, and for you to have the faith and the will to follow the path that will lead you home to Him.

The world in which we live today has worked very hard

to take “the God,” or that which is sacred, out of everything. The Creator is not present in most governments, schools, hospitals, or homes. As a result, most “healing” today does not treat the root of illness. Instead, the person is offered “band-aids” and medication. Such an approach may alleviate a particular symptom or set of symptoms temporarily, however, it does not provide cures for any of the diseases that plague our societies.

Likewise, our experts have no cure for those of us who have suffered severe abuse or those of us who have been forced to witness and/or participate in the horrors of war. We are expected to “learn to live with” the effects of what was done to us by the world and our participation in it, and we feel responsible for the burdens that we carry as a result of these wounds. Yet, such experiences cause injury to the souls of the people involved. I ask you, how can you expect “cures” from illness that is caused by events or circumstances that affect the soul if you remove our Creator from the equation? Is not the soul Heaven’s “area of expertise?”

My American Indian ancestors, as well as the ancestors of many people throughout this world, believed that the state of a person’s body was a reflection of the state of her soul. Therefore, you could not find a cure for what ailed the physical body unless the damage to that person’s soul was addressed. “Medicine people,” or those people who were consulted by the sick when healing was needed, were trained to understand a variety of things.

As it was understood that every disease has its root in an unhealed injury to the soul, understanding the Creator, Heaven, and the spiritual nature of this world was critical. A medicine person also took the time to learn about the medicinal properties of various plants and herbs, and elements of what we classify today as “science,” “psychology,” “biology,” “anthropology,” and “nutrition.” It was understood that in order for true healing to occur one had to help the body, the mind, and the soul.

This perspective is very different than the one shared by modern medicine. In today's world, each of these areas is considered separate from the other. A person can either deal with a disease from a spiritual, physical, or psychological level. In the majority of cases, such an approach is usually minimally effective. Ask any woman who has been raped, tortured, molested, battered, or otherwise severely abused that has managed to overcome her fear of being judged enough to seek professional help. It is likely that the experts she consults will tell her that some of her symptoms can be treated, but that there is no cure for what ails her. Often, she is quoted statistics that support this grim diagnosis. She is told that the idea that there is a complete cure — that she will ever be able to live without panic attacks, severe depression, fear, or rage — is an illusion, at best. She may be told that some of her symptoms can be alleviated with the use of strong medications, which she will need to take for the rest of her life.

I, myself, was one of these women. I survived a great tragedy. Yes, I was still breathing, my heart was beating, and I could speak. However, as a result of what happened to me my body was failing, my mind was lost, and I no longer had faith that the Creator was there for me. I was a mere shell of the person I once was. I could not remember whether or not I had eaten that day, I could not sleep, I was afraid to go out in public, and I hated myself. I did not know how to live, and I no longer believed that I had the ability to be a good person, wife, or mother. As my ancestors would have said, my heart was most certainly "on the ground."

Caring, experienced professionals told me that modern medicine had no cure for me. However, through my trauma, the wisdom of my ancestors called to me ... like a whisper in the wind. At times, I could hear something. "*Our women did not have to live this way*," they said. "*We had medicine for this*," they said. "*Do not forget Us*," they said. Where did these messages come from? Were they more real then the deep depressions that now enveloped me? Were they more real than the bouts of insomnia that kept me up for days at a time? Were they more real than the belief I had that my life was over?

At times I could recall images from my childhood. My grandmother was walking in her sub-tropical garden. It was early in the morning. The sun was rising, and she was singing her prayers in a Mayan dialect I could not understand. She did this quietly, so that only the birds, plants, and the Creator of her childhood would hear. I could remember how real this way of being with the Creator felt. And then the darkness of the present would return and push those images away. I would be filled with terror, once again.

Sometimes, when I was awake late into the night and could not sleep, I could remember the way I prayed to the Creator when I was a young girl. "Please Father, heal these animals," I would plead. The cat with the infected eyes, the dog with a gash in its side, the birds with their broken wings and half crushed bodies. These wounded creatures would allow me to catch them, cradle them, pray with them, and cry for them. Through the trauma, confusion, and self-judgment that was now my life, I could remember these things. When I was small I could not afford the expensive medications or medical procedures that the world said were necessary to heal these creatures. I had "only" prayers, faith, and love. Yet, with these things the Creator answered and healed these suffering animals. These memories swirled within me. More messages came: "*What the world says is impossible is possible with the Creator,*" they said. "*You understood this,*" they said. "*Do not forget this,*" they said.

Yet, my illness was severe. Despite these whisperings from Heaven and memories, I did not believe that the Creator was there for me. I did not have the faith necessary to see the Creator as what He truly is — unconditional love. Because I judged myself, I believed that He also judged me. I did not understand that I was worthy of praying to the Creator for myself anymore. As I internalized these things, my illness worsened. I became filled with rage. I directed this fury toward the people who loved me and tried to help me. Despite this, my husband did not abandon me. He too heard the whisperings of the ancestors, "*The answer is love, and only love*," they said. "*She does not understand,*" they said. "*Forgive her*," they said.

Rather than give up in despair, as I had done, this person who loved me greatly turned toward the Creator. Inside of him swirled the memory of the Creator's great compassion and power. In today's modern world, where God is often something that you read about and only "other people" feel, my husband made a decision that saved my life. He sought out a sacred place, kneeled before the Creator, and made a heart-felt prayer on my behalf. Even though I had let go of the Creator of my childhood — the one who lovingly heard my grandmother's songs and answered my prayers for the animals — the Creator did not let go of me. When I needed him most, He came for me. As a result, my life was changed, forever.

This is a true story about the power of faith, hope, love, and miracles.[7] I would ask that as you read through these pages, you consider opening your heart to the possibility that the Creator also loves you unconditionally and that Heaven is simply waiting for you to grant it permission to intervene on your behalf. No matter what this world has done to you, or what has been done to others through you; the Creator can restore you completely. My story is a living example that the truth will absolutely set a soul free, [8] and that with faith in the Creator, selfless love, and forgiveness, every woman can be healed.[9] Once this is done, you can live as the Creator designed you to be and if you so choose, you can use what you have learned throughout this process to lift others who are suffering.

In 2005, shortly after relocating to a town in New Mexico from California, my family was "hit" by the unimaginable. While eating lunch at a quaint, mountain restaurant, my husband and I met a couple that was eating lunch at the table next to ours. These people claimed to be "spiritual healers" who helped people in need on behalf of a local, religious, indigenous-based non-profit. They told us that this organization was well funded by a wealthy entrepreneur. They handed us glossy brochures and high-quality business cards to prove this.

From that meeting forward, we seemed to "run into them" everywhere. As we were new to town, we were appreciative that they took the time to make recommendations regarding local child-care options, medical care providers, restaurants, reading material, and even fitness centers. Since my husband traveled for business, my young son and I were often left alone in the home. During such times this couple was very attentive to me and to my son. They would invite us over to their home for "play dates" with their own children or to their office, where they claimed to be helping those in need. I had worked with non-profit organizations for years, so the work that they claimed to do "made sense" to me. I decided to trust them.

Within a few short weeks my world began to crumble. To my surprise, my son became violently ill on a regular basis. I noticed that my teeth would often begin chattering and I would shake uncontrollably after eating meals with this couple or having "coffee" — or in my case tea or hot chocolate — with them. I would then often experience gaps in time where I had little or no memory. When I questioned them about this, they used any number of excuses to deflect attention away from themselves. They asked me if I had a history of mental illness in my family, and they told me that I was clearly in need of their "healing services." I was confused and worried, as my son was very sick and local doctors could not understand what was causing him to wake up in the middle of the night vomiting with high fevers.

At the same time, my husband and those who knew me began to notice alarming changes in my mental and physical health. I was rapidly losing weight, suffering from extreme bouts of insomnia, and often had unexplainable bruises and scratches on my back, arms, and thighs. I was paranoid, filled with rage, and felt as though I was losing my mind.

I could not understand what was wrong with me. Flashes of my mother's disturbing mental state came to me and I became frightened. Was I becoming "crazy" like her? I hired a counselor to help. My husband also made me appointments with various medical professionals. By this point, this couple that had originally profiled us to be "easy targets," had time to learn more about us. They had discovered that I had a background in investigative reporting, and that my husband and I had friends in law enforcement and high up in the Federal Government. I now believe that this couple thought I was "onto them" when I began asking questions about our symptoms.

It was later discovered that during this time, this husband and wife "team" was administering drugs to me via my food or drink. Once these chemicals "kicked in" and I was either unconscious or semi-conscious, they would film my body as they and others tortured me sexually and physically. Once it became clear that I was seeking help from medical professionals, their focus shifted toward isolating me further from my husband, family, and friends and destroying my credibility. They began to put more energy into torturing me psychologically. Sadly, as a result of this I even became convinced for a time that my husband was the person responsible for my deterioration. When asked for proof of this, however, I could provide no rational justification, as he was away when the bruises, scratches, and other symptoms appeared. Yet anyone who spent any time with me could see that my terror was very, very real.

I was very frightened. I could not understand what was happening to my body, mind, and soul and I did not know whom to trust anymore. For the first time in my life, I stopped praying. For the first time in my life, I closed the door to the

Creator and His Angels. Because of this, for the first time in my life, I was truly lost. Thankfully, my husband and some friends from a local American Indian tribe did not give up on me. They noticed the alarming changes and symptoms in me and traced them back to my visits with this couple. Such shifts had occurred in the lives of other women in town over the preceding year, and nobody had been able to verify the source. These people loved and prayed for me at a time when I was too afraid to pray for help, myself.[10]

The Holy Spirit has taught me "*no prayer is ever wasted.*" I now know with certainty that God answers every prayer and that He never leaves us. If there was ever a time when I needed God's help, it was now. Not only was my child sick and suffering and my husband beside himself with confusion and grief, my body and soul were dying and my mind was lost. Despite good intentions, no psychological or medical professional could help. They were telling me the truth — modern medicine had no cure for me.

Indeed, despite the sincere efforts of highly intelligent and dedicated professionals, modern medicine currently has no "cure" for those who suffer from severe trauma or those who have experienced drug overdoses. These professionals cannot generate healthy new brain cells, repair a destroyed nervous system, or "cure" panic attacks so strong that they leave you curled into a fetal position, rhythmically rocking back and forth, back and forth, back and forth. They could not take away my shame or self-loathing. Most importantly, modern medicine could not help me to feel God again. It could not "turn back time" for me or for others like me.

Rather than "give up," my husband did what our ancestors used to do in times of great need. These people understood that if you needed a miracle, it was best to go directly to the source. Rather than depending upon this world for answers, he turned to God and to our ancestors in Heaven for help. As our people have done for thousands of years, he climbed a mountain to offer his heart-felt prayers on behalf of another to the Creator.[ii] He chose a mountain that has been considered sacred by American Indians for over a thousand years.[11] Although he did not understand what had happened at this point, he had noticed that my symptoms worsened after I had contact with this self-proclaimed and heavily promoted "spiritual couple." Despite this fact, I was convinced that they were the key to my healing. This is something that they told me over and over, and under the influence of the chemicals in my system and my severe trauma, I believed them. What follows is what my husband and the Holy Spirit have related happened next:

> My husband felt that his life would be over if I died or became further estranged from him through my terrible illness. He got on his knees and asked God to take his anger and to allow him to forgive those who had done something terrible to me. He asked God to forgive him for anything he had done that might have led to this place of grief and illness. He asked God to forgive me for anything I had ever done wrong. He forgave whoever was responsible for this tragedy. My husband felt the anger and pain lift from him completely like a wave. He felt at peace.
>
> Then my husband prayed that God take from him anything that was needed to heal me, even if it meant he were to become sick. He prayed that God give him any task that would result in my being well, even if it meant that he might die. He asked for God to take his life in exchange for mine. He prayed that, even if I were to leave him, he wanted me to be healed and to know

---

[ii] Any man, woman, or child who loves another selflessly and does not have fear can be used as a vessel for the Creator to help another in need. Likewise, the Creator can use certain animals that trust and love a human as vessels for His love.

God's love. He prayed for me, not for himself. As he finished the last prayer, a great light appeared before him radiating energy that pushed him back. Although the brightness of the light hurt his eyes, he could discern the figure of a man inside the light. A man's voice spoke and said, "*God has answered your prayers. Your wife is to be healed and you are to be the vessel for His love. Go to her.*"

At that moment a wave of energy passed from the figure in the light into my husband and knocked him over backwards off of his knees. He lay on the grass stunned and dizzy for a short time. When he sat up, the being of light and the energy surrounding its appearance was gone. He got up, picked up his pack and his prayer stick, and ran down the mountain. By the time he reached his truck and began driving home, he started to become "rational." He started to question his experience. By the time he reached the bottom of the mountain, he had convinced himself he must have become delusional due to the anxiety and altitude. He did not take drugs and had not been drinking, so he discounted that possibility.

Just as my husband came to this conclusion, he felt a wave of energy push him hard on the back of his neck from the back seat. The force was strong enough to throw the top part of his body against the steering wheel and set off the truck horn. My husband swerved and pulled over to the side of the road. His heart was pounding, and tears were streaming down his face. He was crying as a result of the overwhelming feeling he had from the Holy Spirit's presence on the mountain, which was again present in the truck. The same voice that was on the mountain said clearly, "*We are here and your prayers have been answered. Go to her and We will guide you. Listen to Us, and your prayers will be answered. We are here and We are real. We bring the Grace of God for We are His servants, Angels of the Lord."*

Still crying, my husband made his way home. He found me lying on the bed unable to move in any conscious fashion, which had become a "normal" state for me at this point. He placed his hands over me and prayed exactly as the Holy Spirit instructed him to do. He felt a rush of energy pass through him into me, as did I, and for the first time I was lucid and noticeably started to recover.

It is important for you to know that my husband had not been a "perfect" man in his life, just as I had not been a "perfect" woman in my life. We had also experienced our share of challenges within our marriage, as most people do. However, we have learned that a "perfect life" is not required in order to open the door to Heaven for another. What is required is self-less love, faith, and prayer. It only takes a single moment. As my husband has told others, "It is as if you go through life trying to dial the right combination to unlock a safe. You dial and dial. That day on the mountain, I dialed the combination and Heaven could come to help the woman I loved. As a result of this, we all received and continue to receive help. Every day I thank the Creator for answering those prayers."

It was not easy for my husband to turn to the Creator that day. Our situation was dire. According to the world he "had every right" to be filled with fear and anger. The tragedy that affected our family was severe, and my mental and physical health was deteriorating quickly. Yet, rather than embracing revenge, anger, vendetta, or judgment, he chose to "give it to God." As my husband has told me, "I knew that I did not have all the answers. I had gone to medical professionals, federal law enforcement officials, and others. You were furious with me most days. Nobody could bring you back to me or help our son. I remembered the God I knew when I was small. I used to love singing in Latin in the church choir. I loved looking at the stained glass windows. I loved sitting in the woods and meadows. I could feel God there, and I believed that I should turn to Him again," he explained.

My husband's love, faith, and prayers brought Heaven down for me at a time when I did not have the strength to hold onto these things, myself. Once I was well enough to feel myself again, my faith, love for my family, desire to help others, prayers, and will to heal provided the Holy Spirit with the conditions they needed to continue coming. It took me two years to completely heal from my life. Almost as soon as the Holy Spirit began to come to my family in this manner, we began sharing the wisdom we learned from Heaven with others. As Heaven teaches, "*Every gift that God gives to one of His children is to be passed onto others.*"

When my husband and I would pray together and ask for the Creator to use us as His vessels, the messages we received from Heaven were clear and specific. For example, the Holy Spirit would suggest to my husband and me that we find a certain person. At first we were nervous. We were certain that people would think that we were crazy if we knocked on their door and told them that we were "here because an Angel had sent us." However, we had seen the miracles in our own lives and that was enough to propel us forward. Who were we to stand in Heaven's way if others were in need of help and guidance?

Once we had the faith to find and approach the person, Heaven would provide us with instructions as to how to help that person to heal. Based upon these people's prayers and our intent to help them, the Holy Spirit could show us where each person was "stuck" in their healing process and give us the information we needed to help them overcome the obstacle they were facing. While we were in prayer, the Holy Spirit would remove sickness and repair the damage that the obstacle, untruth, or painful experience had caused in that person's body, mind, and soul. I will tell you that the responses we received were always amazing. Heaven knows exactly what is in each of our hearts, and they were sending us to those people who were in need of the Creator's healing Grace. Not one person that we have been sent to has ever closed the door on us. After all, it is his or her prayers that brought us there in the first place.

The miracles, or "evidence of Creator's power," we witnessed during this time were astounding. Cancerous tumors "disappeared" or were significantly reduced in size, people with mental illnesses were "cured," all traces of venereal diseases vanished, and the "infertile" became pregnant. Even those Heaven sent us to who were on the verge of passing from flesh told us that they "felt Heaven," "saw the Angels," "spoke with Jesus," or "felt God" when we prayed with them. They thanked us and often said that they were no longer "afraid to go home to Heaven" if it was their time to do so. All of this occurred without us administering medication or chemicals of any kind, and without either of us physically touching the person that we were sent by Heaven to help.

After about six months of this, the number of people that called us for help or brought their loved ones to us increased dramatically. The word had spread. At this point we prayed very hard for guidance from Heaven. As there were only 24-hours in a given day and our bodies had limited energy, what would Heaven have us do? Clearly each of the people who called us or came to our doorstep was in need. The Holy Spirit answered by suggesting that we create a safe place for people to come together and pray as a group. The Holy Spirit explained that with the prayers, faith, and selfless love that were generated in this room, the Creator could heal the bodies, minds, and souls of those in the room and others around the world who were suffering. They informed us that, "*The Creator would send His children*" as He had already been doing, so there was no need for us to advertise. They instructed us as to the conditions the Holy Spirit needed to work and told us that if we kept these conditions, Heaven would always come.

The Conditions:

1. *We must understand that only the Creator heals, and that the work we are doing is sacred. It is important that we are very clear with ourselves and with others that Creator is the "source";*
2. *We are not to ask for or accept anything for ourselves. This includes receiving no monetary compensation, gifts, "donations," or reimbursements and we cannot be seeking fame or power. We must do this work selflessly;*
3. *All people are children of the Creator and, therefore, all are welcome. There can be no discrimination or judgment, as there is no discrimination in Heaven and there is no judgment in love;*
4. *We must have faith that the Creator is here for us and for each of His children.*

At a time when modern medicine deemed my recovery "impossible" and labeled me a "victim," Heaven graced me with the honor of being able to serve as a vessel to help the Creator to heal others. Helping others in this manner gave me the will to continue with my own personal healing. For the first time in my life, I began to see and understand that I was absolutely not alone in what I had suffered in my life. Women of every age, racial, economic, cultural, and religious group were being "hit" by scenarios and events specifically designed to destroy their souls.

Due to the shame involved in surviving such ordeals, society's judgment, and the fact that we have culturally attempted to remove the Creator from the healing process for the sake of "progress," we have, indeed, reached a place where we have accepted a lie. The truth is that there is a healing process that was created by God, and with it every one of His children can be completely restored. The sorrow and suffering can be replaced with the joy that comes from knowing that you are His child and that you are loved unconditionally. You are already "enough."

Although the process of looking at my life, feeling what was done to me, and forgiving the people who had hurt me and those I loved was very difficult, Heaven explained to me that the wisdom I gained from Heaven throughout this process was mine to share with the rest of the Creator's children, if I chose to do so. This gave me the strength I needed to continue. I had a promise from the Holy Spirit that everything that I had the faith and will to overcome could be shared with others who have been tricked into believing that they are broken beyond repair. Becoming a pure vessel for my Father in Heaven, protecting my family, and loving those who were in need of help became the focus of my prayers. As I applied each teaching to my life and underwent each spiritual "surgery," my wounds healed and I began my return to becoming all that I am.

What does it mean to be "healed" and what does it feel like to live as a woman who is completely healed? When I say that I am "completely healed," it means that the following is true:

A Woman Healed:

1. *I understand that the Creator loves me unconditionally, which means that nothing I could do or others could do to me will cause His love for me to change;*
2. *I understand that the Creator did not do the "bad things" to me that happened in my life;*
3. *I understand what was done to me in my life and why;*

4. *I have forgiven those who have hurt me and my loved ones;*
5. *I have forgiven myself for anything that I have done that was far from Creator;*
6. *I have corrected any behavior that I had that was not close to Creator;*
7. *I understand that I am a pure vessel for the Creator so long as I continue to meet the conditions handed down to me by the Holy Spirit.*

The Creator and the Holy Spirit removed from my body and soul everything that this world did to me to convince me that I was not sacred. As for my mind, my trauma has been processed and the many incidents that were once too horrible for me to face, are now stored as memories that I can use to help others. My determination to be a home for my husband and children, and my intent to bring the "Old Medicine" back to my People gave me the will I needed to reject the things I was taught that are far from Creator so that I could apply Heaven's teachings to my life. Today, I strive to walk the path of the Creator each day, and I am blessed to be able to bring His love and Grace to others.

I am free! Shame, guilt, fear, and anger have been replaced with understanding, compassion, peace, and joy. I can feel my husband and my children, and I am not afraid to love them with everything that I am. I can feel the Creator's love and Grace in my life, as well as the presence of my ancestors in Heaven. While the world tried to convince me that I did not have a place, the Holy Spirit taught me that we all have a very special place with the Creator. It is ours always and forever. Nothing that others do to you or trick you into believing about yourself can change this. The wisdom that I have gained from this process — the Old Medicine — is laid out in these pages. Heaven is "home" for every soul, and every man, woman, and child is sacred, period. This is as Creator made it, and no trick, torture, trauma, sexual violation, law, or cultural practice can change this truth.

When I finally understood my life, I discovered that the Creator had been with me every step of the way. Whereas I had once believed that He had abandoned me or that I had disappointed Him and was being punished as a result, I now understand that the Creator gives every soul the gift of free will. Each of us is free to live our lives in a way that will bring us closer to the Creator or take us farther away from Him.

It is those souls who use their free will to make choices that are far from Creator who make life difficult for others, not Creator. If we hold onto Him, our recovery from such difficulties is inevitable and it will be complete. This healing process helps us to grow closer to the Creator. Every day we have in this world is a gift, for it is an opportunity to help others who are lost. In walking the path of Heaven we, ourselves, grow closer to Him as our love, understanding, compassion, and ability to forgive increases. This is the consequence of loving others unconditionally, however, not the purpose.

Many centuries ago my maternal grandfather's people, known to the world today as the Cheyenne Indians, traded an agricultural lifestyle for a nomadic existence. The answer to their prayers had shown them that their life along the Missouri River, with its stationary homes and an abundance of material possessions, was not helping them to serve the Creator as completely as possible. One by one, families left their material possessions behind, put their faith in Heaven, and ventured forth to the Great Plains region of what is now the United States of America.

There are a number of Angels that the Creator allowed to minister to me during my time of recovery. One of these is a soul known here on this earth as "Black Kettle." Black Kettle was a chief of the Cheyenne people in the 1800s. He is often referred to today as a "peace chief" due to his unwavering commitment to follow the path of God. It is this Angel who the Creator sent to teach me about many of my people's traditions.[12] According to Black Kettle, the Cheyenne people gave up what was of this world centuries ago because God answered their prayers by sending them a great vision from Heaven.

"*Our people did not move from houses to open land for no reason. We had a great vision from Creator that this is how we should live. We made sure that we could carry everything that we believed had value. We did not have many material possessions because it was not desirable to do so. If a man had too many material possessions, he was considered to be someone who was not close to Creator,*" said Black Kettle, explaining the societal belief that if a person had "too much" materially then that person was not doing enough to share his or her blessings with those in need.

I marveled at the amount of faith it must have taken for grandparents, mothers, and fathers to gather their loved ones and leave their possessions, homes, and the river — a reliable source of food and clean drinking water — to follow the guidance provided them by Heaven.

In our home we have a serigraph entitled *Festival of Lights* by the artist John August Swanson. In shades of green, blue, and gold it depicts thousands — perhaps hundreds of thousands — of people coming together from different directions to pray. It is nighttime in the scene and these people, each of whom holds a single, lit candle, cover the rolling hills and valleys. The stars of Heaven shine brightly above them. The light produced by these Heavenly bodies combined with the light from the individual candles on earth illuminate the landscape. As Black Kettle sat with me, he studied this piece for a few moments before continuing with his teaching.

"*Part of our 'religion' was to cover the world as best as we could. The more places we could help make sacred through prayer, the better. We made contact with as many tribes as possible because we believed that Creator wanted us to spread the sacred nature of the world. The world says if you have a lot of 'things' you are a good and strong man. We rejected this because we found the truth. Heaven and earth are made one through prayer, faith, and the selfless love of others. We are all His children,*" said Black Kettle. He lifted his hand and gestured toward the serigraph. His kind eyes scanned the thousands of souls on earth that were depicted, joined together with Heaven in prayer. "*That is the truth.*"

Think of your prayers as telephone calls to the Creator. When you pray, your prayers connect this world to Heaven. Your Father in Heaven always answers your calls, even if you cannot easily hear or understand His answer. In July 2009 God answered a great prayer that I had by providing my family with the opportunity to climb Bear Butte, a mountain in present-day South Dakota that has been considered a sacred place by my ancestors for thousands of years. Black Kettle and his people made pilgrimages to this bear-shaped piece of Mother Earth regularly. I wanted to honor my ancestors by praying for all of the Creator's children on the very mountain that my people traditionally climbed to offer their prayers for their families and the world.

It was a hot summer day. The wind blew gently around me as I changed into my white buckskin medicine dress and put on my beaded armbands. I traded my hiking boots for moccasins and placed my medicine bag around my neck. My husband and children followed behind me as we made the climb. Colorful prayer flags and prayer ties hugged tightly to tree branches and trunks along the trail. Each flag and tie was representative of a heart-felt prayer made to the Creator on behalf of another. The Grandmothers and the Grandfathers had taught me, "*You bring with you up the mountain that which you wish to leave for Creator.*" With each step, a prayer for those who are lost, as I was once lost, and a "thank you" for all of His blessings.

Once at the top, I unpacked my buffalo skin bag and spread my bearskin across the rocky floor.[13] Looking below we could see the world — Creator's world — in all of its glory. My husband and I looked around us as our youngest child teetered back and forth excitedly, a stone in either hand, and our son crouched behind a large boulder in hopes of catching a grass-hopper. Our teenage daughter stared off into the distance, deep in prayer. Indeed, this was Heaven. A prayer for my family, a prayer that all of God's children be given the opportunity to heal, and a prayer that His will be done in this world as it is in Heaven. A prayer that He would provide everything that we would need to help Heaven in its quest to bring His love and wisdom to His children around the world. "*You have brought with you what you wish to give to Creator. Leave it here. You will find His answers all around you once you descend*," said the Holy Spirit.

In many American Indian traditions, one of the most important ceremonies and/or rights of passage is translated into English as "crying for a vision." During this time, a person prepares himself or herself to have an experience with the Grandmothers and the Grandfathers in Heaven. They perform certain prayers, ask for Creator to purify them spiritually so that they can hear His Holy Messengers, and they often go a period of time without food or drink. Most importantly, they bring with them a heart that is open to Creator. "*A person is 'crying for a vision' when they pray with all sincerity that God provide them with guidance from Heaven on how they may fulfill His will here on Earth*," explained the Holy Spirit.

Centuries ago the Cheyenne people and other tribes were given wisdom from Heaven. They responded to this by changing their lifestyle so that they were living according to God's laws, and they taught this way to others. More than two thousand years ago Jesus and his closest followers were given wisdom from Heaven, and their response was the same. Heaven has told me that women of every cultural and religious background around the world are 'crying for a vision.' The eyes and the hearts of the thousands of women that Heaven has brought before us tell me that this is truth.

My sisters, I believe that if you understood what "mountain to climb," you would climb it. And if you understood that Creator always hears your prayers and answers them, you would have faith in Him and in yourself, once again. If you can find the faith and will necessary to go through the process outlined in these pages, at the end of the process you will also understand the truth. This process is "your mountain" and the wisdom outlined in these pages is the "Old Medicine" — a gift to you and those who love you from the Creator and His Messengers. It is the answer to your prayers, as it was the answer to mine.

The truth is that you are a warrior for the Creator. Your Father in Heaven did not abandon you. He did not allow terrible things to be done to you because He was displeased with you or because you were not "worthy" of His love and protection. He did not send you here as a woman to punish you. You are not a slave. You are not "less" because people have taken from you or you were compelled to act in ways that are far from God. You are precious to God, and He would have you understand that you are whole, pure, beautiful, and free. He would have you healed. My sisters, your faith, love, and forgiveness will bring you home. The army of Heaven is here to help. They are with you always, and they are but a prayer away.

"The Creator gives us each a song."

(Ute Indian Wisdom)

Chapter One

God, the Creator of all Life

Bear Feathers, an elderly medicine man, leaned on his walking stick and carefully lowered his thin frame to the ground. The dull ache in his hip served as a constant reminder to him of the difficulties his people had experienced and the love Creator had for them. Many summers ago most of the Nakota tribe had been sick from one of the diseases that arrived with the coming of the white man from across the great water. Bear Feathers had prayed for Creator to allow him to hunt food for his people one last time. During the hunt, his hip had been pierced by the horn of the bull buffalo he had injured and then killed. As always, Creator had granted his prayer for the people he loved with everything that he was.

The eyes of the Nakota tribe were upon him. Although he had lost the sight in his own eyes more than ten winters ago, the heat from the sacred fire warmed his skin and his spiritual eyes showed him everything the Grandfathers and Grandmothers in Heaven wanted him to see. His people surrounded the sacred fire in the shape of a circle. Parents sat cross-legged. Infants were cradled tightly in the arms of their mothers. The older children sat attentively in the laps of their fathers and grandparents. These were his people and he loved them unconditionally.

As his people began to pray, Bear Feathers raised his eyes

toward Heaven and lifted his arms toward the sky in prayer. He asked the Creator of all life to purify him so that he could be a vessel for His Grace and His love. He forgave everyone who ever hurt him or hurt those he loved. He also prayed for God to help the people who were coming to Turtle Island from across the Great Water, for he could feel their fear and confusion. He asked for nothing for himself. Finally, he offered his body to Creator so that his people could receive teaching and healing from the Grandfathers and the Grandmothers. Tears streamed down his face. At this moment he could feel the Grandmothers and the Grandfathers enter his body.[14]

The Nakota people could feel the shift in energy. The love, faith, and prayers of their elder combined with their own had brought Heaven here. The children relaxed and smiled, and the parents and grandparents said prayers of thanks to Creator. These were difficult times for their people and it was hard to keep fear at bay. They listened intently as Heaven began to teach through the body of their elder:

> *There is no fear in Creator. He is love and only love. We are the Grandfathers and the Grandmothers. We are created beings just as each of you is a created being. We are not perfect, but the words Creator grants Us to give you are. Only Creator is perfect. Each of us is a child of Creator. He loves us completely and unconditionally. There is nothing that a child of Creator's can do that would cause Creator to stop loving that child.*

****

Just as Heaven taught my Nakota ancestors long ago during a time of great suffering, the Grandmothers and the Grandfathers began to teach me. Bear Feathers was a soul who lived on this earth in the 1700s. He was a Nakota warrior who so loved the

Creator that he made changes to his life and became a medicine man for his people. He was a man whose faith, lack of fear, and selfless love for his people provided the conditions that Heaven needed to use his body as a vessel. Thankfully, Bear Feathers is now an Angel in Heaven whom the Creator allowed to minister to me. The above story is but one of the many he used to teach me the sacred lessons I would need to heal and to help the Creator to heal others. When the Creator sent the Holy Spirit and individual Angels to minister to me in a way that I could not deny, these Holy Messengers had to start at the very beginning.

It was not that I had never known God, because as a child I understood that He is love. I also believed that the Creator had sent me to this world to serve Him by helping others. I tried very hard to do this throughout my life, however, the world worked very hard to take this wisdom away from me. In 2005 it finally succeeded. What was "of this world" — meaning that which is here on this earth that is not compatible with Heaven — had confused me into believing that I was not worthy of the Creator's love and that I no longer had a place with Him.

Spiritually, I was in "hell." I was not in hell because what happened to me was my fault. I was in hell because I believed the lies that those who tortured me told me, and I, therefore, took responsibility for things that were not my fault. As most women have done at some point, I accepted that the "bad things" that happened to me were a result of "bad decisions" I had made and, therefore, I believed that I must have somehow "deserved" what happened to me. In the midst of my terror and shame, I did not bother to look further. I condemned myself for a situation that had been orchestrated by people who were desperate not to get caught for the crimes they had committed. The Creator did not put me in this place of darkness, terror, and despair. I believed illusion over truth and judged myself as guilty. As a result, I "accepted" the lie that I was no longer worthy of being connected to my Father in Heaven.

Medical professionals stated that there was "no cure" for me even as the memory of what had been done to me slowly returned.[15] As some of the effects of the drugs that were used on me began to wear off and the immediate effects of the trauma subsided, I would get "flashes" of memory. These images and my feelings about them were terrifying and so outside of what I could "cope" with that I would spiral into severe depressions or experience panic attacks. I also experienced moments when I believed that there was no alternative other than for me to take my own life. I did not speak about this to anyone because I did not believe I deserved to. I just did my best to wait until the waves of absolute hopelessness passed. I did not understand how to free myself from the hell that was now inside of me.

When the counselor that I was going to for help asked me to draw a picture of how I felt, I took the crayons that she offered to me and drew a large fireplace, a chimney, and a roaring fire. I used reds, oranges, and yellows to create large flames. I remember experiencing a moment of hope as I drew this picture. I did not have words to describe what was happening to me, and I thought that perhaps I could convey something important through this drawing. Maybe from this picture they could "figure out" what was wrong with me. I made sure that the flames were extra high and bright before I handed my drawing back to the therapist. Later, when we consulted medical professionals, they recommended that I be heavily sedated in order to prevent the severe bouts of depression and anxiety. They told me that over time I might regain some "functionality" in life, but that there was no guarantee that even this could be achieved.

Thankfully, my American Indian ancestors understood that with the Creator every soul could be completely healed. I had understood this as a child. After Heaven came to me and began to help me, I began to believe again in the Creator, Angels, and miracles. I "recognized" the feeling of Heaven and knew that it was what I had been desperately seeking for as long as I could remember. I understood that modern medicine did not have "all of the answers." Only great love and Heaven could save me.

According to one informant, this criminal group had "pumped" enough drugs into me to "kill a horse."[16] I had also been gang raped and otherwise tortured numerous times, all of which had been captured on videotape, "edited" to meet the needs of their customers internationally, copied onto DVDs, and sold along with child pornography and "snuff" videos.

When I was not filled with rage, or curled up into a fetal position crying, countless unanswerable questions plagued my mind. I had the obvious ones, such as, "How could people do things like this to other people?" "How can people watch other people being raped and tortured for 'entertainment' purposes?" and "How is it that such individuals were preying on families and children and not locked away in a prison somewhere?"

I also had the seemingly answerless questions that haunted me, such as, "How can any woman hold her head up in public after having been humiliated and degraded in such a manner?" "How am I ever going to glue the pieces of my broken life back together again?" "How am I ever going to be a good mother to my children?" "How am I ever going to be able to connect to my husband again?" and "How am I ever going to be able to understand and speak about what happened to me?"

It was very, very difficult for me to accept and understand that I had been a "victim" of such a crime. Yet, I could not deny the evidence or the facts. Although I could barely eat and it was nearly impossible for me to sleep, I refused to accept the sedatives that a very kind doctor recommended that I take. I wanted a cure, not something that would trick me into believing I was well if I was not. It was obvious that I was in desperate need of help, yet modern medicine could not offer it to me or to others like me.

I was so terrified and my nervous system so damaged from what had been done to me that, thankfully and miraculously, the

Creator sent the Archangel Michael to place His Grace and love inside of me so I could fall to sleep. This wonderful Angel kindly explained to me that if my brain could not remember to tell my body to eat or help me to sleep, my sickness would only intensify. As this did not serve Heaven, my family, or me, I prayed very hard for the Creator to help me. As part of the answer to these prayers, this loving Angel came to me every night for over a year to help me until I could fall to sleep on my own.[17]

However, the Archangel Michael did not first appear to me as himself. As Archangel Michael later said, "*Had I come to you as a large, eight-foot-tall Angel of the Lord, you would have been on your knees before me the whole time praying with your eyes closed. This was not the point.*" The point was to bring me the Grace of God so I could heal, and in order to do this Heaven had to break through my terror and self-loathing. Instead, the Creator allowed the Archangel Michael and Bear Feathers to work together to help me. I simply knew this "being" and "his" energy as "Bear Feathers," a Nakota medicine man and ancestor of mine whose body Heaven had used as a vessel during his time here on earth.[18]

Despite my pain, fear, and trauma, I felt immediate love for "Bear Feathers." He was the father I had always wanted but never understood that I had. He was humble, patient, respectful, and filled with wisdom. His faith in the Creator's goodness was unshakable. Most importantly, I trusted him. I could feel that he loved me completely. Miraculously, his prayers put me into a deep sleep when nothing else could.[19] He would take the time to teach me about the Creator and Heaven, and he brought with him the Creator's Grace so I could begin to heal. When I asked him what was wrong with me and why I could not sleep, he explained the following to me:

> *You are a warrior for Creator. You have been at war for Him for a very long time. We [the Holy Spirit] are*

here to clean out your wounds. From this point on you will fight differently. The training you received from this world will be replaced with training from Heaven. This is in answer to your prayers and the prayers of others.

So, Bear Feathers was telling me that I had been at war. It most certainly felt that way. His explanation and "plan for the future" sounded good to me. Although modern medicine treated me as a victim, Heaven treated me as a warrior for God who had survived a great battle. Looking back, I do not believe any other approach could have brought me back from the depths of hell. Only the truth could set me free. Only the truth could give me back my dignity. As the individual Angels who came to minister to me explained, our life in this world is very different than we understand it to be. As the Archangel Raphael says, "*There are no victims in this world. We are all warriors for God who come here to fight what is far from Him. We have come to help return this world back to Heaven.*"

Heaven was not saying that horrible things are not done to people in this world. Indeed, they were encouraging me to deal with my memories and forgive the souls who had done everything they could to destroy me. What they were teaching me, however, was to look at this world from Heaven's perspective. According to Archangel Michael, "*The word 'victim' refers to someone that something has been done to and they can do nothing about it. To be a 'victim,' one is simply experiencing existence as 'matter,' he or she is not experiencing life as a soul with free will.*" He told me "*a person cannot always control what the dark chooses to put before her, but every soul always has the opportunity to respond in a way that is close to God [using love, faith, and forgiveness] or far from Him.*"

The Archangel Michael used some examples from different cultures to illustrate his point. One was regarding the Jewish people who were persecuted, tortured, and killed by the Nazis during World War II. He explained to me that the Jewish people were largely pacifists in Europe prior to and during World War II.[20] He said, "*If they had died fighting with guns, would the world remember them as they do? These people were not victims. They were courageous, great warriors in a battle.*" He told me that one of the favorite tortures of those who hurt these people was to gather their religious leaders and order them to pray. They would then shoot these Rabbis in the back of the head while they were talking to the Creator.[21] What did Archangel Michael have to say about this? "*The dark is terrified of God so it devises tortures like this to terrify and traumatize people out of their faith. Even this backfires against the dark. For how much stronger do you think it makes Heaven when people who have every reason to be afraid hold onto God and pass from flesh with a prayer to Him on their lips?*"[22]

Next, he asked me whether I believed Jesus had been a victim. He pointed out that Jesus had been tortured, poisoned, brutally beaten, ridiculed, and nailed to a cross "*just for being nice to people and telling people that God loved them.*" Each of these things was done in an attempt to humiliate Him and make Him doubt who and what He was. Yet, Jesus responded to each of these things with compassion, love, and forgiveness. He even prayed to God for the souls of those who were working so hard to destroy Him as they were doing it. "*Father, forgive them, for they know not what they do.*"[23] Now that is some warrior! At no time did He stop fighting for Heaven and for His Father. He held onto the truths He was teaching people until "the end." As Archangel Michael explained, "*In Jesus living His life the way He did, We [the Holy Spirit] are still able to reach people through Him more than 2,000 years after His passing from flesh.*"

The Archangel Michael also used an example from the history of my American Indian ancestors to illustrate his point. He told me the story of Motavato, or "Black Kettle," a Cheyenne Chief who was born in the early 1800s.[24] During his time here on earth, Black Kettle held onto the Creator in the face of great evil. His ability to do so provided an opportunity for the American public to really "see" what the United States' "Indian Wars" often times truly were — the mass slaughter and decimation of elders, women, and children. According to the Holy Spirit, Black Kettle "*had very good ears for Heaven*," and he loved the Creator and His children. As a "chief," Black Kettle understood that he was a caretaker for the body, mind, and souls of his People.[25]

The Sand Creek Massacre occurred in Colorado on November 29, 1864. It is considered one of most infamous incidents in the United States' wars against the American Indians. The following are excerpts from *Finding Sand Creek: History, Archeology, and the 1864 Massacre* by Jerome A. Greene and Douglas D. Scott:

> At the council at Camp Weld near Denver on September 28, 1864, Evans [the Governor of Colorado] spoke evasively to the chiefs, informing Black Kettle that, although his people might still separate themselves from their warring kin, they must make their peace with the military authorities ... Anxious for peace, Black Kettle and his entourage acceded to all conditions, and [Colonel] Chivington told them that they could report to Fort Lyon once they had laid down their arms.
>
> But the Camp Weld meeting was fraught with "deadly ambiguities." The Indians departed convinced that since they had already been to the post they had made peace, though neither Evans nor Chivington admitted that such was the case. Furthermore, a telegram from General Curtis admonished, "I want no peace until the Indians suffer more" ... Evans notified Washington authorities ... [that] "the winter ... is the most favorable time for their chastisement." Yet, in consequence of the Camp

Weld meeting, Black Kettle prepared his people to accept the conditions and surrender themselves as prisoners of war.

On the morning of November 29, 1864, Colonel Chivington, a former Methodist minister, prepared his drunken, volunteer militia to attack these American Indian "prisoners of war" at their U.S. government-approved encampment at Sand Creek. "Black Kettle, proponent for peace and guardian of his people, reportedly raised an American flag on a pole near his lodge to announce his status, but it was ignored in the heat of the action." The militia used howitzer rounds in an attempt to kill as many men, women, and children as possible. By early afternoon, roughly 150 Cheyenne, Arapahos, and Lakota people lay dead, most of these elderly, women, and children. These bodies became the object of widespread mutilation at the hands of the soldiers.[26] According to Greene and Scott:

> In the aftermath of Sand Creek, as word gradually spread about the brutality of the onslaught, questions arose about Chivington's version of events. The truth shocked and sickened most Americans. In 1865 Sand Creek became the focus of three federal investigations, one military and the others congressional ... The examinations resolved that Chivington and his troops had conducted a premeditated campaign that resulted in the needless massacre of the Cheyennes and Arapahos and that the subsequent atrocities were an abject disgrace.[27]

Had Black Kettle's actions not been close to the Creator every step of the way, the military and government could have found some "justification" for their behavior. Since they had none, the American public could "see" behavior that was far from the Creator as exactly what it is — a "disgrace"- literally "outside of God's Grace." Among the Creator's many miracles that day was that Black Kettle and his wife, who had been shot nine times, were spared. According to the Archangel Raphael, "*If Black Kettle had not responded with peace, love, and faith in the face of pure evil, there would be no Cheyenne blood left on this earth today. What happened to the innocent people massacred on that day was so terrible that the public took notice. Extermination of the American Indian was not going to work. The government had to begin to take another tactic.*"

From the perspective of Heaven, it is clear that there is a great battle here on earth. If we are born into the equivalent of a war zone when we enter this world as the Holy Spirit describes, I needed to understand whom the battle is between and what started such a war. As I grew up attending the Catholic Church, I did have a concept of Angels, demons, and Lucifer, the fallen Angel. However, I preferred the teachings that I received from Bear Feathers to the fear-filled teachings I had received from the church as a child. Bear Feathers first taught me that everything that had life was a part of the Creator and was, therefore, to be respected. This Angel said:

> *Our people understood that Creator is a perfect circle. He has no beginning and no end. He is forever. There is no beginning or end to life. This is because in order to make us, Creator took a piece of Himself and placed it into matter. This is why our people say that all life is to be respected. Every two-legged, four-legged, and winged creature is our brother and sister. Every plant and every drop of water is also "of Creator." Our people have a saying. This saying is "Mitakuye Oyasin." This can be translated as "we are all related." We understand that all life is a part of Creator and strive to treat it as such.*[28]

Next, he explained to me that we are all God's children and

that our Father in Heaven loves every soul unconditionally. Even the people who had tried to destroy my family were children of the Creator. I knew this to be true. In fact, I had always had difficulty understanding how to "*love your enemy*," as Jesus correctly taught, and how to protect yourself at the same time.[29] Growing up with dangerous and violent authority figures, I had no choice but to love those who hurt me. I knew their behavior was not "right," and I had concluded that they just did not understand love. Since I believed I did understand it, I thought I had to try even harder to help them feel love so they could heal and, therefore, stop hurting others and myself.

With the level of understanding that I had at the time, forgiving those in my family who hurt me was not difficult. It seemed clear to me that they were suffering, and I wanted to be close to the Creator and be kind to them. I felt sorry for them because they did not seem able to control themselves. However, I did not know how to help them without putting myself directly in the line of fire. Such people seemed to only be content if they were destroying you, "sucking the life" from you, or if you "covered" for their unacceptable behavior. Bear Feathers taught me to see those souls who are actively doing things to prevent others from feeling the Creator as "bears." He explained to me that we could still help them, but Creator would have us help them differently because at that moment in time, because of their spiritual state of being, they were dangerous. This Angel taught me the following:

Let us look at the bear. The bear is an animal that is made from a piece of the Creator just as we are. We treat a bear with respect, as it is a part of Creator. But we do not get too close to a bear. When our people track a bear, they stay at least one mile away from the bear at all times. To get any closer is not safe. A bear is very fast and can decide at any time that it is hungry. If you

> *are within the bear's circle [territory] when it becomes hungry or scared it will eat you.*
>
> *Those souls who battle against Heaven are bears. I do not say this as judgment of them. Only Creator can judge. A bear is a bear and it will do what is in its nature to do. If you step within the bear's circle it will eat you when it becomes hungry or afraid.*
>
> *Therefore, while you are in flesh you must help bears differently than you help other souls. In order to help a bear, we pray to Creator to help that bear. When we do this we stand outside the bear's circle. We do not step into the bear's circle to help unless the bear sincerely asks for help from Creator and invites us into its circle. Even under these circumstances we pray for help from Heaven before going into the circle.*

For the first time in my life I had instructions on how to help those who were the most lost while keeping my husband, children, and myself safe. The fact that Bear Feathers treated such "lost people" with kindness and respect proved to me that he was telling me the truth about Creator and that he was, indeed, an Angel sent from Heaven to help me heal. I could feel that he was really teaching me about "God the Father," not the judgmental, angry being who punishes souls by banishing them to fiery prisons because they happen to be in the wrong place at the wrong time. Heaven was teaching me about the God whose love I knew when I was a child. This was the Creator my ancestors knew, the God that Jesus illuminated, and the one of which other prophets spoke. As Bear Feathers stated, "*There is only one Creator, yet many ways to worship Him.*"

I began to feel safe enough to open my heart to God again. According to Bear Feathers, the Creator follows the rules He handed down to Jesus more than 2000 years ago and to others throughout the history of mankind's time here. I knew this teaching was truth. The Creator has love, forgiveness, and compassion for all of His children. He really is our Father in Heaven, and serving Him did not mean that I had to accept being beaten, raped, humiliated, or otherwise tortured — often in the name of "love." It did not mean I was a "sinner" just because I had suffered abuse in my life, and finding favor with God did not mean that I was expected to accumulate as many wounds as possible and carry them in a big sack on my back until He decided it was time for the "day of reckoning." I did not have to be a "martyr" and sacrifice myself in hopes of living a life of honor. This was wonderful news!

At this point Bear Feathers asked me a very important question. I can remember it as if it were yesterday. "*Daughter, you are not afraid of Creator, are you?*" Instead of answering, I simply stared back at him. Finally, I nodded slowly and hung my head. Indeed, I had become afraid of God. My rationale for this was as follows: God can do anything, so if He did not prevent these things from happening to me He either did not love me anymore, I had somehow disappointed Him so much that He felt punishment was in order, I was simply no longer worthy of His love and protection, or enduring such suffering was "part of life" and there was nothing that could be done to change this. I had great fear surrounding each of these conclusions.

Bear Feathers kindly explained the truth to me. He said, "*My Daughter, Creator did not make fear. Creator loved His children so much that He gave them the free will to choose to be far from Him or close to Him. The moment a child of Creator walks away from Him, that child experiences the absence of Creator. This absence of Creator is fear. Fear is the opposite of love. Creator is love and only love. You have no reason to be afraid of Creator. Creator did not hurt you or abandon you. You prayed very hard to Creator for the opportunity to come to this world to serve Him by fighting what is far from Him. Those who fight against Heaven had to do everything they could to destroy you.*

Creator sent us to you in this way now as a sign. Your prayers and the prayers of your People have been answered."

More than a year later the Archangel Michael put it to me this way: "*Imagine that you are the general of an army that is here on this earth fighting against Heaven. You know that certain souls who are born into this world have the power to take away a large percentage of your soldiers. What is the first thing you must do? You must target those warriors who are closest to God and try to destroy their connection to Him. You hit them over and over until they do not remember who and what they are.*" This explanation made sense to me and felt right. I knew in my heart that the words used by this Angel of the Lord were true.

So if God is love with an army of Angels assembled to serve Him, then who is the poor being misguided enough to organize a battle against Him? The Catholic Church and other Christian denominations had given me a pretty good background on the fallen Angel known as Lucifer. However, I had my doubts that he was as strong as they gave him credit as being. If he was created by God as we are, then his life force is also "that which is of Creator." In denying the Creator, he was in essence denying himself. This did not sound to me like a particularly powerful foundation. Yet this being was clearly preventing people from connecting to Heaven. Who was this fallen Angel and how much power did he really have?

Before the arrival of the Europeans to North America, the Plains Indian people did not have a concept for "Lucifer" as the Christian Church understands him to be. Culturally at this time, many tribes strove to live their lives in a manner that did not give the dark a place to dwell. These tribes believed in prayer, they did not condone the use of drugs (including alcohol), they considered material greed to be a vice, they did not believe that any man or woman was above another, and they understood that all life was a part of the Creator and should be respected as such. Even the "slaves" that were captured during battle were quickly assimilated into the tribe as equal members, or released.

As a society, they strove to enforce these principles. Therefore, the dark had little opportunity to be more than a mere nuisance to them. As these people did not give the dark a place to "sit" inside of them, it was not able to wreck havoc upon them as it was doing in Europe and other parts of the world at that time. As a result, the closest concept that the Plains Indian cultures and many other native cultures had for "Lucifer" at the time was the concept of "*Iktomi*," a "spider-trickster spirit."[30]

As Bear Feathers explained, it was important to be on the lookout for Iktomi, since he was always looking for opportunities to deceive you into doubting yourself and the Creator. However, he had so little power that one sincere prayer to the Creator could do away with any of his mischief. As this Angel explained, "*If you are trying to pray to Creator and you are having trouble focusing we say, 'Oh, that is Iktomi playing one of his tricks.' Pray to Creator to help Iktomi feel love and you will see that Iktomi leaves you in an instant. Iktomi is no match for the power of love and forgiveness.*"[iii]

The Archangel Michael, who often refers to Lucifer as his "brother," described this fallen Angel to me as a "*small child who is pretending that he is his father.*" He said to me, "*My brother [Lucifer] took everything away from you that you ever valued. Yet despite all of his effort, he was merely able to trick you into momentarily believing that you were separated from God. What you will discover at the end of this process is that*

[iii] Lucifer, the being, is referred to by many different names throughout the world. For purposes of teaching, I will refer to him either as "Iktomi" or in conjunction with those lost souls that support his activities, as "the dark" in later chapters. I find that the concept of this fallen Angel as a "spider-trickster" or as "a force that has intent to push others away from the light" portrays the level of his power more accurately than names such as "Satan" or "Lucifer," which put fear into people. Few people are acting "so far from God" that they give the dark a place to dwell for more than instances at a time. Iktomi only has power to take us away from our path to the Creator if we make a space for him within ourselves. His effect is miniscule, at best, when we walk the path of the Creator.

you lost nothing. My brother works very hard to imitate what he believes God to be, but he does not understand love."

The Archangel Michael confirmed that this world was once Heaven, as is stated in the Bible. He explained that God put four Angels — Michael, Gabriel, Raphael, and Lucifer — in charge of managing this world. One of these Angels and the "army" that served God alongside them, were responsible for "holding" and protecting one of the four sacred directions. Based on a misunderstanding, Lucifer became angry with God.[31] As his anger grew, he became more and more separated from God and Heaven. Since anger is not consistent with the state of being that is Heaven, Lucifer could not stay in Heaven unless he "did the work," which meant analyzing the situation until he discovered the truth, changing any behavior of his that was far from God, strengthening his faith, and exercising forgiveness. Archangel Michael said the following:

> *My Brother was sent to govern this earth with myself, and others of the Holy Host. Since he decided to leave God, his Father has allowed him the free will to retain his knowledge of how we came here to govern and, therefore, how to disrupt it. He is a created being. He is not God, although the part of him that is life is part of God, however small now. He has used this knowledge to create systems to serve his mortality. They, unlike what God has created, are not real. They are failing as they must.*

We have an old, brightly painted Catholic statue in our home. It is a figure of the Archangel Michael standing triumphantly on top of Lucifer, who is portrayed as a black cat creature with a human-like face. Since it was made more than three centuries ago, the sword and shield that "Michael" once held are missing, and most of the plaster has fallen off of "Lucifer's" tail.

As Archangel Michael explained the above to me, he turned his attention toward this statue. He told me that contrary to popular belief, he did not push Lucifer out of Heaven. The Archangel Michael held onto his brother's hand as long as he could before Lucifer chose to let go of it. Lucifer "let go" by using his free will to reject God and love. The battle between Lucifer and Heaven was to help Lucifer find God's love and stay in the state of being we call "Heaven," not to banish him from his Father's kingdom. "*The artist of this piece should have made my likeness with a cross portraying love in one hand and my other hand outstretched toward my brother*," said Michael.

So what happened to this fallen Angel once his behavior was no longer compatible with Heaven and he refused to correct it? Lucifer decided that he did not need God. He decided that this world — the one that God had originally asked him to help manage — would be his home, mere mortality. He would be its self-appointed, mortal master. However, he was lonely, and he quickly realized that he could not be a "master" if he had no "slaves."

Lucifer understood that if he could trick people into believing that they were no longer connected to God, he could postpone their return home to Heaven when they passed from flesh. He would then have these souls as "company." From this point forward Lucifer dedicated his efforts to interrupting the flow of souls returning home to Heaven. According to the Holy Spirit, it is at this time that this world changed from being a part of Heaven (the Garden of Eden) to being "of this world," which it is today. Fear, greed, anger, self-hate, judgment, frustration, lying, shame, guilt, pride, vanity, selfishness, and lust are all elements of "Lucifer's realm." Nice kingdom!

God created Heaven, and this earth as a part of it, but Lucifer's decision to do everything possible to "prevent" souls from returning home to Heaven created the realms the Catholic Church calls "purgatory" and "hell." Purgatory and hell exist because the dark is able to convince people that they are no longer connected to their Father in Heaven. As God did not create either of these two realms, they are merely illusions that the dark has created by using lies in order to trick Creator's children into believing that they are not worthy of going home to Heaven. "Purgatory" and "hell" are nothing more than temporary "holding" places for souls that the dark is able to confuse.

Rape, incest, torture, violence, war, deprivation, addiction, pornography, adultery, lying, hypnosis, brainwashing, drugs (including alcohol), prostitution, and murder were all specifically designed by the dark to convince a soul that he or she is no longer connected to the Creator. Once the dark can trick us into participating in such things and accepting that there is "nothing wrong" with such participation or convince us that we cannot possibly be forgiven for such actions or behavior, he can temporarily change or shift our plane of existence. Those souls who exist in purgatory or hell are able to "hear" and "feel" the dark more clearly than their Creator because their mindset is closer to the dark's at that moment.

However, contrary to what many religions teach, every soul returns home to Heaven. Despite the fact that the dark focuses all of its effort on the destruction of souls, the resurrection of even the most "dedicated" of the dark's soldiers is but a prayer away. The dark works hard to trick people into believing that souls in hell "stay there forever" and a soul in purgatory "stays there for almost as long," yet it is simply not true.[32] According to the Archangel Michael, "*There is no such thing as 'just' prayer.*" The prayers of those in Heaven and here on earth help to release souls from the dark's grasp every day. Raising the dead — now that is an example of the power of faith and prayer!

So, this is the battle. On one side we have the Creator and His Holy Messengers who work tirelessly to help people feel His Grace so they can truly exercise their free will. On the other side we have the dark's army of tortured and confused slaves who dedicate their efforts to frightening people and convincing them that they are unworthy of the Creator's love. You can imagine how quickly the dark's soldiers run toward the Creator once they see the light of Heaven and realize that they are free, can you not?

If your child was kidnapped and abused, and as a result her mind became so damaged that she could not remember that you were her mother, would you stop trying to help her? Would you stop loving her? No? Well, neither does the Creator. Heaven will not give up on any of Creator's children — not even any of the dark. As so many souls are praying to be sent to this world to help return this world to Heaven, this battle will be waged until every soul is freed from the dark's web of lies and returns home to the state of being we call "Heaven."

As the Archangel Michael explained to me, "*There was a cover of a magazine that was made famous during the time of the Vietnam War. It was a picture of a child without clothing running down a dirt road. This child was screaming in terror while the bombs went off around her. People said, 'Where is God in this?' They became angry with God for allowing such suffering to be*," said this Angel, who stated that many people began to think that the war was not an acceptable thing after they saw this photograph. They began to see war for what it actually is, not for what politicians said it was. This Angel explained that after this child passed from flesh and returned home to Heaven, she prayed for God to allow her to help those who bombed her village and all those in the war on both sides that preceded that bombing. "*This 'child' had forgiven what was done to her, and with her love she helped to lift the souls of those who had pulled the triggers, set off the bombs, and directed them in the first place. In such a response, the dark can never win and God's army grows stronger.*"

The Creator does not enjoy seeing His children suffer or hurting one another, yet He loves us enough to honor our free will. He loves us enough to give us the opportunity to grow closer to Him or farther from Him. That is how much the Creator respects the decision each of us made to come here to this world. Although we knew that we would likely experience moments of great pain and confusion due to the dark's efforts and behavior, we also knew that the Creator would not abandon us or stop loving us. His great love even extends to the being known to many religions as "Lucifer," the biggest "bear" that we experience here on this earth. At the point that we have all returned home to the state of being we call Heaven, this fallen Angel can then deal directly with the Creator. As the Archangel Michael has said, "*What price can you put on a soul, daughter? What price on a child of God?*"

This fallen Angel is doing his best to "set up shop" as the Creator. However, his perspective of God is distorted. Remember, he is angry with the Creator and sees Him as a dictator rather than the loving Father that He is. It is this distorted persona of the Creator that this fallen Angel has modeled. So, that guy I described earlier, the "judgmental, angry being who punishes souls by banishing them to fiery prisons because they happen to be in the wrong place at the wrong time," that is the dark's "spin" on God and it is, therefore, not Him. The quicker we let go of that idea the better.

"I am a woman.
I hold up half the sky.
I am a woman.
I nourish half of the earth.
I am a woman.
The rainbow touches my shoulders.
The universe encircles my eyes."

(Taos Pueblo Wisdom)

Chapter Two

The Sanctity of Women

In the springtime by the rivers where our people used to put their tipis and tether their horses, there are purple flowers that come up from bulbs. When there is a late snow that covers the ground, it does not seem possible that these delicate flowers can survive. Despite the elements and the icy snow, they still bloom. They are strong, they are beautiful, and they have good medicine.

You are like this flower, my daughter. I will name you Sweet Flower in honor of this flower.

White Earth

According to Heaven, the terrible events that had just happened to my family did not occur by chance. As Archangel Michael explained, "*The most dangerous thing to do on this earth is to seek God, for when you do so you will be hit continuously by the other side. In this battle one side plays by no rules and the other side plays by very specific rules handed down by God.*" Indeed, I had been openly seeking the Creator my whole life, and the purpose of moving my family to New Mexico had been to trade in a lifestyle I considered to be unhealthy for one I believed was more conducive to helping my family to feel Heaven.[33]

The Holy Spirit told me that if I would commit to doing the work necessary to heal from my life, they would provide me with the tools and opportunities I would need to serve God by helping others to feel His Grace. This was most certainly a great honor and an answer to my life's prayer. In order to provide me with some perspective, Bear Feathers reminded me that during his time here on earth in the 1700s, the people of his tribe prepared their whole lives in hopes of receiving a single visitation from the Holy Spirit or an individual Angel of the Lord. He said the following:

> *Our people understood that Creator designed this world to be Heaven. We understood that our bodies could be used as vessels for Creator. We understood that our prayers connected this world to Heaven. We prepared our whole lives in hopes that Creator would bless us with a sign and help us to find our purpose. Once a person had been blessed with such a sign, they were expected to use this wisdom to better the lives of others.*

I wanted to heal. Although I was not afraid of the Creator anymore, I certainly did not love myself. As some of my memories began surfacing, I could barely handle what I viewed as my participation in this nightmare. I remembered sensing that something was "wrong" with these people and that their behavior was "strange," but rather than running away from them I tried to be kind to them. When they would ask me to meet them at their home to make my "great chocolate-chip, oatmeal cookies" for their child's birthday party or to help them understand some paperwork, rather than follow my gut instinct and tell them "no," I went to help them.

Authorities later explained that this "husband and wife" were seasoned criminals and part of a larger criminal group that used drugs and torture on their victims. I was told that a number of the men, women, and children that they hurt died or became insane from the side effects of the abuse or from being chemically overdosed. As there was a shift in the approach they used on me after a certain point, I believe that they may have thought that I was "figuring things out" due to the questions I was asking. Regardless of whether or not this was the case, they began to tailor the psychological torture used to make me believe that I was responsible for what was occurring to my family.[34]

For most of my life I believed that something was "wrong" with me. Due to the abuse I had experienced as a child and as a young woman, I suffered from low self-esteem. I knew that I needed help, and I was open to receiving it. Indeed, the bookshelves in my home were filled with self-help books and religious texts, and I had invested many years in counseling. Since so many of the things that had already occurred in my life before I met this couple were absolutely not things that I had ever wanted or expected to happen, I already felt that I had failed in many ways. I tried so hard in my life because I judged myself and believed that I had so much to "make up for." I wanted so badly to be "good," yet I was so terrified that I was not. Because I already believed these things about myself, the psychological tactics that this couple used on me "hit the mark," so to speak, and under the influence of narcotics and hypnosis they were exacerbated.

As Heaven carried me back from hell and I began to gain memory, I still could not understand why I had not "figured out" that things were very, very wrong and run to the police after my memory returned of the first assault by this couple. I could not understand the affects of the drugs they used on my mind, nor did I understand the level of trauma that a person sustains from such attacks. Moreover, at this point I feared that I was losing my mind, so I did not know whether I could trust my memories or not. Because of these things, I still held tightly to my self-judgment. Archangel Michael explained to me that a person "*cannot heal from something unless they can speak about it.*"

I had seen by this point that everything this Angel told me was truth. Yet anytime a memory surfaced I became terrified and my mind pushed it away. I simply could not cope with what had been done to me. This is exactly what the medical professionals had said would occur. It is why they had recommended heavy doses of medication and discouraged me from "going there." But if I did not do the work and look at my life, I could not heal. If I could not heal, I could not help my family and others who were suffering.

Despite the fact that I sincerely believed that some of these doctors were trying to help me, instinctively I knew that it would harm me to take the prescription medication they offered me. I simply refused to do so. I did not want my mind to be "tricked" into believing I was well, I wanted to be truly healed. Soon after I made that decision, Heaven came to teach me about the affect that chemicals have on a person's body, mind, and soul. They taught me that at times chemicals can be helpful to help with a physical injury, however, as the Creator designed us perfectly to be able to connect to Him and to our ancestors in Heaven, anything that chemically alters us will necessarily impede our ability to connect to Him.

The Holy Spirit explained that chemicals often stop the healing process designed by the Creator because a person can no longer tell what they are feeling or why they are feeling it. Why would you "look and deal" if you are not able to feel that you have discomfort around an issue or a situation? Bear Feathers taught me that traditionally the Plains Indians did not consider disease to be a terrible thing. As the body was a reflection of the soul, such illness was seen as a "clue" because it helped the person affected to understand that there was something in their life that they needed to address. Once the person had looked, felt, and forgiven, or made the necessary changes to their conduct, company, or environment, the illness would leave the person and they could lead a fuller life. At that point, they were truly "cured" rather than simply having their symptoms momentarily addressed.

Bear Feathers explained that simply because a society or a group of people decides at a moment in time that the use of certain substances is acceptable, this does not mean that the chemicals are not harmful to people and that they do not have serious spiritual, physical, and mental side effects. This Angel used the word "alcohols" when referring to prescription medication, "illegal" drugs, chemicals taken from plants that are used in ceremony, beer, wine, and hard liquor. Bear Feathers taught me the following:

> *Mankind was perfectly designed by Creator to hold Him and what is of Him. Traditionally, our people understood how to create the conditions within themselves necessary to connect to Creator. His love entered from the top of our heads and exited from our hearts. It came directly from Heaven into us and from us into another.*
>
> *Later, when fear came and prevented our People from feeling Creator in the same way, Iktomi offered us alcohols as a substitute. He tricked us into believing that what we felt while the alcohols were in our body was the Grandmothers and the Grandfathers when, in fact, we were feeling and hearing the souls who no longer have physical bodies who are lost and confused. Such alcohols actually prevent Us [the Grandmothers and the Grandfathers/the Holy Spirit] from entering a person. They do not allow Us to help answer their prayers.*

Bear Feathers paused, and tears fell from his eyes. He told me that it pained the Grandmothers and the Grandfathers greatly to see the tricks that Iktomi plays on Creator's children. He explained that people across this earth once understood that the Creator designed mankind to live connected to the Ancestors in Heaven, but over time this wisdom had been lost. He told me that he knew my prayers and if I truly wanted to help the

Creator's children it was important for me to keep my vessel pure.

"*You will meet people who will tell you that the alcohols are helpful, that they will make you spiritually stronger, or that they will help you to hear Us and heal. Know that this is not the truth. This was not our way. Creator already made us just as we needed to be. Alcohols only serve to give Iktomi space inside of you that is meant for Creator. Our people understood this and did not traditionally try to connect in this way. Keeping a connection to Creator and the Grandmothers and the Grandfathers is done with faith, selfless love, and prayer. There are no short cuts with Creator*," said Bear Feathers.[35]

This humble Angel from Heaven lifted up his arms toward the Creator. He said prayers in his Nakota tongue — one for each of the four directions. He then announced that the Grandmothers and the Grandfathers wished for me to know the story of the White Buffalo Calf Woman. In this, I would understand more how these Plains Indian ancestors of mine came to know the Creator so well. Here is the story of the White Buffalo Calf Woman, as told to me by the Grandmothers and the Grandfathers:

****

The People were lost and there was great hunger and deprivation across the land. The People prayed to Creator for understanding and wisdom for how they should live so that all things would become in balance. Two hunters were seeking game out upon the prairie when there was a great storm and the sky seemed to speak to them with its roiling clouds and light. It was as if the Thunder Beings, themselves, were coming to earth.

From the base of this great cloud, in the distance, there stepped a beautiful woman. And as she walked towards them, the light danced around her. The People needed to learn how to be so that all their relations could live in balance and harmony as one with them.

Because the People were still learning, one of the braves said to the other, "A woman walking alone on the prairie can be taken." He said that he would take her. And the other cautioned him. "This woman is wakan[iv]*. To do such a thing would be against Creator." But the other man would not listen, for his head was full of this world and he did not know how to be right before Creator.*

So, the brave moved to grab this woman, and to take her body, and the great cloud with roiling light descended once again. And there was a clap from Heaven as if the Thunder Beings were speaking. And when the cloud lifted, there was nothing left of the man who had approached this woman in a non-sacred manner. The remaining man knew what he had already known — that she was wakan, and that she had been sent by Creator to answer the prayers of the People and to teach them how to be.

The very beautiful woman spoke to him in a clear tone. "I have been sent by Creator to give the People their hoop[v]*, such that they can learn to be the way that is right before Creator." And she asked him to go and prepare the People, for she would bring them wisdom from Heaven and give them seven sacred ceremonies so they would understand that they too, were wakan. She said that if they honored these ways, they would always be able to connect to the Grandmothers and the Grandfathers in Heaven and to the Great Spirit, who*

[iv] "Wakan" in he Lakota language means "sacred."

[v] The "hoop" for the Plains Indian people refers to "the journey they are supposed to take here during their time on this earth."

brought all things life and who gave them this, so they could truly live again.

He ran ahead to the village, assembled the People, and told them what he had seen and what had happened. He told them they must make a place among and within themselves for this woman. This they did, and she lived among them and carefully taught them the ways of Creator and how to be here, among all His Creations, and one with them. She taught them that they also were wakan.

And she gave them the songs, the dances, the seven sacred ceremonies, and other wisdom, so they would always know how to be. One day, she rose in her white buckskin dress, and she smiled and gently put out her arms. She said to all the People, "Creator is calling me home, and it is time for me to return to the place where the Grandmothers and the Grandfathers dwell in the middle of each of the sacred directions."

As she walked onto the prairie, the People were very sad. And they asked her not to go. And she said, "I must, and I will always be among you, and you will know me when you sing the songs, dance the dances, and honor Creator, the Ancestors, and all their relations. For you will feel me, and know that I will bring you visions, just as I have at this time."

As she walked, a great herd of tantaka[vi] *appeared, as if out of nowhere, and she walked into the herd. The People were worried that she would be trampled, as these creatures swirled around her and embraced her as if she were one of them. And they saw her turn into light, and from light, into a buffalo that changed color four times until it was a brilliant white. And they heard a voice*

[vi] "Tatanka" in the Lakota language refers to the animal we call "bison" in English.

clearly say that this was a sign from Creator, and that when her People saw the white buffalo returning they would know that she was coming back and that Heaven, once again, would descend here and that Creator would bring good things for all the People.

And they saw her rise up and everyone knew that she had never been a woman among them, and that she had descended as an answer to prayers of the People and the Ancestors from Heaven so that the People would know how to live and so that the People would know that she would be coming again. And as she disappeared, eagles followed her so high that they became dots against a darkening sky. And the People also knew that they, too, were signs that Creator had sent so they would know that their prayers would be heard and carried to Him in Heaven.

****

A few evenings after Heaven shared this story with me, God blessed me with my first visit from White Earth, an Angel who had been a medicine woman for the Cheyenne people from a time before the Europeans had come to the Americas. She explained to me that there was a type of earth that was white, which the Cheyenne considered sacred. It was used in ceremonies to honor *Maheo*, [36] the Creator of all things. Her people painted their bodies and faces with it during prayer. She explained that the Holy Spirit named her after this sacred earth.

She explained to me that the Ancestors, or Angels, are created beings of light that move very, very quickly. She lifted her hand and moved her finger in the shape of a spiral and said that this symbol, the spiral, has been carved into stone and wood, and painted or drawn onto other objects since Creator first placed mankind on this earth. Even today, it is present on many of the objects we buy and sell, and many of the characters in children's movies are decorated with this symbol. It is what Angels look like from mankind's perspective — one way that Creator allows them to show themselves to us to help us to understand that we are not alone.

She also explained that since Angels move so quickly, something for them to "sit in" is often helpful when Creator sends them to this world to help Him to heal His children. White Earth stated that Angels can sit in "*anything that holds life or once held life*" and she taught me that certain materials are particularly good vessels for holding the Grandmothers and the Grandfathers, such as the "white earth" after which she was named, rock crystals, pipestone, jade, limestone, and water. Of course, one of the strongest vessels for holding Heaven is a person when they love someone or something selflessly and have no fear. Another very strong vessel is an animal that trusts and loves completely.

"*Our people understood how to amplify the power of Heaven by praying with and joining spiritually with many of Creator's creatures, such as the buffalo, the horse, and the dog. The horse was not 'transportation,' it was family, and a link to help the People to connect to the Ancestors above*," said White Earth, explaining that these animals were treated with honor and respect and in return, when there was great need, they would often willingly give up their vessels and allow the Holy Spirit to enter them and work through them to help a person, family, or community.

White Earth was unlike any woman I had ever met. She was an Angel of Creator, yet she appeared to me as one of my people's medicine women. She spoke with authority, yet she never raised her voice. The fact that she was a virtuous woman who loved the Creator was obvious. Unlike Bear Feathers, I was not immediately at ease in her presence. This was not because she did not feel like she was from Heaven. On the contrary, not only was it clear to me that God had sent her, it was also clear to me that she understood exactly what had happened to me. The explanations of events in my life that I used in order to "cope" with what had been done to me were not true, and I could see the compassion and empathy in her eyes when she looked at me. Her eyes were my clue — whether I liked it or not — that I had a great deal to look at, feel, and forgive. On top of this, I had suffered abuse at the hands of my mother, which made it difficult for me to trust a "mother figure."[37]

White Earth was here to help me to understand and "speak about" what had been done to me, and to clean out my wounds. She was here to teach me that being sent by God to this world as a woman was not a punishment. She was here to teach me that God did not make me physically attractive because He hated me. She was here to help me understand that women are proof of God's great power, and that they are strong vessels for His love and compassion. She was here to show me that in the past my People had a "good and honorable place" in their societies for women who had the courage to heal from the wounds they received during this battle between Heaven and earth, and who wanted to serve the Creator by helping others. These "medicine women" brought the Grace of God to those in need, and their wisdom and teachings helped all to grow closer to their Father in Heaven. White Earth was here to teach me that I was God's daughter sent here from Heaven as an answer to prayer.

Yet, I was terrified to see and feel the terrible things that I believed I had done. I was afraid to look at all the times I had "not been perfect" in my life. I had not yet told my husband many of the details I had started to remember about my life, nor could I deal with them. White Earth explained the following to me: "*My daughter, We [the Holy Spirit] are here to tell you that what happened to you in your life was not your fault. You did not want these things to happen. You are beautiful and pure in the eyes of Heaven. We are going to heal you completely. This is a gift from the Creator.*"

She explained to me that God blessed her by allowing her to help Him heal women around the world. She said that God had heard my prayers. He knew that my intent was to help others who were suffering by sharing the wisdom I gained from Heaven. Although I was afraid of what I knew White Earth understood about my life and the "mother figure" she represented, I was also in awe of her. I had never met a woman who understood she was sacred, or "of God," the way White Earth did. I wanted to feel like that, myself.

As I did not have a mother figure in my life that I believed I could model and still be close to God, White Earth humbly asked that I consider her my "spiritual mother." She said, "*Every soul sent here by Creator has a set of spiritual parents. At times such souls pray very hard to be sent here to Mother Earth to serve together. Other times the parent helps and loves their child from Heaven. In your case, your spiritual parents are both helping you from Heaven. However, Creator has now blessed us to be able to communicate with you in this way.*"

Although it was still nearly impossible for me to feel for myself, I could see that White Earth had great love for me. My suffering moved her to tears. It had been a long time since I had cried for myself. For a woman to be able to cry for herself she has to see things as they truly are. For a woman to be able to cry for herself she has to take down the barricades, or "blocks," around her heart and soul. For a woman to cry for herself she has to understand that she is a child of God with free will, not a slave. For a woman to cry for herself she must have a safe place from which to look at her life, see it for what it truly was, and forgive. Heaven had come to provide me with each of these things.

According to White Earth, "*There are two instances when Creator sends life. One is when there is great need and the other is when there is great love. Whenever Creator chooses to send life to a woman, the soul that is sent is always a gift from Heaven.*" She also stated that there is "*no such thing as a 'bastard,' as Creator is Father to us all.*" She explained that during her time here in this world as White Earth, most American Indian tribes did not use "blood" to determine whether or not someone was a member of their tribe. She said that for many tribes, membership was determined by a person's "heart" and their willingness to follow "the way" or "spiritual path" of the tribe.

The Archangel Raphael later explained that most American Indian tribes understood that there were three ways that God sent children. "*A child can be sent by God to a woman and carried in her womb, an adult[s] can adopt a child who does not have a caregiver, or two souls can 'recognize' one another spiritually and decide, together with God, to love each other in this manner.*" As each of these was blessed and made possible by God, one way was not considered "less" than another.

As White Earth taught me, when helping women to heal, "*The woman determines the order.*" I wanted to love and trust White Earth. However, in order to do so completely I could feel that I needed to heal from the damage done to me by the actions of my mother in flesh. Clearly, this is what my soul needed to deal with first. At the suggestion of Bear Feathers, my husband, brothers, and some of our local American Indian friends had helped me to erect a medicine tipi in the mountains behind our cabin.[38] Although I had always loved churches and other structures used by people to worship God, in my heart I wanted a simple place to pray — a place where it was just God and myself — no distractions. To my family and me, this tipi was beautiful. I named it "Bear Feathers Lodge," and my prayer was that it be a place of healing for many.

One fall morning, I sat with White Earth in the medicine tipi in the mountains. As the birds sang and the wind blew through the trees, we talked about my experiences with my mother in flesh and other members of her family. This Angel of the Lord explained to me that I had experienced "*the most difficult thing to heal from.*" White Earth said, "*A long time ago incest was handled in a very specific way by the Lakota, Nakota, and Dakota people. They understood the spiritual purpose and consequences of incest. They understood that it was the attempted murder of a soul. Therefore, those in the tribe agreed that the punishment for such behavior had to be so severe that people would not take the risk. If a man abused a child in such a way, he was killed. If a woman did such a thing, she was banished from the tribe and made to wander alone. This meant almost certain death for her.*"

White Earth explained that she was not condoning the killing of another — only God could decide when a soul's experience here on this earth was finished. However, she wanted me to understand the seriousness of what had been done to my brothers and me in the eyes of my ancestors. "*When a father does such a thing to his daughter or son, society and even the child can sometimes get their head around it and say, 'Well, sometimes men are sick and they do such things.' Yet, when a mother does such a thing to a child who came out of her womb, it destroys the very fabric of society, the child, and the family unit. It is so contrary to the nature of what God created that the child lives believing it has nowhere to go. There is nobody in flesh for that soul to trust.*"[39]

As I went through my childhood memories, White Earth confirmed them. Yes, I was afraid to put my head under water because my mother would pretend she was going to rinse the shampoo from my hair and, instead, hold my head under water until she "felt like" letting go. Yes, my mother really did sexual things to my body and would tell me she was being a "good mother" because she was "preparing me" for what men would do to me. Yes, after she would do these things she would tell me that I was "so bad" that I "made the Angels cry." Yes, she allowed others in her family to "use" me as they wanted. Yes, she enjoyed humiliating me by taking me for physical exams to male doctors and having them "focus" on my genitals while she laughed behind their backs at my obvious discomfort. Yes, yes, yes.

White Earth also addressed the large gaps in memory that I had experienced throughout much of my life. This Angel explained that a soul "*cannot remember what it cannot abide in.*" She explained that many, many women are not able to remember the incidents of abuse that occurred in their childhoods and in their lives because their brain will not allow them to recall what is too terrible to face. However, their bodies, minds, and souls will exhibit the symptoms of everything that they experienced. Although every single memory is stored in the mind, the brain will not allow a person access to certain incidents — those that are "unspeakable" — until the person is in a place in their lives where they are safe enough and willing to face what occurred.

In my case, I could remember the events that occurred directly before many of the incidents of sexual abuse and what occurred directly after the acts. Of course, I also had very strong uncomfortable feelings and negative reactions toward certain people. There were uncles who sent chills up and down my spine when they walked past me and brushed against me, and cousins that could send waves of shame through me when they looked at me inappropriately. I also became filled with rage when my mother made sexually suggestive jokes or gestures. However, as I still had to live with and love the people who did these things to me as a child, my brain helped me to "cope" by simply storing the remaining details in another place in my mind until I was safe enough to access them and begin to piece together the truth.

White Earth explained that our world does not understand the spiritual nature of what we call "trauma." She defined trauma as: "*The aftermath of an event or series of events that creates fear and the inability to process situations in a manner that allows the woman to stay connected to Creator [God]."* This Angel added the following:

> *Trauma is Creator's way of protecting a soul from that which is so overwhelming the mind and body may not be able to handle the truth of what happened and continue to function. Yet the mind is designed to keep trying to heal such wounds and steadily continues to bring forth memory in a manner that such memories can be processed through understanding their true part in a soul's spiritual growth. This can be seen as very painful for people, and all manner of methods are used to "suppress" such memory. This is only necessary because a spiritual or "of Creator" explanation is lacking from much of the present societies' health care practices.*

White Earth explained that in my case, I had a great deal of difficulty remembering the level of violence that people used against me in my life. As it was "the unspeakable" for me, I would simply "go away" mentally and "return" once it was "over." Although I believed her when she told me this, I was having a hard time understanding how it was that I could not remember feeling many of the blows that were dealt to me in my life. There was an incident in particular that I had in mind when I was asking my questions.

When I was about 8-years-old, my brothers and I had been left with one of our favorite aunts while my mother went to the store. This aunt was allowing us to jump off the kitchen table onto a pile of sofa cushions that she had stacked up on the floor. As I was taller than my brothers, when it was my turn to jump off of the table, my head hit the ceiling lamp and it shattered into pieces. Although I had cuts on my head, I was terrified — not because of the blood trickling down my face, but because I knew that I would be beaten for what "I had done." My anxiety was so strong that my stomach was in knots and I was doubled over in pain. By the time that my mother had returned from the store, I was in a fetal position on the floor. I "went away" as I saw the belt buckle come toward me. I "came back" after the beating was over. The blood on my head was now dried, there were bruises in various places on my body, and I was alone in my bedroom. I recalled the feeling of gratitude I experienced at that time knowing that it was "over."

White Earth patiently and lovingly answered my questions, however, it was not until years later that I would truly see this process "in action." It was early one morning, and I was feeding our herds of Native American horses and buffalo. Although I normally did not do this, I decided to carry a full bucket of grain through a horse pasture. I figured that the herd in this pasture was "busy" eating the grain I had just poured for them, and I would have time to cut through their pasture and make it to the buffalo herd before they finished. However, that day some of the horses finished eating their grain in record speed and they decided to follow me. As they closed in around me trying to get to the grain in my bucket, the lead mare in the herd nipped the backside of a little paint mare that was between her and the bucket of grain in my hand. As the little paint mare shot forward, I knew that I was going to be trampled by her.

The next memory I have is of being on the ground. My bucket was rolling down the pasture, and the horses were eating the grain that had spilled around me. Although I had the bruises on my body to "prove" that the little mare had trampled over me, I did not have memory of her actually stepping on me and I could remember feeling no pain while it occurred. At that moment it "clicked" for me. I said a prayer of gratitude to Heaven for both helping me to escape that incident relatively unharmed, and for helping me to truly grasp the lesson that they had begun to teach me years before in my tipi in the mountains.

Although in the beginning of my healing process I could not

feel for myself, I could feel for my brothers. When they were abused when we were children, I knew it was wrong and it made me very angry. I remember believing that if such people were abusing me they would not "have time" to hurt my brothers. The Archangel Michael gently explained the following: "*If a parent will do such things to one child, they will do it to the others.*" This broke my heart, as I had been able to "cope" with what my family had done to me because I believed some good came from my "taking the hits." I saw myself as having sacrificed to protect my brothers from the unspeakable. Thankfully, God answered my prayers and sent the Angels to begin helping my brothers to heal.[40]

To help me to deal with the feelings of disgust, shame, and self-judgment that I had regarding the sexual abuse I suffered as a child and a young woman, the Archangel Michael came to speak with me one evening. As I was reviewing the things that White Earth had taught me, and the memories that went along with these concepts for me, this Angel said to me, "*Daughter, it is not possible for a child to 'have sex.' A child is not biologically able to understand sexual assault as anything other than violence or participate in it in the manner that society understands. I would ask that you listen to me closely,*" said the Archangel Michael. "*When a child is sexually violated, it is no different than someone taking a baseball bat and hitting them in the back of the head. It is violence, period.*"

As I thought about this, I realized that I would not feel shame if someone hit me on the head with a bat, and I would not be confused as to the fact that it was violence. Clearly it would not be "my fault" if someone made a decision to do that to me. If that was the case, then I needed to work hard to shift my understanding of the effect of sexual abuse on a person. As I was praying about this, White Earth appeared. This Angel said, "*Daughter, there are no shortcuts with Creator. We are all here to learn to be closer to Him. The Holy Spirit asks that you allow yourself to feel everything that you could not feel when these things were being done to you. We then ask you to forgive those who gave Iktomi a place inside them so that the dark could do these things to you. Once you have done so, We will remove the pain and fear from your body, mind, and soul and repair any damage that was done."*

She explained to me that my mother in flesh had suffered greatly as a child and as a woman. As a result of having everything taken from her at a very young age, she believed that she had no choice left but to do to others what had been done to her. In her sickness, she believed that love meant "exercising power over others." If I wanted to understand what had been done to her throughout her life, I needed only look at her actions toward us. She was simply "recreating" what her caregivers and others had done to her. Her mind was "stuck" at the place she experienced these traumatic, childhood events.[41]

My maternal grandfather had blood from the Cheyenne, Arapaho, and Comanche people of the Great Plains region of the United States. The Holy Spirit had done an excellent job of teaching me about my ancestors from the Plains Indian people. I now understood that they had great faith and had the wisdom to know that all life was sacred, or "a part of God," and that they were connected to Him and to the Ancestors in Heaven. Although my maternal grandmother worked hard to be a "good Catholic" by attending mass many times per week, crocheting intricate cloths for the local church altars, and reading the Bible on a daily basis, it was clear to us that she was still Mayan at heart.

On hot summer days, as she was crocheting and watching "I Love Lucy" reruns on her small, black and white television set, my grandmother would stare longingly outside of her living room window at the colorful plants and flowers in her lush garden. If we were lucky, she would tell us stories about her childhood home, a tiny, jungle village in the Yucatan. This village was within walking distance from the ancient ruins of her Mayan ancestors. As a small girl she was trained in the spiritual healing ways of her people. Soon after this she was sold into slavery and forced to convert to Catholicism. Despite her new religious training, as an adult she would still agree to help the sick when modern medicine failed to produce satisfactory results. As a child I witnessed these traditional healings, which took place in a back bedroom in her home.

I knew from my studies in school that the Mayan culture had a strong spiritual and religious foundation. Archeologists and historians know that the Mayan civilization, which is considered to have been one of the most advanced in the history of this world, abruptly declined between 1300 and 1500AD. However, they do not understand the reason this occurred.

According to Archangel Michael, "*The priests became too powerful and those who were praying heard from God through the Holy Spirit that it was time to stop. Building a great civilization for man is not creating a great civilization for God. Imagine the faith it took to take apart an entire civilization to try to find and repair the part that was broken. At a certain point they [the Mayan people] decided that God controlled them and they did not control God. They sealed up their temples and became simple hunters and farmers again. They got rid of the high priests and each person communicated directly with God.*"

If this was true, as I knew it to be, what had happened to change this level of faith and commitment to God? What was it that had turned people who would sacrifice everything to do what they believed to be right and to not cause harm to another into people who orchestrated the environment in which my brothers and I had been raised?

According to the Archangel Raphael: "*If you are trying to understand the state of a person, community, or nation and you are having trouble doing so, then you have not gone back far enough. It took five generations of terror, slavery, rape, starvation, torture, manipulation, and brainwashing to create the circumstances you and your brothers experienced within your family.*" If I applied this information, stepped back and took a "bird's eye view" of some of my family members, their behavior, responses, and choices no longer seemed to have "come out of nowhere." Many of the stories told to me by my grandmother, mother, aunts, and uncles now began to make sense. They, themselves, were also forced to survive in circumstances that were very far from God. [42]

White Earth explained: "*Children learn how to love from their parents and others around them. This is as Creator made it to be. Your mother watched those around her and from their actions, behavior, and words she learned that love meant 'doing things she did not want to do.' She learned that her value was in her adequacy as a sexual object. She was a little girl who wanted to be close to God. Iktomi worked very hard to convince her that such a place was no longer available to her.*"

Could I understand this little girl? Yes. Could I forgive her? Absolutely. Were my children and siblings physically far enough away from her and her family so the cycle could be broken? Yes. As the Archangel Michael said, "*God has great compassion and love for such souls. We call them 'little lost ones,' and when they finally break free from my brother's [Lucifer's] hold, we carry them gently in our arms to Heaven.*" This made me happy. I had done all I could do to love my mother in flesh and help her feel God's Grace. I had confronted many of those who had abused her on her behalf. My husband and I had removed my brothers so that she and her family could no longer hurt them. My children were safe. I could now forgive her and other family members completely, since I understood what they had done and why. I could now "give them to God," while continuing to pray for their souls each day.

The next few days were very difficult. White Earth had removed the "block" that I had put up inside myself to cope with these events.[43] According to the Holy Spirit a "block" is "*the false need for self preservation of an individual's life through failing to look at behavior of themselves or another and how it truly impacts the world.*" Now that this block was gone, the pain was so overwhelming that I was nauseous and my stomach ached. I could not even answer simple questions. I was afraid to open my mouth because I did not want to burst into tears.

It was going to take time for me to internalize the fact that what had been done to me when I was a child was not my fault. In order to "cope" I had lived with the belief that what had been done to me was "not so bad" and that those who hurt my siblings and me simply "did not mean" to do what they had done. To know that my mother and her family had orchestrated scenarios with the intent to hurt, confuse, and destroy us — as they themselves had been hurt, confused, and destroyed — left me stunned.

The pain crashed into and through me in waves. My joints, jaw, and lower back ached. As White Earth explained, "*The soul always knows the truth, but Iktomi uses techniques to trick the mind and the body. When the mind, body, and soul are out of balance a person becomes 'sick.' What you are experiencing now is your body and mind's reaction to what really happened. Your mind, body, and soul are becoming aligned with regard to what was really done to you. You have rejected the lies that were fed to you and the tricks that were played on you. Your mind and body now understand what your soul already knew to be true.*"

Now that I had "done the work" in this area by "looking," allowing myself to feel what really happened, and forgiving those involved, the Holy Spirit could remove the illness that had settled into my mind and body as a result of having accepted my abuser's version of what had occurred.

With White Earth's help, and the help of the Corn Maidens she brought with her,[44] I allowed myself to feel what it was like to be completely dependent upon a woman who was severely spiritually and mentally ill. I allowed myself to feel what it was like to be a little girl who is violated by her uncles and cousins and is physically beaten and blamed for it by the grandmother and aunt she tells. When I had experienced this and forgiven these people completely, these Heavenly Angels repaired the damage that was done to my body, mind, and soul.

Over the next few weeks my sadness and grief were replaced with love and compassion. I knew that God was helping my mother and her family, and in sending White Earth, He had ensured that I had everything I could have ever dreamed of having in a mother. God sent this lovely Angel to teach me more about my ancestors and the sacred nature of women. White Earth taught me about Sweet Medicine, the prophet that God sent to the Cheyenne people long ago at a time when they had been lost. I was surprised at how similar certain aspects and details of his life were to what I understood to be true about Jesus. However, now I understand that God is always consistent, as are the conditions necessary to bring Heaven to this world. God does not waver, and when His children are suffering He always sends help. The story of Sweet Medicine as told by the Holy Spirit is as follows:

****

Long ago The People were lost. It had been a long time since they had felt Maheo in their lives. There was a young woman who understood that she was a pure vessel for Maheo. In a dream Heaven came to her and told her that she had been chosen and "Sweet Root" would come to her. She did not understand what this meant. She had never been intimate with any man, yet in time it became clear that she was with child.

When it became time for the child to be born, the young woman went alone to a nearby river and built a hut out of reeds and grass. When her baby boy was born, she said a great prayer to Maheo asking that He bless her child and keep him safe. She was afraid that if she returned to her village with the child that he would be abused by the other people in the village.[45] *She cleaned and wrapped her baby and left him for someone else to find.*

Soon after she left, an old woman came. The old woman followed the sound of the baby crying until she came to the little grass hut. As she was childless and had longed to be a mother, she was overjoyed to find the baby. She named him "Sweet Medicine" after the sweet root that makes a mother's milk flow, which surrounded the little hut where he was born.

At a young age it became clear that Sweet Medicine was different than other children. His first recorded miracle occurred when he was ten-years-old. During this time there was a drought and his people were starving. He prayed for Maheo to turn a hoop, which he had fashioned from an old, tattered buffalo hide, into a buffalo calf to feed his starving people. Since he was pure of heart and asked nothing for himself, Maheo answered his prayer.

A boy's first hunt is an important milestone. When Sweet Medicine killed his first buffalo calf, an old chief approached him and demanded the skin for himself. As Sweet Medicine had plans to use his first hide for spiritual work, he offered the old chief some of the animal meat instead. The old chief took both the meat and the hide, and a fight between the two ensued. Still, Sweet Medicine refused to part with the hide.

As a result, the enraged chief and his followers chased Sweet Medicine out of the village. Sweet Medicine prayed to Maheo for guidance, and Maheo led him to a sacred mountain. Today, this mountain is called Bear

Butte and it is located in South Dakota. Sweet Medicine entered a cave in this mountain. There, the Grandfathers and the Grandmothers ministered to him. For the next four years they taught him the laws of Heaven. The Grandfathers and the Grandmothers gave him sacred arrows and medicine to bring to The People.[46] *When it was time, Sweet Medicine packed the sacred arrows and some sweet grass and headed back to his village.*

When he arrived, Sweet Medicine saw that his people had suffered greatly while he had been gone. The people were dying without Maheo in their lives, and the buffalo had left them because they were not respectful. Their bodies and souls were starving. Sweet Medicine began to teach them the medicine, as the Grandfathers and Grandmothers had instructed him to do. With the application of these teachings the Tsistsistas, as the Cheyenne call themselves, came to be.

****

White Earth explained to me that Sweet Medicine lived on this earth a very long time. When he returned to his people from Bear Butte, he encouraged them to leave their homes in the Great Lakes region and led them out into the Plains. She explained to me that the Cheyenne became missionaries. Indeed, they were nomadic as the history books describe, but they were not moving from place to place simply to follow the great herds of "buffalo."

The Cheyenne people believed that they could best serve the Creator by spreading the way of life — the path of God — that was handed down to them by the Holy Spirit. They believed that every soul, whether it was here on Mother Earth in spirit or in flesh, was a child of Creator. The Cheyenne understood that their bodies were vessels that God could use to help others in need. Every place they stopped was honored with prayer, and the people they encountered were gifted with "medicine" from the Grandmothers and the Grandfathers/the Holy Spirit. They had been taught how to create the conditions to bring Heaven here, and they were working hard to share this with the rest of God's children.

White Earth explained that one of the teachings the Grandmothers and the Grandfathers instructed Sweet Medicine to return to his people was the wisdom that women were to be honored, as they were sacred vessels for Creator. She explained, "*The most difficult thing to do on this earth is to come as a woman. Women are the center. From the time that human beings were put here on this earth by Creator, new souls entered this world through our bodies.*" White Earth said that this does not mean that men are "less," it simply means that women have a unique covenant with God.

> *Creator gave only women the power to bring forth life. Whether a woman does so or not does not change the honor and covenant that Creator gave to her. In this world it is very difficult to understand that being born a woman is very much proof of Creator's love. Our capacity as women to feel love for our children is very close to that which Creator feels for us. Our capacity to be a home, both physically and spiritually, for our mates is also proof of such love.*

So, if women had a special covenant with God, why were so many females around the world treated so badly? Why did many cultures treat their grandmothers, mothers, and daughters as if they were "less" and "unworthy?" Why were women often labeled as "deficient" in intellect, ability, and strength? Why were they treated as if they were burdens to society rather than gifts from God?

White Earth paused and looked me straight in the eyes.

"*Make no mistake, daughter, the dark is waging a war against women.*" Despite the seriousness of the statement she had just made, this Angel of the Lord was at peace. It was clear to me that she had complete confidence in God's ability to heal all. I realized that God must have sent her here to help not just me, but all of His daughters. I wondered whether or not God had just deployed the equivalent of a "secret weapon" in sending her to the world in this way at this time. She continued:

> *In this iteration, women were designed by Creator to be vessels for both His life and the lives He brings here. For a man to understand that Creator and His Holy Spirit may occupy his body is a leap of faith and understanding. For a woman, she understands her body will as it is designed, be occupied by both her mate and her children. It is hers to share within her free will, and through such will, that of Creator.*
>
> *This does not mean that women as souls are greater than men. It means that the dark must urgently destroy this link between the very manner in which Creator embodied women here and Creator in Heaven. If he does not, it is a very rapid realization for women to know Heaven and Creator's Grace here. Thus, the lesson you brought from Heaven and have heard from me your whole life is correct. If the women are healed, so returns the world to Heaven.*

White Earth used the example set by of some of my ancestors to teach me how a community functions when the role of women is understood and respected. She explained that the Cheyenne women were known throughout the plains as being virtuous women. As I would find out later in my research, women literally were the "center" as White Earth had taught me. They were the heart of the family, and they were responsible for the spiritual education of the children.

According to George Bird Grinnell in his book The Cheyenne Indians: History and Society, "The women of the Cheyennes are famous among all western tribes for their chastity[47]... the women have great influence. They discuss matters freely with their husbands, argue over points, persuade, cajole, and usually have their own way about tribal matters. They are, in fact, the final authority in the camp."[48]

According to Archangel Michael: "The people understood that the majority of perceived learning took place between birth and five years of age. Concepts such as respect, working together, selflessness, community support, and the behavior that created cultural cohesiveness were all primarily learned by a child through participation with his or her mother and observation during these years."

Until the age of five, the children of most American Indian tribes spent the majority of their time with their mothers, aunts, and grandmothers. It was the women who taught the children about their Creator and about who and what they were. After the age of five or six, young boys began to spend the majority of their time with their fathers, grandfathers, and the other men in the tribe, while the young girls stayed close to the women.

What did these young children learn while in the company of these women? In a community such as the Cheyenne, where it was understood that a woman was sacred, the children learned how to live here on earth while still being connected to Heaven. Each morning started with prayer, and each night ended in the same manner. Children were taught that they could "hear" the Grandfathers and Grandmothers in Heaven if they conducted themselves in a loving manner, but not if they were afraid, angry, jealous, dishonest, or otherwise disrespectful to the life around them. The state of being that is Heaven could be achieved here on earth, one simply needed to create the conditions with her actions, thoughts, beliefs, and intent.

"The Cheyenne women had 'societies' just like other tribes around the world. However, after Sweet Medicine brought Our [the Holy Spirit's] teachings to them, these societies changed in nature. The women now strove to be 'the best wife' or the 'best mother' they could be by applying all that they learned from Us [the Holy Spirit] and each other. Throughout the history of this earth, We [the Holy Spirit] have come to God's children all around the world," said Archangel Michael. "The Cheyenne were among those peoples who changed their lifestyle, customs, and religious practices to ensure that We [the Holy Spirit] had the conditions necessary to keep coming."

With these teachings about what it meant to be a woman and about the history of some of my ancestors, the Holy Spirit and individual Angels of the Lord helped to heal a deep wound that had been lodged in my body, mind, and soul since I was very young. As a child, there were many times when I longed to be anything but what I was — a hungry, poor, frightened, brown girl without a place and without the obvious ability to effectuate change. Now that I had the facts, I was beginning to see my childhood and myself differently. I now understood that I descended from people who strove to bring God's Grace to others, and who had great faith and love for the world. Many of my ancestors understood the responsibility that God had bestowed upon women and they, therefore, worked hard to allow them to be everything they were.

According to the Holy Spirit, every soul here in this world was sent as an answer to their own prayers and the prayers of others in Heaven and on earth. If this was true, I not only had a place with God in Heaven, I also had a very special job to do for Him here. I realized that I must have had great love, compassion, and faith to ask to be sent as a woman to help a family in flesh that was in such need of Heavenly intervention.

As a wife and a mother, I was the "center" of my immediate family. I now had the opportunity through my responses, actions, intent, prayers, and the examples I set for my children, to break a cycle of abuse and deprivation that had crippled generations of people. This abuse was so severe and continuous that it managed to convince honorable, reverent, and spiritual people that they were no longer connected to their Creator.

Heaven was now helping to give me an opportunity to put an end to Iktomi's perceived "reign" by exposing his tricks and lies. This realization hit me hard. I marveled at the power of God, got down on my knees, and prayed for God to give me the strength to continue with my healing. Since the Holy Spirit was willing to help me, I intended to leave no wound left unhealed.

"When the sun died,
I went up to heaven and saw the Creator
and all the people who had died a long time ago.
The Creator told me to come back and tell my people
they must be good and love one another,
and not fight, or steal, or lie.
He gave me this dance to give to my people."
(Wovoka, Paiute Indian Prophet,
regarding the origins of the Ghost Dance)

Chapter Three

Vessels For God

In order to heal, women have to understand that they did not make the choices that they believe they made. If you do not believe that you exist, or you believe that you exist only to serve others — you are a slave. A slave does not have free-will. A slave is taught by the world that she is not a person, and that she does not matter to Creator. This is a lie.

White Earth

It had been another day filled with the Creator's miracles. White Earth and Bear Feathers requested that my husband and I help with a family that was in need of Heavenly intervention. Once we agreed to serve in this manner, they told us that the Holy Spirit would send this couple to us. We were to help to deliver God's answer to their prayers and the prayers of their "circle" of loved ones in Heaven and here on earth.

White Earth explained to us that the idea that any person has that he or she is ever alone is merely an illusion created by Iktomi, as every soul has a "circle," which is comprised of souls in Heaven and here on earth who are always helping that person with their love and prayers. She also confirmed that every soul here on earth has at least one Angel that serves as his or her guardian. This is one of Creator's many gifts to help His children navigate this world, and to find their purpose and their path home.

Sure enough, about an hour later we received a telephone call from a person who knew this family, gave us their telephone number, and asked us to contact them because they needed help. Within two hours, this husband and wife were seated before us. According to medical experts, Anna[vii] had stage-3 ovarian cancer and she was expected to "lose" her battle with this disease shortly.

Although I had just met Anna and her husband, I instantly felt a connection to them. Without any outward display of emotion, Anna relayed the details of her medical diagnosis and shared with us some of her alarming symptoms. Her husband told us that they had four young children. He added that Anna had suffered through many miscarriages and had also "lost" other children. At his mention of this, I saw a flicker of pain cross her face. As we began to pray with this couple, Anna began to cry. She could feel the Holy Spirit in and around her and wanted to know what it was.

We explained to Anna that God had asked us to find her, and that what she was feeling was His Grace as brought to her by His Angels in Heaven. At the urging of White Earth, we told Anna that what had happened to her in her life was not her fault, and we asked her to share more about her life and about the children she had "lost." Anna described her own mother's belief that her daughter would "grow up to be a terrible mother." She spoke of relationships with men who threatened to leave her when she told them she was carrying life. These men also told her that she should not have a child because she would be a "bad" mother and "ruin the kid." In a panic, she did what they asked and aborted the life that God had sent to her. This happened

---

[vii] "Anna's" name has been changed along with some of the details of her condition in order to protect her privacy.

more than once. After she shared these details, Anna looked into my eyes. I saw great sorrow, fear, and confusion. "You see, my mother was right. I *did* turn out to be a terrible mother."

After our first meeting with this couple, Bear Feathers came to speak with me. I could not get Anna's suffering out of my mind. I had not seen a murderer seated before me; I had seen a woman who did what she did because she believed she had no choice. I could feel her self-loathing and believed that if she left this world now the cause of "death" would be a broken heart, not "cancer."

I had learned by now that God and His system "make sense" when viewed from the perspective of Heaven. The Holy Spirit had also taught me that the concept of free will is incredibly important. So if Anna had "chosen" to abort some of the children God had sent to her because she was backed into a corner and could see no alternative, it would appear that she had not been given an opportunity to exercise her free will at all. To make a "choice" a person has to understand that they have options.

Bear Feathers sat quietly as I gathered my thoughts. "*Daughter, your feelings about this are correct. What was done to this daughter [Anna] was not her fault. Starting from when she was very small, her mother in flesh told her over and over how bad she would be as a mother. She told her this so many times that she [Anna] finally believed it to be true. Many of these men understood this about her life and used it against her to get the outcome they wanted*," said Bear Feathers. He explained that God only holds a soul accountable for the choices she makes when she exercises her free will. "*Therefore, a person cannot exercise her free will if she does not understand that she has it.*"

Bear Feathers explained that God gave every man, woman, and child here on earth and in Heaven the gift of free will.[49] Because of this great gift, each of us has the freedom to make choices that will help us to move closer to God or farther away from Him. We are all children of Our Father in Heaven, and only He is above any of us. If one person wishes to control another person, that person must use tricks and lies in order to convince the other that there is a power imbalance. Once a person believes that they are "under the authority" of another other than God — even for a moment — their soul is exposed. This is the necessary condition for what this world refers to as "hypnosis."

Bear Feathers used the following example to illustrate his point: "*If a husband comes home to his lodge every day for many winters and greets his wife by saying, 'You are a fat pig. You are no good. You are nothing without me,' over time she will begin to see herself not as she actually is, but as he tells her over and over that she is. She will begin to live not as Creator made her to be, but as she believes someone who is 'no good' would live,*" said Bear Feathers.

According to the Holy Spirit, in order for hypnosis to occur "*someone has to consent to give the power to control their actions to someone else other than God. The limit of what can be done under hypnosis is only the limit of the power the person gives. Hypnosis talks to the soul.*"

Can you guess which being is desperate to "talk" to as many people's souls as possible? Remember, in order to "trap" a soul in purgatory or hell, Iktomi, the spider-trickster spirit, must convince a soul that he or she is separated from Heaven. If Iktomi cannot trick souls in this manner, he has no "army." If he has no army he is "alone" in this world. At the point that he is "alone," it will be clear — even to him — that he must face God and the consequences of his actions. Iktomi works very hard to create the conditions that will leave a soul open to hypnosis. This fallen Angel will do anything he can to get a person to "give" his or her consent.

I can tell you from personal experience and from helping others in their healing process that Iktomi fights very dirty when it comes to devising scenarios to trick a person into believing that someone other than God has control over her. Iktomi only needs a moment to cause spiritual chaos. According to the Archangel Raphael, "*rape, violence, and incest*" are tricks commonly used by Iktomi and those he works through to create the illusion of authority and power over another. Once a person believes she is "less than," "controlled by," or "at the mercy of" another, any comments directed at her by this "authority figure" have the same effect as hypnosis and/or brainwashing on the mind, body, and soul. These comments are directed "straight to the soul."

Many of the world's "experts" on hypnosis, including psychologists, medical professionals, and law enforcement officials, claim that a person "cannot be hypnotized to do anything that he or she does not want to do." What these people do not understand is the extent to which tools and techniques — such as drugs (including prescription medication and alcohol), rape, violence or the threat of violence, lies, and manipulation — are commonly used on women to weaken their resistance and get them to spiritually relinquish their free will to another. Therefore, the opinion held by these experts is at the very least dangerously misleading.[50]

If hypnosis "*talks to the soul*" as the Holy Spirit teaches, then it is impossible to understand it unless you look at it from a spiritual perspective. It is critical to understand what happens when Iktomi (or "Lucifer," as Christianity often refers to him) convinces a person — even for a moment — that someone other than God has authority over her. At the moment that a person in flesh believes that she is at the mercy of another person, this fallen Angel does one of the only things he is able to do in this world. He directs souls that are trapped in purgatory or hell, who experienced the same thing during their time here on earth, to this person so that they surround and "fill" her.

It is this spiritual component that ensures that the effects of hypnosis on a person are so powerful. Iktomi has tricked the person in flesh into "opening" their soul and mind to an idea that is far from God. Once they do this, he immediately "links" them to other souls who share this belief system or have a shared emotional experience. Iktomi uses these lost and confused souls to reinforce the idea that is far from God that he has just tricked the person in flesh into accepting. When the Archangel Raphael says, "*The idea that we are ever alone is an illusion,*" he means it!

Have you ever wondered why battered women return to their abusers? Why do women whose bodies are dying from malnutrition still diet and exercise obsessively? Why do recovered drug or alcohol addicts suddenly relapse when they were "doing so well?" Unless the spiritual component of the hypnosis that was used on these individuals is addressed, they cannot be completely healed. Any progress will be temporary, at best. The "lost souls" Iktomi linked these people to are real, and they must be released and helped to return home to Heaven. Once this is done, the person in flesh can exercise her own free will to reject the belief system that is at issue. This is why people with faith in God can be healed when others who suffer from the same afflictions are not. By putting their faith in God and praying for Him to intervene in their lives, they are "dealing" with their challenges on a spiritual level. God and the Holy Spirit can help these lost souls to return home, as they are the spiritual experts and love these souls completely.

Archangel Michael explains the above concepts in the following manner:

> *"The modern medical experts of the world do not understand the human brain. There is a large part of the brain, the usage of which they cannot account, nor comprehend in its complexity. A significant part of the brain's function was designed specifically by God to hold Us, what different cultures refer to as 'The Holy Spirit', 'Holy Host,' 'Divine Presence,' 'Grandmothers and*

Grandfathers,' or 'Enlightened Beings from Heaven.' We pass into you and through this union you become one with Us, part of the Holy Host of Angels, just as it is for Us in Heaven. God specifically designed mankind to join with and hold Us, for as this world was once completely of Heaven, so must mankind be in its Creator's design 'completely of Heaven.'

Each person can in an instant create the conditions of Heaven inside themselves and we will come and be one with them in Love. Fear, anger, confusion, judgment, self-loathing, recrimination, hate, and selfishness are not of God. Such negative manifestations of God's gift of 'free will' are of the part of this world that has been turned from God. They are the consequences of a non-alignment with God and Heaven. When people choose to engage in such emotions, they are using their free will to tell Us of the Holy Spirit that We are not invited to join with them in body or spirit. As We are servants of God, We only follow the free will of all of God's children. This is the command of the Creator and is as much a law as that of 'gravity' for you. It is the way We are in Our state of being.

Those beings that have turned from God do the opposite. They seek to influence and control people by using such negative emotions to further draw people away from the peace and power that is joining with the Kingdom of Heaven. This is all the power that the dark truly has, to create through misdirection of 'free will' the absence of the state of 'close to God.' This is the first battle. When space is not made for Us in a mind, those that stand against God in spirit can fill this space with lost souls. Unlike Us in the Holy Spirit, such lost beings do not leave upon the command of their Host. Each person must recreate the conditions of Heaven inside themselves in order for them to leave and to regain their natural state of Heaven. This is the second battle. Each person must then keep this state of being with Heaven such that lost souls will not have a compatible home any longer. This is the third battle. These battles for control are never waged alone, as we stand with all of God's children in love and with all of the power of Heaven every step they allow."

Let us use Anna's story as an example. Like all children, when Anna was very small she was completely dependent upon her parents. Since the relationship between parents and children is naturally one that involves the issue of authority, it is critical that parents try to foster an environment in which the child understands that she is a child of God and that she has her free will. This occurs when a child understands that she is loved, respected, and safe. If, for whatever reason, a parent is not able to do this, it is very easy for Iktomi to create the conditions necessary to spiritually hurt the child by working through that parent.

Remember, the Holy Spirit teaches that every woman is born knowing that she has a covenant with God. Her soul understands that God may choose to use her body as a vessel to carry another soul into this world. It is critical that every child's body be respected. However, because of this covenant, females who are sexually violated are particularly at risk spiritually. If there is no intervention on her behalf, Iktomi has the "foundation he needs" to continue to chip away at her soul throughout her lifetime. If she is tricked into believing that she has not kept her covenant with God, her self-esteem is damaged in a way that this world understands to be beyond repair. Of course, as many cultures once understood and as the Holy Spirit has taught, with faith that God is here for her, prayer, and will, every woman can be completely restored and her wounds healed.

Anna's mother often drank alcohol and was angry when she would tell her daughter that she would be a "terrible mother" and that it would be "best if she never had children." Such words delivered under these conditions frightened Anna. Therefore, at such times Anna believed she was "at the mercy" of her mother. During these instances, Iktomi had the spiritual conditions he needed to be able to link her with many, many lost souls who also believed that they were "terrible mothers" or who had actually done "terrible things" to their child/children during their time here in flesh.

Imagine being in a crowd of hundreds of people who are walking west when you, alone, are trying to walk east. This is how difficult it is to exercise your free will when lost souls are pushing you in a particular direction. This is peer pressure to the extreme. In times of crisis, Anna would often do things that were inline with behavior one might expect from a "terrible mother" not because she was a bad person, but because she was being influenced by all of her "companions" in purgatory and hell. Also, in Anna's case, as she had a very protective nature, she was trying to "love" her unborn children by protecting them from what she believed to be the biggest threats of all ... herself and fathers that did not want to take responsibility for them.

Due to the disorienting affect that these lost souls have on a person, the first thing that the Holy Spirit asks us (my husband and me) to do when someone is brought to us for help or they send us to find someone, is referred to as "clearing," "cleaning," or "taking people home to Heaven." This concept traditionally existed in American Indian cultures, Celtic traditions, and elsewhere in the world. In the Bible most of the miracles Jesus performed involved "raising the dead" or releasing souls so they could return to His Father in Heaven.

According to the Archangel Michael, "*Ninety percent of all healing is taking people home to Heaven.*" This is what Anna felt when we prayed with her and her husband the first time they met with us. Our prayers literally brought Heaven to Anna and to those with her who no longer had a body and were "lost." Once these lost souls felt the Grace of God, they left Anna and went with the specific Angels who God sent to help them return home to Heaven. Once they were removed from Anna, the Holy Spirit could begin working directly on her body, mind, and soul.

Bear Feathers explained that Anna's body was "dying of cancer" not because God was punishing her for killing her children, but because she accepted responsibility for having made choices that were far from God when she, in fact, had not done so. Anna had been "up against" men who manipulated the situation with the intent to secure a particular outcome. These men knew that Anna did not have the financial resources to support a child. They threatened to leave her and not support the child financially or emotionally if she did not terminate her pregnancies. These threats, combined with the hypnosis used on her as a child by her mother, are what tricked Anna into believing that she did not have her free will to "go against the crowd" that Iktomi had linked her to over many years.

According to the Holy Spirit, Anna was physically ill because there was an imbalance between what her body, mind, and soul understood to be true. Anna's body was simply "doing its job" by making it obvious to her mind that this "imbalance" was serious and needed to be addressed. "*If this daughter [Anna] decides to look deeper into each of these instances she will find that she never truly made a 'choice' to take the life that Creator sent to her. She was put into situations where she was made to believe that she did not have free will. She did what she did because she believed she 'had to' not because she 'wanted to,'*" said Bear Feathers.

This Angel of the Lord explained that once Anna understood this, she could feel what was done to her and let go of the pain and fear she was holding surrounding her belief that she had made choices to take the lives of some of her children. Next, she could forgive those who hurt her and her children. Finally, she could forgive herself for decades of self-condemnation. Once this was done her body, mind, and soul would be healed. God would also grant the prayers of her children in Heaven by allowing her to feel their love for her. The fault in such instances lay with those responsible for manipulating the situation to get the desired outcome, not with the woman who was forced — physically or psychologically — to undergo the medical procedure.

He paused after explaining this to me. As I am sure was his intent, the wheels in my mind were turning. From what I had just witnessed and learned today, it was becoming clear to me that I, myself, needed to revisit my own experience with my "lost child." Although I thought of this child often and had asked God many, many times to forgive me for taking the life He had sent to me, I could feel that the Holy Spirit wanted me to "take another look" at the circumstances surrounding my first pregnancy. "*Daughter, when you are ready your mother will come to help you with your next healing. Go with Creator*," said Bear Feathers, before exiting my husband's body and returning to Heaven.

I had always loved children and had a fierce desire to protect those who, like my siblings and me, were being treated in a manner that was far from God. Indeed, my own brothers at times looked to me as a mother figure, and I worried about them as I imagined a mother would. All children have dreams, and the following were mine: a) I would become a nun and dedicate my life to relieving the suffering of the poor[51] or b) I would marry the husband God sent for me. He would be the only man I would "know" intimately and we would have six children together. I would become a doctor so I could travel around the world and help people to heal.[52]

Thankfully, I had always enjoyed school. The colorful classrooms, opportunity to learn, and the chance to receive positive feedback from adults was a blessing. I also appreciated the state-sponsored lunches and welcomed the escape from my dark home life. Most importantly, I believed what my teachers taught me — with hard work and dedication I, too, could have "the American dream" and bring it to my family.

At night, as I lay in my bed too afraid and filled with anxiety to sleep, I would talk to God. What I truly wanted was for my family to "get better." I came up with a plan. I would do well academically and work hard so that one day I would be able to afford to help my mother, father, and siblings.[53] Once my mother did not have to "worry" about money, I imagined she would embrace counseling, get the help she needed to learn how to love, and be the mother my brothers needed.

Looking back over this, it was still hard for me to understand how a young woman whose childhood dreams were to serve God and protect His children could end up in such a difficult situation. What had occurred with my "lost child" was so upsetting to me, that I told my husband-to-be about it on our third date. I could feel that he was a good person, and he was clearly intelligent. I wanted to be completely upfront with him. I was also hopeful that he could help me to understand the situation, as I was still very confused. "When I was 23-years-old, I became pregnant and had an abortion." This statement did not match with who I felt I was as a person. Nevertheless, like Anna, I had taken responsibility for it and accepted that it was a choice I had made.

As I began to pray for help, White Earth appeared before me. As always, her eyes were filled with compassion and love. Although I searched hard to find signs of judgment, there were none. I was ready to heal from this wound, but I was not sure where to begin. "*Daughter, a soul begins to die the moment it takes responsibility for something that was not its fault. Your son is here in Heaven with us. He would like you to know that he likes the name you chose for him. He would like you to know that he is sorry that people did bad things to you. He loves you, and he is here to tell you that it was not your fault,*" said White Earth.

This time, there were tears. I had "felt" all those years ago that my baby was a boy, and I had named him "Michael" after the Archangel Michael, the Angel I understood to be a Heavenly protector. I had even asked the nurse at the abortion clinic if I could keep the sonogram picture they took. Although my child was no bigger than a lima bean, he was my baby. I held onto this picture until it was taken from me.

Since I believed that I had been responsible for what had occurred, I did not believe that I "deserved" to mourn the loss of my son. All I knew was that I did not have a safe environment in which to raise him, I had no resources for medical care or child-care, and I was afraid of his father. As a child I promised God that my own children would be provided with a good, clean life and that they would not grow up hungry or afraid. I could not bear to have my son suffer the way I had. Because I could not figure out how to protect him, I "gave him back" to God.

By explaining to me that what had happened was not my fault, White Earth and my son were giving me permission to look and feel. I knew from my previous healing experience that it was important for me not to be afraid. The less fear I had the easier it would be for me to access my memories. As the Holy Spirit explained to me, part of the brain's "job" is to keep us functioning and alive. Therefore, it will not allow us access to memories that will overwhelm us or otherwise incapacitate us. If a person is "too afraid" during this process, it will take them longer to get their memories. In such a case, it is important for a person to pray for God to help her to overcome her fear so she can proceed with the healing process.

Although it had been almost a decade since the time of my first pregnancy and I now lived in a different state geographically, I still occasionally had nightmares about "running into" my unborn son's biological father.[54] The thought of such a scenario still caused chills to run up and down my spine. During this time in my life I had felt like a caged animal, not a human being with free will who had control over her body, mind, and soul. When I discovered I was pregnant, I called and visited people who I believed had the resources to help me. I was devastated when they refused to help and encouraged me to terminate my pregnancy. I had no credit, no support system, and no resources. I did not know how I would be able to protect my unborn child.

When I was small and needed help, I would often walk a block from our house to the local Catholic Church. With my eyes closed, I would open the Bible and point to a section. I would then open my eyes and read "my answer from Heaven." During this pregnancy I did the same thing many times. For a reason I did not understand at the time, my head was "feeling funny," I was unable to focus, and I was not able to feel Heaven as I usually could.[55] I did not understand until later that this man put drugs into my juice so that I would not "run" or be able to think clearly during this time.

One day after I had returned from the local church, "without my answer from Heaven" yet again, this man and his father were waiting for me at the door of the apartment where I lived. They pressured me to abort my child. They pointed out that I had no health insurance at the time and no money to pay for medical care for my child or myself. They knew that I had just quit my job, which is where I had met this man, because I believed the work environment was dangerous.

Despite the fact that their family was wealthy, they made it clear that they would not help financially if I chose to have the child. They also told me that they would not support adoption and that they would seek full custody if I chose to carry the child full term. As they talked, I felt sick to my stomach and terrified for my child. I did not believe that I could successfully "hide" my child from this family, and I knew that there was no way that I could afford — let alone win — a court battle against them.

The thought of having to surrender my child to such people was unbearable.

This man and his father then walked to the sidewalk where they spoke privately. When his father left, this man walked me to his car, drove me to the abortion clinic, paid for the procedure, stayed there to ensure it was "done," and drove me back to the apartment when it was completed. I remember feeling dazed and disoriented during the month after the procedure, and I would look at the sonogram picture many times each day. I often felt like crying, and my heart was very heavy with sorrow. This man raped me many times during the weeks that my body was recovering. By this point, I knew that nothing I said or did would stop him and I did not know how to get away.

It had been a long time since I had allowed myself to remember these details. However, White Earth was with me and I knew that it was safe to do so. Now I understood that it was not my fault, and that I had never been given the opportunity to make a choice regarding my child. My fear lessened and I was able to see things more clearly. In reviewing these details and being honest with myself about how terrified and heart-broken I was at the time, it was easy for me to understand that I had not been given the chance to exercise my free will. To also understand the effects that the chemicals he put into my body had on my mind, body, and soul truly helped to set me free.

"*Creator sends life when there is great love or great need. In your case, Daughter, you were fighting a battle. Many things were being done to you that were far from Creator. You were beginning to lose faith in yourself and in Creator. Your son came as a gift from Creator — a sign to remind you that Heaven is with you and that you are not alone*," said White Earth. This Angel explained that in instances of great need, God often sends life as a means of helping to preserve and heal the body, mind, and soul of the woman who is being hurt by the impure intent and actions of another.

"*In your case, you knew that something was very wrong, but Iktomi used chemicals, violence, and lies to keep you confused. Your son loves you very much. He has been part of your circle of loved ones for a long time. He prayed hard for Creator to give him the opportunity to help you in this way*," said White Earth. This Angel of the Lord proceeded to teach me that all life is sent to this world from Heaven. As it lives and grows inside the mother's womb, she is literally a "vessel" that God has chosen to use to "hold a piece of Heaven" for the world. Every moment that she is not afraid, this little soul (or very big soul in some cases) is working hard to repair the damage Iktomi, and those who served as vessels for him, did to the woman and to help her keep her connection to Creator.

"*Even if the woman does not carry her child to term, for whatever reason, the soul [child] has often already done what Creator sent him or her to do by the time it leaves this earth and returns to Heaven*," said White Earth. She explained that a woman who has experienced a "miscarriage" or an "abortion" is still a mother to the soul who prayed for God to send him or her to this world. "*It is hard for a woman who has 'lost' a child not to experience a sense of grief. However, once she has mourned, it is important for her to understand that nothing was truly lost. She is still a mother. Her child is serving Creator, helping her, and loving her from Heaven.*"

These concepts brought me joy. My son had understood that he was a product of rape, but he had come to help me understand that Heaven was with me. As White Earth taught me, "*Why does Creator sometimes send life in a situation of rape? Because sending life to a woman, even for a short time, is one of the greatest ways that Creator can communicate love. A child of rape is not a child of violence, but Creator's transforming such violence into love, itself.*"

To describe my son as "courageous" seemed to me to be an understatement! My son was still with me, and I needed only to decide whether I wanted God to give me another opportunity to carry him into this world. According to White Earth, my son Michael was happy serving God from Heaven. However, he would be honored to return again to this earth through my body if I wished. As I was "the mother," the decision was mine to make from his perspective.

I could feel my son around me. He felt wonderful, familiar, and strong. I realized from this experience that he had most likely been the soul helping to carry me, and all of the pieces of my broken heart, all of these years. I knew that nothing would make my son happier at that moment than to have his "mama" healed. I was ready to give to God that which was not mine to carry.

White Earth asked me to bring her a braid of sweet grass, lie down on my bed, and pray. She explained to me that both my American Indian ancestors and my European ancestors traditionally considered this winter-hardy, vanilla-scented grass sacred, and it was used to help spiritually and physically cleanse a person, room, or home. As I prayed, I felt cool sensations in my abdomen, heart, and chest. My head and limbs felt heavy. As this Angel "worked" she talked to me about what God was instructing her and the Corn Maidens to remove, repair, and replace.

White Earth explained to me that when something traumatic happens to a person and she is filled with fear, Iktomi is able to cause injury to cells in the body for as long as that fear is present. After the violence or the threat of violence is over, the injured cells remain. If the body is scanned from Heaven, these injured parts literally look like dark bubbles and are spread throughout the bloodstream, organs, bones, and tissue. Each time the blood circulates through the body, whereas it once flowed freely and uninterrupted, it must now "deal" with these dark bubbles by going over or around them. Iktomi understands that when this occurs, the brain and other parts of the body are yet again, reminded of the traumatic event. White Earth explained to me that part of what I was feeling was the removal of these "bubbles."

Next, my Heavenly Mother reminded me that once I was healed from this, God and the Holy Spirit could use me as a vessel to help heal other women and girls who Iktomi had hurt, tricked, and confused in this manner. After she had gathered the negative "energy," which was stored in my body and soul as a result of this experience, and released the lost souls who Iktomi had "linked" to me, White Earth picked up the braid of sweet grass from a side table.

"*Daughter, We [the Holy Spirit] would ask that you watch carefully. Your Father in Heaven would like to make sure that you understand, once and for all, what you were up against during this battle.*" As she lit the tip of the sweet grass braid, it burst into flames and curled into the shape of a large, black spider. This surprised me, as sweet grass normally burns gently before the flame dies, leaving columns of sweet-scented smoke to rise from the blades of grass. "*Daughter, your Father in Heaven asks that you find it in your heart to forgive Iktomi and those who allowed themselves to be used as his vessels.*"

"Oh, the comfort, the inexpressible comfort of feeling safe with a person, having neither to weigh thought nor measure words, but pouring them all right out, just as they are, chaff and grain together, certain that a faithful hand will take and sift them, keep what is worth keeping, and with a breath of kindness, blow the rest away."

(Shoshone Indian Saying)

Chapter Four

Mary Magdalene and Archangel Michael

My daughter, "virtue" is a state of being created by action and faith. A woman cannot always control what the dark chooses to put in front of her. It is how she responds to what is placed in front of her that determines her virtue, not whether or not someone has physically entered her body or forced her to do things to their body.

Mary Magdalene

One day, shortly after the Holy Spirit asked us to begin regular prayer sessions for the public, "Bear Feathers" told me that Heaven had something important to share with me. I was speechless as my spiritual father told me that he and my spiritual mother were, in fact, known to the world by different names. He told me that God had deemed it time for them to appear to me as the Archangel Michael and the Angel Mary Magdalene. He told me that Bear Feathers would continue to pray for me from Heaven, as he had great love for me. He explained to me that my mother had experienced life here on this earth as "Mary Magdalene" and later in the Americas as "White Earth," so her "feeling" would remain the same.

Truthfully, this information left me feeling very disoriented. I had learned to trust again because God sent His love to me through "Bear Feathers" and "White Earth." It took me days to make this adjustment in my mind and to let go of my impulse to be upset by this sudden "change." The Archangel Michael explained to me that God had determined that it was time for them to "*gather their own*" and begin the process of returning this world to Heaven. He told me that there was no limit to what God could do through any of His children here on earth, and that now was the time to allow my mother in Heaven to continue helping me with my healing process. It was time to "step it up," so to speak.

The following day God graced me with my first visit from White Earth in the form that was familiar to much of the world — Mary Magdalene. I remembered a little bit about her story from the Bible, as well as from a portrayal of her that I had once seen in a movie. This movie had been shown to me in a Catechism class when I was in my early teens. I remembered that the portrayal of her had upset me so much that I had stormed out of the classroom, yet at the time I did not understand why my reaction had been so extreme. Sure enough, when this Angel of the Lord came to speak with me, her "feeling" remained the same, as I had been told it would.

"*Daughter, you have sensed from the beginning that I understand your experiences and can help you heal from them. The world does not understand my story. The dark worked very hard to distort the truth. Yet, I kept returning to this world, as God willed it to be. It is time that you hear my story,*" said Mary Magdalene, as she proceeded to share the details of her life.

"*I was born in a small village near Galilee. My family was considered to be very religious and well respected. One day a group of bandits raided my village. I was eleven-years-old at the time. My sister escaped, but I did not. They did terrible things to my body and left me for dead. When these men had finished with me, I made my way to my home. Yet, when I saw my family, they would not look me in the eye. I did not understand what I had done wrong. As nobody in my village would help me, I left to seek help to heal from what had been done to me. But everywhere I went, the same thing happened,"* said Mary Magdalene, wiping the tears from her eyes.

Although I still had trouble feeling for myself, I most certainly felt for this Angel. I could picture a young, vulnerable girl — hungry, battered, terrified, and traumatized — wandering from village to village looking for somebody who had the wisdom and compassion to help make her whole again. I knew that child very well. I knew that child better than I wanted to admit to myself.

"*One day a woman in Galilee opened her home to me. She offered me food and a bed. After I had a night of rest, she told me that she would continue to feed me if I would lie with the men and women who patronized her brothel. I was very hungry and had no place else to go. For the next ten years I was forced to lie with between nine and thirteen men and women a day. However, every night I would stare outside my window and pray to God to ask for His forgiveness and His help. One day, I heard a great deal of noise on the street. I went to the brothel door to see what the excitement was about. There was a man who was surrounded by a crowd of people. This man left the crowd and walked over to me. He got down on His knees before me and told me that I had the most beautiful soul He had ever seen. This man was Jesus, and from that moment on my life was forever changed,"* said Mary Magdalene.

Mary proceeded to tell me that Jesus's unconditional love for her and faith in God, combined with her faith and will to heal, allowed the Holy Spirit and individual Angels of the Lord to use Jesus's body as a vessel to help her to understand her life, forgive those who had hurt her, forgive herself, and heal. I marveled at the faith it must have taken for this young girl to continue praying to God through so many years of torture, and the strength it must have taken to overcome the judgment and condemnation she received from her community. I was grateful that God had sent such a powerful answer to her prayers.

Mary explained to me that during the time that she was here on this earth more than 2,000 years ago, a woman was considered "unclean," even if what was done to her body was clearly "against her will." After a girl or woman was raped, as occurred in her case, the community would shun her and treat her as if she was "less than human" because they believed she was no longer virtuous. This gave people the "excuse" they wanted to justify treating such women in ways that were against God. However, God had sent Heaven to release her from the lies the world had told her and to teach her the truth.

"*My daughter, if there is a woman who has not experienced rape, as Heaven understands rape to be, then I can say to you that is a lucky woman. However, whether or not she has experienced such a violation is not a measurement of her virtue. It is how she responds to what is done to her that determines virtue. Does she try to find love and forgiveness? That is the question,*" said Mary Magdalene. She explained that the dark has "*waged a war against women*" and knows that attacking "*what is sacred*" is the best way to ensure that women become confused and believe they are lost to God.

And what did this Angel of the Lord do with this wisdom from Heaven while she was here on earth? The Archangel Raphael summed up her response as follows: "*Who do you think brought the women to Jesus so they could heal? Galilee was a small place where many, many of the people there had hurt her. Yet, she rose each day to help such people to understand that God loved them unconditionally and they were forgiven for their sins.*" He delivered this information to me during a conversation we were having regarding my initial hesitancy and fear regarding sharing the details of what had happened to me in my life with the world. At that time I could not understand how I could possibly help God to resurrect souls by using my "imperfect" life as an example. However, Heaven had suggested I do so and I had come to trust the Holy Spirit completely.

It was obvious to me that the various Angels that God sent to help me had a deep respect for Mary. Even the Archangel Michael considered it a "*great gift from God*" that Mary was able to come to help me understand my life, and to teach me about the tricks the dark and this world play on women. I was even able to feel her energy clearly when she first came to me as White Earth at a time when I was most afraid, "blocked," and numb. Her strength and proximity to God was undeniable to me.

It was at this time that Mary issued us a request from the Holy Spirit. She requested that we hold two prayer sessions each week, and that one of these sessions be designated solely for women and their children, if they wished to bring them. She stated that Heaven would use my husband's body, and at times my body, as vessels to help those present. She reminded me that when a person loves selflessly, he or she is in a state of being that is compatible with Heaven and, therefore, the Holy Spirit can enter them and use them as vessels to help others. So, in fact, at times the Holy Spirit would be using each of the people in the room to help others in the room and others around the world.

She explained to me that in order for a woman to heal, she needed a safe place from which to do so. "*With our love, faith, and prayers, Daughter, we will create this place of safety for them. God has willed that it be so. He is coming for them as He came for me and for you*," said Mary, her hands clasped together as if in prayer. I could feel her excitement and her joy.

Another Angel appeared to provide more details. He presented himself as a Native American warrior, but he did not offer his name. He explained that it was "*only important to know him as a humble servant of Creator*." He explained that the Plains Indians had "lance carriers." These warriors were not only physically strong, but they were also specially trained in "spiritual warfare." They not only carried very tall, sharp lances, they also knew how to fight with the strongest weapons in existence — love, faith, forgiveness, and prayer.

Traditionally, at least one lance carrier stood at the door of the medicine tipi or ceremonial site while a healing was taking place. Some of these ceremonies or prayer sessions lasted for days, and in some cases even weeks. Throughout this time, these lance carriers used their prayers and love to keep the space around the medicine person/people and the person/people receiving healing from Heaven, both physically and spiritually pure. They used their intent and spiritual wisdom to keep Iktomi at bay. They also prayed for Creator to help any lost souls that were with the medicine person or the "patient" to return home to Heaven. This Angel requested that one of my brothers serve as the lance carrier for the women's prayer group. He was to be seated by the doorway at the back of the room and "*do what he came to this world to do*."

One evening soon after we began these prayer sessions for women, I received a telephone call from Laurie[viii], a woman who was suffering from cervical cancer and extreme lower back pain. She had heard about the weekly prayer group from an old friend, a woman who called her to tell her that "the Angels" had cured her of Lyme's disease. As Laurie found this hard to believe, she arranged to meet with her friend at a local café. Sure enough, Laurie could see that her friend's hands, once nearly frozen into a twisted position, were now "perfectly normal" and she noticed that her friend seemed "more loving and less fearful and angry."

Laurie told me that her friend had handed her a piece of paper with our telephone number written on it, and asked her to "promise to call." Her friend had explained that these prayer groups were free-of-charge, that all were welcome, and that

---

[viii] "Laurie's" name has been changed, along with some of the details of her situation, in order to protect her privacy.

nobody was asked about their religious affiliation or whether or not they even had one. She explained that anyone who came was asked to sit and pray for those in need. At times these sessions lasted up to five hours or longer, as the Holy Spirit stayed until the last person was given the opportunity to sit before them. She had explained to Laurie that everyone was free to leave at anytime, but said she was often "surprised" at how much time had passed when she finally gathered her belongings to leave and glanced at her watch.

"So, I am not sure how this works, but I am calling like I promised her I would. I could really use some help. I have been to medical doctors and holistic doctors. My insurance will no longer cover any of my treatments. I am nearly out of money. I have run through my savings, and I am sorry to say that there has been no improvement," said Laurie with a sigh. She explained to me that most days her lower back pain was so extreme she had to spend the entire day in bed, and her most recent medical tests showed that the cancer cells in her body were still growing.

The Holy Spirit had taught me that it is important to treat the "root" of a problem and not simply the symptoms that manifest as "sickness" or "disease" over time. Therefore, I began to ask Laurie to share some of the details of her life. White Earth had taught me that the affects of rape often manifest in a woman's body in three ways: breast cancer, cervical cancer, and extreme lower back pain. As Laurie had two of the three, it seemed clear to me that the cause of her illness was sexual abuse. However, when I told her this she paused.

"I don't see how that could be possible. You see, I married my first love when I was 19-years-old and we stayed together for twenty-four years. We divorced last year and have three children together," said Laurie. She told me that the divorce had been very difficult for her. "He left me for another woman, and no, I don't have any idea how long the affair had been going on," said Laurie. I could hear her crying quietly as I told her that Heaven was here to help her. I asked her to pray for Creator to heal her, and I told her the date and time of the next group prayer session. She thanked me for my time and told me she would be there.

When I hung up the telephone, Mary requested that I find "*something to write with and on.*" She asked me if I understood what "rape" is. Although Heaven had taught me that I had not made the choices I believed I had made, I had to admit that I did not fully understand what the Holy Spirit meant when they told me that "*what happened to me in my life was not my fault*" and that I was "*pure in the eyes of Heaven.*" I certainly liked hearing them tell me these things, but I could remember many instances in my life, including my first experience with a "boyfriend" when I was seventeen, that were confusing to me. In such instances I knew with certainty that I had not "given my consent." However, because I knew the person who was "doing the taking," he told me he loved me, and he denied that he had done anything wrong immediately following the incident; my mind had accepted that I "must have made a choice to be there."

Mary sat patiently as I rattled off a definition of rape. "Rape is a violent, sexual act that happens between people, at least one of whom does not give her or his permission." As it was unusual for Heaven to suggest that I get a pen and paper, I got ready to write. "*It is very simple, Daughter. From the perspective of Heaven rape is 'have to' instead of 'want to,' and there are many, many scenarios the dark has designed to trick a woman into believing that she gave her consent when she, in fact, most certainly did not,*" said this Angel of the Lord, before pausing to give me the time I needed to finish writing the words she brought from Heaven.

"*And if a woman did not give her consent, if she did not exercise her free will to make a decision to share her body with another, then the incident — no matter how horrific, no matter how perfectly designed to manipulate and confuse — does not touch her soul. She remains pure in the eyes of Heaven, and she has not broken her covenant with God,*" said Mary.

I continued to write without looking up from my notebook. Was Mary saying what I thought she was saying? Was it true that all the "taking" I had experienced in my life did not "count against me" from God's perspective? Was it true that God had designed such a perfectly fair system that there were "no short-cuts" for any of His children? Was she telling me that a woman's soul remained pure even if she could not physically fight her way out of a dangerous situation, and even if she was being manipulated but did not understand this at the time? I could feel my vision beginning to blur as I finished writing down her words. I did not look up from what I had written. I could not look up from what I had written. I did not want to cry.

Why had nobody — no doctor, religious person, counselor, or female authority figure — ever told me this? I had spent years of my life carrying the pain and fear that goes hand-in-hand with believing that I had disappointed God and myself. I had come to a place in my life where I no longer believed that I was worthy. Each of these experiences had left me feeling like a part of my heart and soul had been changed, forever. I believed that there was nothing I could do to "heal" any of these wounds, as I could not "go backwards" and undo what had already been done. Once my body had been taken, I believed that my virtue had also been taken.

I knew that I did not like what these people had done to me, but as I did not believe that there was anything I could do about it at the time, I tried to love through it. As I had not physically beaten them, tried to kill them, or successfully prosecuted them, I had learned to see myself from the world's perspective. I must have somehow exercised my free will to make these "choices," or I must have been so "stupid" that I somehow brought these situations upon myself. Either way, I had accepted that it was my fault and that something about me was bringing these scenarios upon myself.

"*So, this Daughter whom we sent to you just now, the one this world calls 'Laurie' — you noticed that her body holds sickness that is often caused by the act of rape. Yet, she worked very hard in her life to be a 'good woman' and do the 'right' thing. She worked hard to be the 'perfect' wife and mother. She told you, herself, that she married her first love and stayed with him until he left her recently. She is speaking the truth. So how is it that her body holds such sickness?*" asked Mary. If Laurie's intent had been pure, and she married a man she loved, then it did not seem to me like her own actions or intent could be the cause of her sickness.

"*This Daughter was honorable. She loved her husband greatly. Yet, what happens when one person in a marriage is sincere and the other is not? What is the affect on a woman's soul when the soul she commits to is not committed to her? I have just taught you that when a man or a woman manipulates a situation to create 'have to' instead of 'want to' in order to gain access to another person's body it is rape. A person can be raped with or without a piece of paper that says she is married,*" said Mary.

This Angel of the Lord went on to explain that Laurie's ex-husband was someone that this world would consider to be a "catch." He was older than Laurie, a locally celebrated athlete, and he came from a "good family." He had known Laurie's family and believed that she would be the kind of woman he could "bring home to his parents." He knew that she was a "good girl" that was "saving herself" for marriage. Society had taught him that the outcome, not the process, is what mattered most in life for a man in his position. As his father often told him when he was small, "Son, show me a good loser and I will show you a loser."

He made the decision to seduce Laurie knowing that by doing

so he could achieve the outcome he desired. He used alcohol to "loosen her up" and "had sex" with her in the back of his car during one of their dates to a drive-in movie. Afterwards, as she was crying, he told her how "great" it was that she "decided to make love" with him that night. He told her that he loved her and that what just happened would "bring them closer." This is something he had done before to other girls, so he knew it would "work" with her. Laurie was confused, as she did not remember having any intention of being sexual with him.

"*From Heaven's perspective, this daughter was clearly raped. However, this man and society gave her only two options to choose from, neither of which was true. By using alcohol and manipulation, this man created 'have to' instead of 'want to.' However, 'rape' was not one of the options that Laurie was given the opportunity to choose from. As she was taught by the world that rape 'looked differently' than what she had just experienced, what just happened had to be either 'love,' or she was a 'whore,'*" said Mary.

As Laurie knew that she was not the type of person who would share her body with another person "lightly," he had "said all of the right things," and he was celebrated within the community, her mind determined that it must have been "love," and that "sharing" her body with him was a "decision" she had made. Once her mind accepted this, she proceeded in the relationship as a virtuous woman in love would — she gave him everything and created a world around him. This Angel of the Lord explained that Laurie's soul understood that rape had just occurred. However, her mind and body were tricked and confused by the chemicals and the manipulation. As there was an imbalance between what her body, mind, and soul understood to be true, the seed for sickness was planted.

"*Shortly after this occurred, this man proposed marriage to Laurie and they were legally joined. Throughout their union he was unfaithful to her many, many times. He also asked her to do things with him sexually that made her uncomfortable, yet she comforted herself by telling herself that these things were done 'in love' and 'under the sanctity of marriage.' So, even though Laurie was honorable in her commitment to her husband, she was actually being raped over and over again. She experienced the trauma that occurs with repeated rapes, and he continued his lies and manipulation of her,*" explained Mary, without even a hint of judgment in her eyes for either of the souls involved. As Heaven had taught me many times, "*only God can judge, as only He understands what is in the heart of His children*" and clearly this Angel had mastered this teaching long ago during her time here in flesh.

Mary taught me that in order to help Laurie, it was important to help her to understand the truth and to help her to feel everything that goes along with it, as painful as this would be. Once she had the courage and faith to do this, Heaven would come and remove the disease and any other damage that occurred as a result of her experiences. She encouraged me to share parts of my healing process with her, as this would help Laurie to understand that she was not alone in her suffering and that with God, all things could be completely healed.

This Angel from Heaven then asked me to encourage Laurie to forgive the souls that hurt her. She said that although many people in this world see forgiveness as weakness, there is nothing but strength and the power of God in this action. "*Daughter, 'forgiveness' does not mean that you liked what someone did to you that was against God or that you 'approve' of it. It means that you hold nothing against them. You have 'given it to God.' The act of forgiveness is incredibly important spiritually, as it severs the link that fear, anger, and hate allow Lucifer to create between souls,*" explained Mary. She reminded me that although there was rarely justice from the perspective of this world, "*God's process is a perfect circle.*"

"*Most importantly, We would have her understand that*

the actions and intent of this man did not — and does not — diminish her or her love in any way. For more than two decades her prayers, faith, and love helped this man, her children, and her to feel God's Grace. Heaven honors her for finding love in her heart for someone whose actions toward her were often far from God. Once she completes God's process, we would suggest to her that she begin to pray for her soul mate, as he is praying for her," said this Angel of the Lord.

Mary explained that a "soul mate" is a soul that is a part of your "circle of love" from Heaven. At times such souls agree to come to this world to serve God at the same time in order to help each other to realize their purpose here. Such souls, when they find one another here on this earth, have the potential to help each other to get very close to Heaven very quickly. They bring with them to this world their love for one another from Heaven.

"*This daughter's [Laurie's] soul mate is here on this earth and he is praying for God to intervene in his life. He would benefit greatly from everything that she will learn throughout the process of healing from her life*, explained Mary. She reminded me that although God does not like when his children suffer and it is important to help those who are in such a state, there is no experience that cannot be overcome and used to help another. As the Archangel Michael has said, "*Everything that Lucifer does to a soul can be turned against him.*"

Now that I had enough information and understanding to help Heaven answer Laurie's prayers, this Angel of the Lord returned to the topic of this world's view of "rape." I wanted to know how it was that the world's definition and understanding of rape was so much more complicated than Heaven's. It seemed that a woman could not get any "closure," at least from the world's perspective, unless she successfully prosecuted her rapist in a court of law. Yet, the exact same case might be successfully prosecuted in one state or part of the world and "lost" in another, and countless women choose to "opt out" of the legal process because they are unable to psychologically cope with "going back there" again. Mary Magdalene explained the following:

> *"There are two kinds of laws. There are laws of God and those of man. Those of man depend upon the time, history, country, culture, religion, political system, country system, people's willingness to enforce the law, and people's perceptions. Therefore, the laws of man are subjective and they are irrelevant to what is real.*
>
> *People impose law in an attempt to control and to direct. It is a political tool more than anything else. You can achieve the end result through not making law, making a law badly, making a law well, or choosing whether or not to enforce it. Because it is a political tool, any of these conditions may change at any time. Therefore, they are not real. They are only temporary. They are only relevant for a particular woman for a particular place at a particular time.*
>
> *So, the 'world law' has received a sanction through global treaty that rape as a tool of war in genocide is a crime and, therefore, against the law. But this does not say very much because you still have to establish what 'rape' is for each woman, for each place and each time."*

If this was the state of mankind's legal systems, then it seemed to me that women and those who loved them needed some help from Heaven to be able to determine for themselves what had or had not been done to them so that they could heal. They needed a definition of rape that was real and consistent, no matter the country, political system, religious affiliation, or societal opinions on the topic.

According to Heaven, there is a way for every woman to completely heal from anything that the dark manages to "throw at her." Yet, if the world's definition of rape varies so greatly and the tricks to convince a woman that she gave her consent have historically been difficult to detect, I did not know how a woman would be able to understand which incidents in her life "qualified" as rape and which did not. How would she be able to determine the incidents, relationships, or experiences from which she needed to heal? Mary sat patiently as I finished recording her words. I looked up to see this Angel nod her head in understanding. Mary continued with her teaching:

"In seeking the way to heal those who came to this earth in female form, you must address what rape is, itself, away from what it may mean to a legal system, a culture, a religion, or a society. Remember, God created all women with a covenant with Him. It is this covenant with God that is at issue first, and a woman's feelings about that. Rape is 'have to' not 'want to.' It is upon this frame that you can build back the heart of a woman who has suffered and whose soul is in pain and seeking to heal.

Different societies may say 'have to' is good. You may be seen as honorable, such as when a husband is chosen for you. In some societies this is the only way a woman can be considered honorable. But this does not change the effect on her soul and her feelings. 'Have to' is not free-will; 'want to' is free- will.

We will build a matrix — a questionnaire — that each woman can use to understand each relationship they have had and whether it is rape or not, and if so, how she can heal from that. This matrix is universal. The outcome may or may not result in what is considered a crime of rape in the country at issue.

The difficulty with rape is that the entire relationship and all the factors above come into effect. We are seeking to strip those things out and analyze the encounter from only the perspective of Heaven. From the perspective of what it does to the soul. We will use the term 'spiritual rape' so there is less confusion."

Mary returned my focus to what had occurred to Laurie in her life. She told me that she wanted me to pay very close attention to the women the Holy Spirit would be bringing to the prayer groups. She reminded me that God would be "sending His daughters," and she said that such an opportunity for Heaven to work directly in this manner with His children was a great blessing. "*Make no mistake, Daughter, we are going directly into battle to help return them to everything that they are.*"

This Angel of the Lord explained that Laurie was far from alone in her experience. Mary stated that many, many women throughout this world had, in fact, married their abusers — some in an attempt to try to legitimize what occurred and "make Holy" that which they understood God made to be sacred, others because they were tricked and did not understand that the intent of the other was not pure, others because the person treated them as their own caregivers had when they were small and, therefore, they believed that such treatment was love, and others still because they wanted to be seen as honorable and virtuous in the eyes of their community. Mary paused to make sure that she had my full attention before continuing:

"*No relationship of any kind entitles anyone to a woman's body, mind, or soul. There is no place for such control by a man or woman over another. If a woman is with a person who has raped her at one time, then it is very unusual for her to ever subsequently give her consent in that relationship, as fear is now a factor in subsequent encounters.*

If a woman has been raped by others, then similar

gestures made by another person may lead to great terror and little more would be required for that woman to give up and stop fighting. In other words, the effect of these types of rape are cumulative in nature and the filter through which a woman sees herself forever changes, unless she understands.

And then once they understand, they can hold their sorrow close to their heart, but it no longer holds them. It no longer keeps them away from God or who they are. So, rejection of that which is 'of man' and embracing what is truly free-will or not is in no way a legal analysis. It is giving women that which is theirs — a true freedom to 'want to' and never to 'have to.'"

(The following is an Encounter Questionnaire from Heaven to help each woman to determine for herself, whether or not a sexual encounter qualifies as "spiritual rape," which has the affect of an assault on her soul. Please circle "yes" or "no.")

Definition of rape: *Any physical contact or verbal contact of a sexual nature that is directed toward a woman without her wanting to have such contact.*

1. Was violence used? YES or NO
   (Heaven's definition of "violence" is as follows: "Any physical contact or verbal contact designed to frighten or threaten a woman to comply.")
2. Was any threat of violence used? YES or NO
   (Please apply the above definition of violence when answering this question. Violence or threat of violence can be physical touching, force, emotional yelling, using threatening tones of voice, making threatening gestures, using threatening words about the woman or those about whom she cares, or using/threatening to use

any weapon or anything that the woman believes can be used as a weapon. This includes blocking her exit, isolating her so she cannot get away, and restraining her in any way physically, emotionally, or mentally. If any of these things were done in order to produce a sexual encounter — then it was a rape — as the woman was responding to these things. Each of the above listed things influences a person's free will, and without a woman giving her free-will the encounter is rape.)

3. Was lying or any kind of deception used in order to induce a woman to give artificial consent or in order to put her in a place where the above violence or threat of violence could be used in order to rape? YES or NO
4. Did an authority figure, such as a mother, father, uncle, aunt, grandparent, husband, extended family member, religious figure, or societally accepted leader (such as a doctor, lawyer or teacher) use his/her position of power to make the sexual contact "have to" and not "want to"? YES or NO
5. Was the woman, through her circumstances, deprived of sustenance (food, water, shelter, sleep, or the necessities of life in order to create "have to" instead of "want to"?) YES or NO
6. Were artificial stimulants given to the woman such as drugs, alcohol, etc. to create "have to" instead of "want to"? YES or NO
7. Was hypnosis, brainwashing by a group, or societally sanctioned abuse used to create "have to" instead of "want to"? YES or NO

   (According to Heaven, this question also addresses physical changes made to the body, such as initiations, or other forms of mass hypnosis. For example, if a woman cannot bear children or be married without being vaginally mutilated, this is considered "mass hypnosis" as the woman is provided with no choice but to endure this if she wants to be considered a "good" woman.)

8. Was she in a relationship with anyone where her wishes were not respected as to whether she wished to engage in sexual conduct or not? YES or NO

"Humankind has not woven the web of life.
We are but one thread within it.
Whatever we do to the web, we do to ourselves.
All things are bound together.
All things connect."

(Chief Seattle — Duwamish Indian)

Chapter Five

We Are All Connected

God made women perfect and holy, and no act of violence by any being against them can ever change their sacred nature as created beings. Once women understand this, and understand that there were consequences to falsely accepting the lie that they were somehow changed away from God, than they are healed and free.

Mary Magdalene

The women's prayer group that Mary requested we hold each week felt very different to me than the prayer group that was open to men, women, and children. Not only did the energy from Heaven feel slightly different, the fact that Mary came to teach many of the lessons made them incredibly powerful. At the times that she would share parts of her story, there was rarely a dry eye in the room. Women who were otherwise poised, contained, or even distant during their daily lives, would connect to parts of her story, even if they could not yet feel their own pain or see themselves in her.

It was clear to me from watching the reactions of the women who attended these sessions and witnessing the miracles that occurred as a result, that all of God's daughters benefited greatly from experiencing this Angel's wisdom, love, and compassion. She was their spiritual mother, too. Our hearts all seemed to be asking the same questions: Are we worthy of the Creator's love anymore? Did these things that were done to us or through us really change us forever? Is there any goodness left inside of us? Does the Creator really love us? And for many of us, do we have to remain here on this earth anymore?

According to the Holy Spirit (the Grandmothers and the Grandfathers), the definition of suffering is: "*When a person cannot feel God because of something that they, themselves, are doing or something that others are doing to them.*" It was becoming obvious to me that I was not alone in my suffering, as these warriors had also experienced moments, or long periods in their lives, when they also could not feel their Creator. Although I had certainly not been blind to the pain of others in my life, I had come to believe over time that I had "failed" more than most people, and that most women were a lot happier or more fulfilled than I was.

My mother in flesh and her family had always taught me to "keep quiet" about the things that happened in our home and to "keep my head down" while enduring abuse. I was physically beaten or sexually assaulted when they discovered that I had truthfully answered the questions my teachers at school asked me. No, I had not eaten dinner the night before or breakfast that morning. Yes, my uncle touched me "down there." And yes, my grandmother hit me with the belt and that is why I have these bruises.

When these beatings occurred, they became more severe if I fought back, tried to run, or tried to scream for help. Over time, I figured out that if I could manage to stand still, go limp, and show very little emotion, the bouts of abuse seemed to come to an end more quickly. Sadly, I tried to numb the horror that I felt by adjusting my mind set so that such incidents would seem less terrifying and almost "routine" in nature. As I looked back and remembered these things, I felt very guilty — almost humiliated — by my response.

Thankfully, the Archangel Michael came to help me to heal

from this. This Angel explained the following to me, "*There are three responses that a person can have when in trauma or great fear. Fight, flight, or freeze. The one that a woman implements in her life — until she is healed — will be the one that she was 'allowed' to have in her household when she was a child.*"

This Angel explained that if a little girl fought and her abuser reacted by lessening the pressure, then that would be the response that she was likely to carry forward in her life. If she could flee, and such movement helped to relieve the pressure from her abuser, then that would be the response that she carried forward. If the family structure supported "freezing," then she was conditioned, or trained, to respond to an assault in that manner.

As my mind processed this information, many things began to shift inside of me. I shed many tears — a river for all of the times I should have cried but did not understand that I had the right to do so. To know that I was not responsible and that there was a physiological reason why I responded the way that I did helped to release more memories and emotions. Even though I "froze" during the majority of my assaults, according to Heaven my response did not mean that I liked, wanted, or deserved what others had done to me in my life.

This explanation matched perfectly with the way I had felt — literally frozen in terror. I could remember times when I wanted to scream, and I physically could not do so. I had been confused and sickened by this response. I wondered why I was not more like the female action heroes that pulled out a weapon, or executed karate moves to bring their attackers to the ground. Instead of fighting back in these ways, I had done what the women in my family taught me to do. If I was physically backed into a corner and could not talk or think my way out of the situation, I endured in silence in hopes of getting out alive and in one piece.

After the assault was finished — if I even understood that

it had been an assault — I would gather myself together, blame myself for not having been smart enough to avoid the attack, and pray for forgiveness. In the times that I did not understand that I had been assaulted, I would work hard to turn the encounter into "love." Needless to say, these responses confused me, and I could find no self-help book or counselor that had been able to give me an explanation that would help to relieve my shame. No matter what the person had done to me, the thought of hurting them "back" caused me great pain. It had always been this way for me.

However, thankfully and by the Grace of God, Heaven had answers. As Mary explained, "*To a woman's mind, 'allow' is the same thing as 'cooperate.' The dark understands this very well. It is important for a woman to separate the 'allow' from what actually happened. That is the trick.*"

The word "cooperate" hit the nail on the head for me. The times that I had not physically fought back or successfully avoided the assaults, I had felt like I had "cooperated" and that I was, therefore, responsible in someway for what had occurred. Because I believed I was responsible, I did not believe I "deserved" to pray for God to remove the pain or to protect me from what was happening. In some cases, when I knew my attacker, I tried to legitimize what had occurred. Although I could not control what was often done to me, I had always understood that sharing the body with another is a sacred thing. Because I could not control what was being done, I felt like a failure as a woman. As I believed I somehow was at fault — even though I could not logically figure out how that would be the case — I would try harder in those instances to be kind to the person who had taken from me.

My mind went back to the times in college when people had made fun of me because I was "different." Unlike the majority of the other students, I did not have a support system, and I was only able to afford to attend the university because I received scholarships, minority grants, and work-study jobs. I was very grateful to be there, and I did not take my education for granted. While other students were "cheating," I was trying very hard to master many of the basics that my struggling public school in California had not had the resources to teach me. Even though I did what I could to disguise the obvious — by lightening my hair and focusing on my European ancestry when I was asked about my ethnicity — it was clear that I was a native woman.[56]

As my freshman year in college began, so did my introduction to a world that looked polished and sophisticated on the outside but was soiled and rotten on the inside. Chills went up and down my spine as I remembered the time that I believed I was attending a study session. I was excited about the invitation because I was looking forward to making some new friends. My arms filled with books, I made my way to a dorm room on the first floor of the building. Once I entered, one of the young women present handed me an open can of juice. I remember some of the other students smiling and laughing as I took a drink.

After what seemed like a few minutes I began to feel lightheaded and sick to my stomach. As I sat down in a nearby chair, I noticed that some of the people who had been in the room were whispering to each other. Some were leaving. As the door closed behind them, one of the boys locked it. The bed was pushed in front of the door and the volume on the stereo system was turned up. A sickening feeling came over me, and I quickly tried to determine whether or not I could "talk my way out" of the situation or otherwise escape. When I realized that I could not, my "head went down," and I froze. I understood all too well what was about to happen. The smell of smoke and alcohol in the room frightened me. Mentally I "went away." Yes, my body was physically there, but my mind was elsewhere, and my soul was as boarded up and protected as I could make it. Ah, yes ... the "allow" had indeed felt like "cooperation" and it weighed heavy on the heart.

My shoulders sagged forward from the weight of these memories and my body was shaking. I had severe pains in my stomach. I had been terrified, and when I was in those situations I believed I was small again. I was locked in my mother's house with nowhere to go and no choice but to submit and get out in "one piece." Mary lovingly guided me back with her wisdom. "*My daughter, 'cooperation' is a way to preserve the vessel long enough for the soul to heal from what was done to it. What person who was being raped would not 'cooperate' if they understood that it was critical for them to save their life and preserve their vessel? Although the nature of rape is misunderstood in this world, the soul understands what the threat is. The soul knows that if it 'cooperates' it can preserve the vessel and always heal afterwards from what was done to the body. Remember, although the body and the mind can be tricked by the dark, the soul always understands.*"

Later, when I read through books about rape and other violent crimes written by FBI experts, forensic specialists, psychologists and psychiatrists, and spoke with Federal authorities, the consensus of these worldly experts was in line with what Mary was teaching. Even many of the experts on criminal behavior in this world seemed to be in agreement — if a woman managed to survive a sexual assault, she was to be respected and the methods that she used to do so (whether it be fighting, running, "cooperating," pretending, or manipulation of the attackers emotions) should not be questioned, as using them did not make her responsible for the crime. It did not mean she "wanted" it or that she was "responsible" for it, it meant she was doing what she had to do to make it out alive.[57]

As for the women who tried to love those who hurt them, Mary explained that she also responded the same way during her time here on this earth. One day, she asked the women present to move as close to her as possible. She wanted to make sure that everyone could hear her words if they wanted to. Women who were seated toward the back of the room came up to the front. They filled the chairs and whatever space was available on the floor. Some were even perched along the windowsill.

This Angel proceeded to tell us that she understood very well what it felt like to look into a mirror (or in her case a lake) and be disgusted by the reflection that stared back. She understood what it was like to bathe and bathe and still feel soiled. She described what it felt like to be trapped in a brothel, dependent upon the owners for food, clothing, and shelter. Her only "companions" were those who were paying money to have the "right" to destroy her body, mind, and soul. Many of us cried when she reminded us that she was forced to lie with between nine and thirteen men and women a day for more than ten years. In trying to love through this, the beauty of her soul had been preserved. "*My daughters, 'cooperation' is a self-preservation mechanism. If the soul has to hate, part of it dies. If it does not have to hate and can, instead, find love — it will be well.*"

Through these teachings, Heaven was able to help me understand that I had not "deserved" or "wanted" what the world had done to me any more than Mary had, or than these other women had. As for the humiliation I had felt at trying to love through the abuse, Mary taught me the following: "*Humiliation is the acceptance of what has been done to you as opposed to what is being done to you. To be humiliated, one has to allow it. Humiliation can only be if we do not see or understand the intent.*"

Among the many magical gifts that Heaven gave to me to help me to heal were two horses, a red roan mare and her new baby foal. They were gifts from some Native American friends of ours who kept our family in their prayers during this time. When these people prayed in a pure manner, they could feel Heaven's suggestions. They sensed that I "needed something more." I named the mother horse "Nakota Wind" and the little white, creme, brown, and black filly "Cheyenne Faith."

The truth was that I was afraid of most things because throughout my life I could not predict when something bad would happen. I no longer trusted my judgment, and I was scared that people were going to lash out at me for no apparent reason. Therefore, I was constantly "on guard." And if I was afraid, Heaven could not answer my prayers and perform the healing work I needed to have done. My fear blocked their ability to enter me and fill me with God's love.

Thankfully, Heaven knew that my fear would be replaced with love when I was around these beautiful and sensitive creatures. Although the world may not have believed they were worth much, I had come to love them fiercely. I cried quietly to myself many times as I brushed Nakota's reddish mane, and rubbed her face and belly. In order to heal, it was critical that I allowed myself to feel what had been done to me. Much of this part of the process occurred in this mountain meadow with this mare, her foal, and the eagles, ravens, and other birds that swirled above us. I was very honored that this protective mother would allow me to share her space and spend time with her baby. Somehow, even though I did not know much about her story, I could tell that she understood what I was feeling.

A few months after she came to live with us, I watched her charge a full-grown, male black bear that entered the little mountain pasture that we had cleared and fenced for her and her baby. It seemed to me at the time that this bear was after the two-month-old filly that stood near me in the field. As the rest of my family ran to the cabin for cover, I reluctantly heeded their calls and went with them. I wanted to stay and help, but I realized that this spirited mother had the situation under control. Nakota loved her baby completely — and in doing so, fear had no place in her. This bear stood on its back legs and roared as this mare charged him — once, twice, three times. Miraculously, the bear sniffed in the air, roared, and turned to leave. To be able to watch this mare's love in action was breathtaking.

The Archangel Raphael used this mare to help me to understand how powerful the gift of love actually is, and the effect of conditioning on a person. This Angel said, "*You can feel that this horse understands you. I will tell you that she most certainly does. This horse is what your people called a spirithorse. When a person cannot connect to Heaven for whatever reason, such a horse will spiritually take you on its back and carry you to Us — the Grandmothers and the Grandfathers. Your people — the Cheyenne, Arapaho, Comanche, Nakota, and the Mayan — understood this powerful medicine. They also understood that the spirithorse could only help you to connect to Heaven in this way if it chose to do so with its own free will. You cannot 'make' a spirithorse love you in this way. Nothing you can take from her or do to her can make her do this. Real 'medicine' from Heaven cannot be taken, bought, or sold. It must be gifted from the heart.*"

Indeed, I could feel that something very important was happening in and around me when Nakota looked at me with her intense, loving eyes. There were times when I felt the weight of the healing process on my shoulders, and I would quietly wonder if I could make it to the next step. Could I stomach one more memory? Could I stand to see people's real intent and love them through the truth? During these times, as I stood in the meadow with Nakota and Cheyenne, I would pray for Heaven to help me. I needed the Creator's help so that I would not give up this fight. At first it surprised me when Nakota would also bow her head as if in prayer. When this occurred, I felt peace and I knew that I was safe. It was as if Heaven was taking its arms and wrapping them around the three of us.

The Archangel Raphael continued, "*We brought her to you with great purpose. Would it surprise you to know that Nakota was also beaten, starved, and forced to do things that she did not want to do during her lifetime? The people whom you received her from loved her, but they could no longer care for her as they wished to do. Do you remember what their daughter told you about this horse? She told you to watch out because she was 'crazy.' I ask you, is she crazy with you?"* I shook my head "no" to his question. Indeed, this horse was nothing but kind and patient with me — a woman who had no experience with horses whatsoever. Although I had always loved animals, we could not afford to feed them or care for them properly when I was young. When we did have them, my family would inevitably "forget to buy food for them" or simply put them into a box, drive them to a field, and leave them there.

"*If you take this beautiful horse and you beat her each time she tries to do what she was designed by God to do rather than what you want her to do, in time, she will not understand that she is a spirithorse anymore. She will not remember that she has medicine that is powerful enough to carry those she loves to Heaven. This horse, Daughter, was also trained to 'freeze.' She was beaten if she tried to run, and starved if she tried to fight. This was the state of the place where she was born. Your world calls this 'training.' Heaven calls it what it is — that which is against God,"* explained Archangel Raphael.

I knew in my heart that nothing this mare or her spunky filly could do would ever justify a violent response from a person. Had I known what Nakota had been through or had any horse training experience from this world, perhaps I would have viewed her differently. However, since I went by her "feeling," I had immediately understood that I had nothing to fear. She was a gift from Heaven through people who loved me. So, to me she was sacred, period. Since I approached her as such, she made the decision to love me back with her own free will. And in this, time and time again, she carried me on her back to the Ancestors in Heaven. The times when I was "about to give up," she would connect to me spiritually and give me the strength I needed to continue on. In my allowing her to be what God made her to be, all of the effects of the "training" the world had given to her and to me were falling away. I pictured Nakota in all her glory as she fearlessly charged that hungry black bear to protect her baby and me. I could not help but rejoice, for if she could do it, than so could I.

I could see now that to many of the people in my life I had been little more than an animal who required "training." They were going to do what they wanted to do, period, and they were not about to let my free will "get in the way" of that. It did not matter to them whether what they wanted to do to me was close to God or not, or whether I would even consent. I could see the truth in this lesson during the women's groups. With my own eyes, I witnessed what such youthful conditioning did to a woman, no matter which of the three responses she had been "allowed" to have. I saw the "fighters," the "runners," and the ones who, like me, had been trained to "freeze." Although we may have responded differently based upon our training, we all had something very important in common. Not one of us had liked having our free will — or our voices — taken from us. Not one of us had truly given our permission for many of the things that had been done to us. And if we had done so, it was based upon a false understanding of what love truly was.

In my life, the training I received from my grandmother, aunts, mother, and the men who surrounded them, had convinced me that I was isolated and deserving of the suffering I experienced. Yet, Heaven was teaching me something completely different. By creating a safe place where women from different ethnic, religious, economic, and cultural backgrounds could sit and pray together, Heaven was allowing me to see with my own eyes that what I had been taught as a child was simply not true. The idea that any of us was isolated was a lie. We were all connected, and other women could understand my feelings because they, too, had experienced the agony of having things done to them that were against their will. They, too, knew what it felt like to have something taken from them that they valued greatly.

As the women walked through the doors and the prayers began, many believed that they could finally put their guard down — a brief respite from the battle. At times you could hear sighs in the room as Heaven lifted the tension, anxiety, and fear from their tired shoulders. Life here on this earth had been painful, and in many cases disappointing for many of the women who made their way to the small office space we rented. They braved the elements — rain, heat, snow — and even angry roommates, friends, religious leaders, and spouses — to come together, pray, and ask for help.

In this, I could see Heaven restoring hope to those of us who were brave enough to find our faith in Creator again. These Holy Messengers were gently and lovingly lighting the candle that each of us carries within our hearts. We are born into this world with our candles burning brightly, and the dark works tirelessly to extinguish our light while we are here. With faith, prayer, and love Heaven can reach inside and "reconnect" each of us back to our Heavenly home and family. The candles I saw being lit once again were beautiful!

After praying about it I realized that what had initially surprised me about seeing women of all ages, economic backgrounds, religious traditions, and ethnicities joined together in love and prayer was how "right" it felt. Although most religions end up excluding those who worship Creator differently, this gathering of warriors felt powerful. If I listened to what my heart was telling me, as I was learning to do with Heaven's help, it was clear that our differences made us stronger when we "put down our swords" and came together in prayer and love to join with Heaven. We were all connected, or as my Nakota ancestors say at the beginning and end of every prayer, "*Mitakuye Oyasin*," we are all related.

As Mary explained to me, "*The point of what the dark did to you was to convince you that you were alone, without anyone to love you or help you. In fact, you were never alone. God was always here for you, and We (the Angels in Heaven) never left your side. However, because of your fear and the chemicals your family sometimes put into your body, you could not feel, see, or hear Us. The two biggest blockers to feeling Heaven are fear and chemicals. The dark uses these things to trick a soul into believing that they are disconnected from Heaven."*

As each of these women came before Mary, Michael, or one of the other Angels sent by Heaven to help, the truth of what the world had done to them was easy for me to see. Although at times it was still difficult for me to forgive myself and to break the habit I had of self-judgment, I did not judge the women who came before the Angels. It was obvious to me, both because I could feel their hearts and because I was able to hear the answers Heaven gave to their questions, that they were good women whom Iktomi had tricked. I was certain that God loved them and had sent His Holy Messengers as an answer to their prayers.

The Angels gathered women who were dripping in diamonds, carrying expensive designer purses, and had hair that was perfectly styled. They brought elderly women who came with their canes, shawls, and prayer cards. They called to those who wore exotic cloaks, had European accents, and dancing eyes. And there were women who had bruises, swollen lips, and wore old sweat pants or jeans. No matter the outward appearance and characteristics — they were all Heaven's warriors.

Despite what the world had done to each of us, Heaven did not see us as the hopeless failures we sometimes believed ourselves to be. We were warriors with battle wounds, and Creator's messengers were here to tend to our wounds and send us back into battle healed and with "all of our tools." No more did we have to fight blindfolded and with one arm tied behind our backs. If we chose to fight on Creator's side, then Heaven wanted us to understand that they would stand with us whenever we were aligned with God.

In the office space that we rented in which the prayer groups were held, we had a replica of a 19th century spear hanging above one of the doorways. The shaft of this spear was intricately beaded. The artist had used red, blue, white, black, and yellow beads to depict a design that was called "the eye of God." Lakota Indian artisans had used this design on weapons to remind the person wielding it that the Creator was watching. The tip of this spear was beautifully carved out of pink obsidian stone.

The Archangel Raphael used this spear as a visual example to illustrate the concept that Heaven was trying to help us to understand. "*Look at this spear. It is strong and beautifully crafted. Think of Us — the Grandmothers and the Grandfathers — as the shaft. You, the souls here in flesh, are the tip of this spear. When your will is aligned with Ours, and together we are aligned with God, Our Father in Heaven picks up the spear and throws it perfectly every time. We are all one when we are aligned with His will.*"

Although many of the women present came to receive help with a physical problem that they, themselves, were experiencing or someone they loved was experiencing, there were many who simply came to offer their prayers and help. Such women asked nothing for themselves. However, when they approached the Angel sent by Heaven to help, the Angel would smile, thank them for their wonderful prayers, and remind them of the fact that "*everyone who comes receives help from Heaven.*"

With that, the woman would close her eyes, pray, and Heaven would enter her. Outwardly, as this occurred, her face would soften — years would peel away. Some would cry, some would radiate peace, and some would laugh with joy. There was one woman, in particular, whose face changed so much when Heaven entered her that she looked to me like the likeness of "La Virgin de Guadalupe," the apparition of Mary that had appeared to an Indian man in Mexico centuries ago. She was beautiful! Heaven was home, and the Creator was bringing it "down" for each of these women.

Mary explained to me that as much as my love and faith were being used by Heaven to help the women in the room and others in need, the Holy Spirit was also using the love and faith of these women in the room to heal my body, mind, and soul. She reminded me that with the Creator, it was always a perfect circle. She told me that there was more that the women needed to understand about rape and the effect it had on the woman, the family, and the community. This Angel of the Lord said the following:

> *The act of rape is, with purpose, an act to take the sacred and turn it to the profane. The physical act is only violence, yet specifically targeted to an area of the body that otherwise brings forth and shares the sacred. The purpose of rape is to take a woman away from God and to keep her from understanding that she can hold the sacred. The flesh may be damaged, but in most cases it can and does heal. It is the wound to the soul that causes the most damage, for it can last the longest, even into passing from flesh if unhealed.*
>
> *Rape is an act that strikes at the woman and those she loves. A man that cannot keep a woman he loves safe from rape believes that he too cannot connect to Heaven and is unworthy before his Creator. Children that witness such acts are brought into fear and confusion, their mother's trauma thereafter not allowing them to know peace until healed. The community that has such occurrences within it, whether housing "rapist" or "rape subject" is impacted by both the fear of it happening to others, and living with the only partly functioning consequences of the lives that have suffered under it.*
>
> *This is only possible because the nature of rape is violence upon the sacred and, therefore, violence against what God created and keeps holy. It is, therefore, a*

spiritual attack in a battle against what is of God and that of darkness.

Sure enough, when I began to research rape and how it had widely been used as a tactic of war throughout the history of mankind, I could see that it was indeed a tool the dark was using to destroy, not just the woman, but the entire family and community. Heaven had taught me that the dark uses different tactics to destroy a woman than it does to destroy a man.

For a woman, what is at issue is her covenant with Creator. She understands that she is to keep herself pure in case God chooses to send life into the world through her. If the dark can convince her that she has broken this covenant whether or not she actually has, then the destruction of the soul begins. For a man, if he cannot keep his covenant with Creator, which is to protect those who carry the sacred — the women — then the destruction of his soul begins. I could now see how rape allows Iktomi to destroy souls at a very rapid rate. Since he has limited power, it is a highly effective weapon of war.

As the Archangel Michael explained, "*There are three points to doing something that is far from God to another soul. The first is to get that person to hate, and in doing so to create a place for those souls who are in purgatory and hell to sit while that person is still in flesh. The second is to send that person to hell or purgatory once they are no longer in flesh, and the third is that if the dark can achieve the first or the second, that soul cannot help others in spirit or in flesh. Remember, this is simply battle. He (Lucifer) is trying to take soldiers of God out of the battle by capturing them and turning them into soldiers of his own.*"

I could see in my own life, and in the lives of these women whom Heaven had gathered together, that Ikotmi was "going for blood," so to speak. He was fighting for his very existence. If none of us chose to give him a space inside of ourselves — if we could replace the fear with love, faith, and understanding

— then he had no choice but to vacate our space. When enough of us did this, he would have nowhere to go but "up," back to his Father in Heaven. All of his "conditioning" and "training" could be undone for each of us as quickly as it had been undone for my spirithorse, Nakota, if only we had the conditions necessary for us to feel our Heavenly home.

By providing this mare with an environment in which her free will and her nature were respected, her baby was safe, and she was surrounded with love and prayer, she was able to see for herself that the doors to her prison had been opened. Once she realized that, she chose to throw fear out the window, and she successfully fought her "bear" with love and faith. Rather than attack her, the bear decided to turn and walk away. The bear's desire to "take" what she loved most was no match for a fearless mother who was brave enough to love unconditionally. Despite everything that Iktomi had done to her, Heaven's love had restored her to the spirithorse she was born to be.

As the Archangel Michael explained to me, "*The dark works on a person every day they are here in this world. The dark chips away at a person's soul in order to confuse them into believing they are no longer sacred. However, all of the damage begins to fall away when We — the Holy Spirit — are able to help that person to feel God's love and understand that We are here for them. So, I ask you, who has the real power? The dark works a lifetime, yet God needs but one moment.*"

So, this is what Heaven was doing for me, and for each of the people it was gathering. Once we had the opportunity to feel the Ancestors in Heaven and understand that we were, indeed, feeling our Creator, we could "remember" that feeling and call it back again and again. We too, could shed the training from this world, and replace it with training from Heaven. If we were provided with understanding and given the conditions we needed to live as what we actually are — sacred beings that are made in the image of our Creator — we too would heal and be able to stand in the glory — and protection — of love.

Once I had come to this conclusion, Mary nodded her head in approval. She wanted to make sure that I understood what Heaven was teaching us about the nature of the battle and the part that rape, and other forms of "taking," played in this war. She wanted to make sure that I could understand it for what it was and "let it go." This Angel then continued, "*Rape, therefore, must be recognized by a woman as what it is in order for her to be healed. It is an attack in a spiritual battle against those that were designed by God to hold life, itself. There are no 'victims' in a rape, only warriors for God seeking to protect that which He made sacred and beautiful.*"

I believed what she was saying, and I could feel the humiliation and shame lifting from me. It was not I who should have been carrying the burden that comes with having intent that is far from God, it was those who had organized and committed the assaults. "*What God created to both share and bring forth life, itself, cannot be 'taken' in a rape. It can only ever be given in love. The wound of rape is, therefore, only of flesh if women understand this. Such warriors need not be ashamed of injury in battle, for battle by its nature will result in injury. Rather than living in shame, they should be held up as surviving an attack meant to do more than just injure but to destroy a soul's connection to God and Heaven and to pass such lack of connection onto the next generation.*"

I could feel the candle inside of my heart. Heaven had reached inside of me and it was now burning brightly again. I now understood that Creator was love, and that He had never left me. I also understood that the scars I carried were mere battle wounds, and that the war in which I fought was a noble one. I knew what side I was on, and the shame that I carried throughout my life for trying to love "bears," no matter how hard they had bitten me, was now gone.

Tears rolled down my cheeks. However, these were not tears of pain, but tears of gratitude. I realized that I had been simply doing my best to survive all of these years. With Heaven's help, I finally had answers to the questions I carried in my heart. I could feel the energy shift around me and I knew that the Archangel Michael was present.

Archangel Michael: "Daughter, do you think that Jesus 'survived' or 'lived?'"

Me: "Well, I imagine that he did both."

Archangel Michael: "No, Daughter, the Jesus that the world has come to know did not just 'survive,' He lived."

Me: "Well then Father, what is the definition of 'living?"

Archangel Michael: "Ah, Daughter. That is an excellent question and one that Heaven is very happy you asked. 'Living' is knowing the truth and loving through it."

"It does not require many words to speak the truth."

(Chief Joseph, Nez Perce Indian)

Chapter Six

Living With the Truth

An important part of understanding where a woman can go is letting go of where she has been. Women do not need to be afraid to see their lives for what they were, Daughter. We are here for them, and God [Creator] never left them.

Mary Magdalene

As I had the faith and courage to trust Heaven and continue to seek the truth, my life looked less and less the way I had believed it to be. Before Heaven came for me in a way that I could not deny, I feared that I was a soiled, broken woman who had disappointed Creator. Now, I understood the truth. I was a dedicated warrior whose love and faith had the power to act as a beacon for countless others whom Heaven was reaching out to help.

Surely I would not deny a soldier who had been sent to war on behalf of his country the treatment he needed for the wounds he received in battle, nor would I look at him with anything other than compassion and gratitude. I now understood that it was important that I offered myself the same courtesy and respect as I would to such a soldier, as I shared and understood the wounds of battle, myself. However, the war in which I fought was not between two countries, but between what is "of God" and what is "far from God." As Mary reminded me, "*The most difficult thing to do in this battle is to come to this world as a woman.*"

It seemed to me that this gentle yet powerful Angel was determined to fortify Creator's troops who were fighting on the "front line." One of the first women that Mary requested we find was a young woman named Kim[ix]. This Angel gave me a picture in my mind of a local shop and told me that I was to go there and find "the woman." She said I would recognize her by her feeling, and that I was to tell her "Heaven was here for her." She asked that I tell her, on behalf of the Grandmothers and the Grandfathers, that she was "not crazy," but that "it is what the world had done to her and was doing to her that was crazy." I was to offer her whatever spiritual help she needed, and to tell her the truth — that what had happened to her was not her fault and Heaven would like to remove it completely from her body, mind, and soul — if she so wished.

My husband and I drove to the shop, and sure enough, there stood "the woman." Her eyes were large, and I noticed that her hands trembled slightly as she dealt with the customer at the cash register. She reminded me of myself before Heaven had come for me and I could not help but love her. She stared at me as I approached her. I smiled, and told her that an Angel from Heaven had asked me to find her and to bring her a message. As I repeated the message, Kim burst into tears. Over and over she whispered, "Thank you, thank you." We gave her our telephone number. Thankfully, by this point I did not question Heaven's suggestions. If I had the faith to trust and implement them, it was always more beautiful than I could imagine.

As the weeks went by, Kim called to ask me questions. Yes, she needed help, as did her children. She was in an abusive relationship, and she had been with Johnny — the father of her

---

[ix] Kim's name and some of the details of her life have been changed in order to protect her privacy.

children — since she was 14-years-old. Johnny hit her often, screamed obscenities at her, and made her do sexual things with him that she did not want to do. She wanted me to know that she was not complaining about this for herself. She told me that what bothered her most was that Johnny would do many of these things to her in front of the children. This upset her so much that she could not sleep most nights.

When I asked Kim why she felt that she needed to stay in such a relationship, she told me that she was worried that he was abusive toward her because she was "broken" and "not doing a good job" as a mother and a partner. She paused and struggled to get the words out. "I have problems, and I am sure that people think I am crazy. When I was small my father ...did things to me. It happened for a long time."

Kim proceeded to tell me that her father had molested her for many years, and her mother had not protected her. Instead, she told Kim that she was "crazy" when she told her about it and exhibited symptoms of the abuse. When she was 14-years-old, she met Johnny. He gave her drugs and "had sex" with her. Kim was desperate for the pain to stop at home, so when he continued to give her drugs, she accepted them. She had noticed that with the drugs in her system she seemed to be able to "forget" about what her father had done to her and what this man was doing to her. As "no" had never been an answer that anyone respected, she believed that her only choice was to self-medicate so she could cope with what was happening to her.

"You see, being that way with Johnny was better than being that way with my dad. Anyway, we are still together, and I try. Every day I try, but I am scared because my head doesn't work sometimes. I am scared that I am 'crazy,' just like my mother said I was. And I just don't want to hurt my children. Please help me so that I do not do something that will hurt them," said Kim. Her anxiety was palpable, and she was speaking at a rapid speed. It was clear that she was terrified, and when I had last seen her I noticed that she was dangerously thin and had scarring on her wrists. My husband and I agreed to come to her home and pray with her and her children the following day.

In order to help her, Heaven came to teach me about the affect that drugs have on a women's free will. In order for Kim to heal, it was critical for her to understand the truth, which was that she had never made a choice to be with Johnny at all. Between her father teaching her that she did not have the right to her own body, and the drugs that this young man fed to her, Kim was living the life of a slave, not a woman whose free will is being respected. So, even though she was working hard to be a "good partner" to Johnny, her anxiety, fear, and anger came because the foundation of their relationship was not what her mind believed it to be and because her soul knew the truth — that she was trapped in a place that she did not want to be.

The energy of the group of Angels that came to help teach this lesson was distinct. They explained that they were technically a sub-group of the Holy Spirit, whose mission was to "seek to unlock souls who have been injured because of biochemical damage done to the vessel." I was amazed at this, as I had not realized that Heaven had committees or groups that work together to solve problems and focus on particular issues.
They explained the following:

> *All that is resolute is of the soul. The soul at once abides in Heaven, and abides in the body of women and men on this earth. The effect of drugs is to cause a separation between the connectedness of the soul to Heaven, which is its anchor, and that of the world, which is its battle. The chemical effect on the mind is to create an alternative reality rather than that of Heaven and, thus, the resolution of a soul grown not just in life here, but in life in Heaven, is set adrift.*
>
> *The practical effect is to break down the will and,*

therefore, the free will of the individual to truly make a decision or to understand that a decision has been made at all. In effect, it creates a slave to a conscious slave master, rather than allowing for the true battle to be fought. Thus, the influence of drugs often renders the battle over before the woman even knew there was one to fight.

So, according to Heaven, when drugs are in a person's system, it is very difficult for her to exercise her free will to make a decision that is aligned with what her soul truly desires, as the chemicals serve to sever her spiritual connection. Therefore, she does not have access to "all of herself" in order to make a real choice. With the chemicals inserted into her system, she is significantly weakened.

According to the Archangel Michael, "*With the right combination of drugs and circumstances the dark can trick people to go against their nature because they cannot remember or understand who or what they are, physically where they are, and in what time they exist. Frequently, women who experienced abuse when they were children revert to that emotional age as adults or adolescents when they are under the influence of such chemicals.*"

The next afternoon, we arrived at Kim's home. It was small, yet tidy, and the neighborhood dogs greeted us with barks and howls. Her son and daughter ran out to greet us. I could tell that her daughter was wise beyond her years, and that her son, Matt, was his mother's quiet protector. He hid under the kitchen table as we spoke with his mother. While we prayed, I could see that although Matt had been pretending not to notice us, his eyes had closed and his head was leaning against a chair. He was breathing slowly and deeply. The Angels were working on this "little man," just as Kim had prayed would happen.

The next morning we received a call from Kim. She told me

that she was confused about something that her son had dreamt about the night before. She said he had told her that he could see "people in white dresses with wings" around her when she had been praying with us. These people told him that they were here to help, and that he did not have to worry. Matt said that three of these people had come to him again while he was sleeping later that night. He announced to Kim that she needed to "get your things ready" because they were going to "pick you up Momma and take you for a drive in their flying car."

The following week when we returned to their home, we delivered Heaven's answer to Kim as they had requested. Heaven had asked us to explain to her that her son could see them clearly. Since he loved his mother completely and worked hard to protect her, it was respectful for them to explain to him what they would be doing. As they would be performing "repair" work on his mother, at times they would need to enter her and bring parts of her "up to Heaven" to answer her prayers and heal her body, mind, and soul. When the Angels had told her son that they would be "taking her away" at times for this, he had assumed that they would be picking her up in a "flying car" and taking her on a trip.

Kim laughed at this explanation for a few moments before her hands started to tremble again. Her lips began to quiver, and she quickly reached for a box of tissues. As the tears rolled down her face, she told us that things were getting more difficult at home. She said that Johnny was starting to bring other women into the bedroom and demanding that she participate. She wanted to love him and "do a good job," but it seemed to her that nothing that she could do for him was ever enough. "He always wants more. It's like he won't stop until I have nothing left that matters to me. To tell you the truth, I am having a hard time keeping it together," said Kim, with a look of hopelessness in her eyes.

The feeling in the room shifted. We told Kim to try and

relax, as Mary was present and she wanted to help her. Kim leaned back in her chair and closed her eyes. The tears flowed down her face. Her son ran toward her from the other side of the room. He took one look at his mother before gently taking the box of tissues from her hands and returning it to its place on the side table. He nodded to us solemnly and left the room so that the "lady in blue" could help his mother.

I could feel Heaven's love for Kim and her children as they worked. Kim had met Mary before at the women's group, so she knew her feeling and trusted her. This Heavenly mother spoke to her, "*Daughter, I have told you parts of my story. This world made me a symbol of fallen women. Yes, I was in hell, but not because I did things to put myself there. I was in hell because I accepted what others told me about myself as truth. Yet, these things were lies. I was very 'popular.' I was adequate at my job. This does not mean that I wanted to do the things I was doing, or that I liked having to do them. What this meant is that I did not understand what was happening to me and I believed I 'had to' instead of 'wanted to.'*"

At this, Kim opened her eyes. Heaven had gotten her attention. "*When the world does everything it can to destroy you and you can still find love for the world, that is close to God. That is an Angel. Is it wrong to love you father? No, to love is never anything but 'of Heaven.' It is the way in which he taught you to love him that is wrong, and this, my daughter, is most certainly not your fault. I ask you, are there any fallen women here?*" asked Mary. Kim looked at this Angel. She looked at me, and at her daughter who was watching television with her son in the next room. She shook her head "no." She then caught her own reflection in a small mirror that hung close to the front door. Kim then looked down at her hands. Shame was etched across her face. "*The answer, my daughter, is 'no,'*" said Mary.

Kim was still looking down at her hands, which trembled in her lap. Slowly, she pushed one shirtsleeve up over her wrist, and then the next. We could see that she had a fresh scar on her left wrist. The blood had coagulated, but the cut had been deep. As always, Heaven had arrived just in time. "I don't know why I do these things. I don't want to do them. I want to be here and fight for my kids, but sometimes I get so scared that I wonder if they are not better off without me. Is it better to have no mother than a crazy mother?" asked Kim. I was impressed with this young woman's courage. From the world's perspective she could not have been more vulnerable, yet here she was, baring her soul — and all her perceived failures — to us and to Heaven.

"*Daughter, we would ask that you listen carefully. The people who hurt you were not after your vessel. The ones who are hurting you now are not after your vessel. They were, and are, trying to destroy your soul. Do not hate the vessel, for it is that which allows you to work with Us — the Angels — from here. The vessel is not why they were targeting you in the first place*," explained Mary. This Angel told Kim that it was critical that she feed the body properly, as God gave her — and only her — this vessel. Mary explained to Kim that when she ingests the chemicals that Johnny gives her, her mind becomes confused as to what is real and what is an illusion.

What this Angel explained helped me to understand one of the things that had happened to me during and after the attacks I experienced in New Mexico. This criminal group had administered drugs to me without my knowledge and I had, indeed, lost touch with reality. Although I am naturally tall and slender, I dropped weight rapidly during this time. When my husband would express concern that I was not eating, I literally could not understand what he was so angry about. Although I looked like a skeleton with big, sad eyes, I could not see this when I looked in the mirror. I was convinced that I was eating regular meals and that he was simply over-reacting. I could not see reality and I could not feel that I was hungry. The Angels later explained to me that it can take months for the chemicals to completely exit the body, so a person can have such side effects throughout that time, and longer if the brain suffered more permanent damage.

Mary explained to Kim that God did not give her a beautiful vessel because he hated her or wanted her to suffer while she was here in this world, rather, her vessel was beautiful because it was created to match the beauty of her soul. "*What does the world expect an Angel to look like? It expects an Angel to be beautiful. So, if God were to send such a soul here to this world in a body, it would be likely that the vessel gifted to her by Creator would also be beautiful,*" said Mary.

She explained that contrary to what the world teaches, a woman's body is important not because of the way it looks on the outside, but because it houses her soul. In doing this, it allows her to have the experience here in this world that she prayed to have before she was sent to this earth. It can also be used as a vessel, or a holding place, for the Holy Spirit if the person's will is aligned with that of Heaven. She went on to explain the following:

> *There are two ways in which you can attempt to destroy that which is of God. The first is to believe that if you take women away from men that you can prevent men from sinning and create the conditions of Heaven this way. The second is that you can create a false view of women and expect that people who do not understand can then create the conditions for God.*
>
> *Some cultures in the world take the first approach. They take women and protect them and hide them and then give them to a man. Most of the time this is not free will, so women will feel raped.*
>
> *Other cultures take the second approach. They make a woman be something that she is not. They make her feel inadequate, and make her have false everything. If you are not yourself, and your body is distorted and*

destroyed in order for you to be worthy of being loved, what does this say about God? If being outwardly pretty is the base from which you see yourself, then that is not right. God created all women to be beautiful.

I was very grateful that Mary took the time to address this. Growing up in California, I had been taught early on that physical beauty was what mattered most. Little did I know that the pictures of the Hollywood starlets were all heavily airbrushed and that most of them had to endure painful surgeries to alter their physical appearances so they would be considered "marketable." I also had not understood that a number of the leading men were often filmed standing on boxes or wearing platform shoes in order to make them appear taller and more masculine. As we did not have money growing up, I often had only one extra change of clothing that was clean, and most of what I owned was second-hand, stained, and ill-fitting. Instinctively, I knew that what you looked like on the outside mattered less than what you were like on the inside, yet being bombarded by such images and ideas made it very difficult to hold onto this knowledge. Mary explained that the dark was still using the same techniques today, as it did thousands of years ago, to confuse women as to the purpose of their bodies. She explained the following:

Billboards, magazines, and movies today show women in a certain way to cause men to desire them, and women to want to be like them because men desire them. And if men are successful in the material world, the implication is that they can possess such a woman as this.

This is the same thing they did in ancient times. Long ago in the fertility culture, they took a prostitute, a slave, a woman who had no choice — like a temple virgin. They gave her to a man without her consent. This man could mate with her as a symbol for the coming year's harvest. The priests used to hold her up every year to incentivize the men to work harder. These men would do so in hopes that they would be awarded the right to take her. She was beautiful, so the other women sought to be as desirable as she was. By this, they were trying to take the Christ — the love of God — out of the world.

Kim had been listening closely to Mary's teachings. She leaned over to make sure that her children were still in the next room watching television before asking her next question. "And Mary, what about ... you know, the women? I am confused. One of the women that Johnny brings home is a lady I considered to be my friend. Sometimes I am so mad at him that if I have to be with one or the other, I almost think I would choose her. What is going on with me?" asked Kim, holding her head in her hands as she sobbed. "Does this happen to other women, too? What does this mean?"

The compassion that this Angel of the Lord had for Kim was palpable. She waited until Kim's sobs lessened before continuing, "*My daughter, we have come to you at this time for many reasons. It is important that you understand that the dark can use either a vessel belonging to a male or a vessel belonging to a female to prevent a woman from exercising her free will. I have taught you that rape is 'have to' instead of 'want to.' So, tell me. Is what is happening to you in the evenings after your children have gone to bed 'have to' or 'want to'?*" asked Mary.

Kim stared back at Mary and then she turned to look at me. I nodded encouragement to her, in an attempt to help her to understand that she was safe to speak the truth. "It was not my idea, Mary. Johnny says things like, 'you have always wanted this' and 'you like this, I know you do.' When he says these things my stomach hurts and my head feels dizzy. It is like I can't say 'no' to him anymore, but I don't want to do these things," said Kim. "I just want to be good and make him happy."

Mary calmly explained the following:

Anytime a person prevents another from exercising her free will, it is against Creator. There are many ways that women can be confused into believing that they are what this world calls "bi-sexual" or "homosexual" when they are not. One of these ways is that a man with whom she is intimate can compel her to have a sexual experience with another woman, even one that is her "friend." In doing so, he is using such a woman as a proxy to rape her. Therefore, such an experience does not change her in the eyes of Heaven.[58]

Another complication is that once "done," some women decide they must be "bi-sexual" or "homosexual" for such an encounter to have happened at all and they can become trapped in a lie. This is not unlike marrying your rapist where you decide that it must be "love" since you "had intercourse" with them. Neither is true.

Another issue is that society rushes to judgment on such issues, with certain aspects condemning the woman for her "willful act" and other aspects holding her up as part of "gay society." In most cases, neither is true, and it is very difficult for a woman, once she has experienced such events, to get nonjudgmental assistance in order to understand how "it" could have happened and what it means for her life.

Frequently it means that she now believes that neither men nor women are a "safe" place for her, which can further isolate her. If she is "not gay" and not able to understand how it happened, she is just left to suffer in silence, frequently as in the case of a rape from a male "friend." If a woman has nowhere safe and unbiased to go to get help to deal with the event, it means she cannot make sense of what happened, process it, forgive it, and let it go.

As we were preparing to leave Kim's home, it pained me to think of what she might endure that evening after Johnny returned. I could remember that feeling, myself, for at various times in my life I had been as physically trapped as she was. Such a big world, and so few safe places for a woman to go. I gave her a big hug, and told her that she was loved greatly here on this earth and in Heaven. Kim thanked us, and her children jumped up to give us "high fives" and ask us when we were coming back to see them. We promised them "very soon" and reminded them that the Creator loved them.

That evening as I was saying my prayers before bedtime, the Archangel Michael appeared to continue the discussion that Mary had begun earlier that day regarding the importance of the vessel — or human body — here on earth. As the Archangel Michael explained it to me, there are three ways in which Angels can work here in this world to serve the Creator. The first is that the Angel can move around and temporarily enter into vessels when the necessary conditions are present. The second is that an Angel can be born into a body in conditions that closely mirror those in Heaven (such as in a family setting that is truly healthy where the child is protected, nurtured, and taught the true nature of Creator.) The third occurs when such a soul is born into a body in conditions that are very much "of this world" (such as in a family or environmental setting that actively makes a place for the dark with their beliefs, behaviors, and their level of fear.)

In order to illustrate this point, this Angel spoke with me about Joan of Arc, an illiterate, peasant girl who was born in a small village in eastern France in the 1400's. At a time when her country was under the control of the English and the French people were suffering, she began to receive visions from God through visitations from the Archangel Michael, and the Angels known as Saint Catherine, and Saint Margaret. Guided by her Heavenly visions, this young girl followed their suggestions and, with their help, managed to orchestrate a meeting with the then uncrowned French king, Charles VII.

In a private meeting, Joan prayed with him as the Holy Spirit had instructed her to do. As her intent was pure, Heaven could use her as a vessel to reach the future King of France. Based upon this experience, Charles granted her request. He allowed this teenage girl who had "Heaven behind her" to travel at the head of the French army wearing the equipment of a knight. At a time in Europe when women were not considered equal to men, this young girl — who prepared for battle with prayer and entered into battle without weapons — helped the French troops win several important victories during the Hundred Years' War.

The Archangel Michael explained that Joan was already an Angel in Heaven when God answered her prayers and sent her to this world in a body. He told me that Joan was born into a household where the conditions closely mirrored Heaven, as her mother had great faith, worked hard to protect her, and loved her greatly. "*Her mother created the conditions that Joan needed to hear Us, the Holy Spirit. One of Joan's favorite things to do was to sit in the fields of lavender and sing and pray to God. Because she had no fear, and she had complete faith, we were able to come to her and she could see and hear Us,*" explained the Archangel Michael.

Contrary to what the world understands, or what she understood at the time, the purpose behind what Heaven asked Joan to do was much larger and far reaching than simply helping to coronate a king. "*At that time in the world, the Spanish, the Portuguese, and the British all took a 'conquerors' view of the Americas. However, the French, over all, took more of an 'alignment' view. For them, it was less 'conquer' and more of an interest in working with the people who already inhabited these continents. If the French had been able to be convinced to follow the conditions outlined by God, rather than following a secular approach, it would have changed the balance of power in Europe, and through that change the impact of what the dark had planned for the Americas,"* explained the Archangel Michael.

However, once Joan left her home and was sent out to bring what she understood to be God's message to the rest of the country, she became faced with what was "of this world." Because she did not understand how to live and fight in conditions that closely mirrored hell or what the true "game plan" was, fear began to enter her. When this occurred, she became confused and could not hear the Heavenly Messengers clearly when they came to help her. It is at this point that the dark began to close in on her.

"*Through her faith, Joan helped to change Europe at a time when it was suffering greatly. She was — and is — a very strong warrior for Heaven. However, the risk in coming to this world as an Angel in a body who is born into conditions that closely mirror those of Heaven is that when you are finally sent into battle with what is 'of this world,' it is very difficult to fight fear during the onslaught the dark puts before you because you are surprised and confused,"* explained the Archangel Michael.

He explained that although it is a big risk, many Angels attempt to serve on this earth in the third manner. They pray for God to send them to this world into a body, and into conditions that are very much "of this world." "*To be sent in this way also requires great faith, as it is very likely that the dark will surprise you and confuse you enough at an early age that you cannot remember who or what you are. In such cases, your caregivers — if you have any at all — teach you that 'love' is something that it is not. However, if this soul can find the faith to reach for Heaven through this darkness and find and hold onto what is true, then they are able to serve as the strongest vessel that we have here on this earth. At this point, it is very difficult for the dark to trick them, as it has already 'played all of its cards,' so to speak,"* said the Archangel Michael.

What Heaven had just taught me helped me to put a lot into perspective. I could remember wondering as a small child why I had to live in a household that exhibited so much abuse, fear, and anger. At that time, I knew such things were wrong, but I also knew that God did not make mistakes. This confused me, as I did not feel that many of the people in my house were truly my family. Their behavior was strange and disgusting to me. It felt so contrary to what I understood to be right. I was not a jealous person, but I do recall being envious of a girl I knew whose family seemed to be genuinely loving and supportive. I had wondered if she knew how truly blessed she was.

As a child, I spent many hours sitting in my small, makeshift garden praying about this dilemma. I simply could not understand why God had put me where I was. Sometimes I was so angered by the things that were being done to my brothers and I that I would push an old, wooden crate up against the sagging fence that bordered the back of our house. I would use this crate to climb onto our aging roof. Once at the top I would scream at the top of my lungs. "I hate this place," I would yell, over and over. Sometimes, I would even scream obscenities. I could not remember if I was screaming them out to anyone in particular. I did feel badly when this happened. I suppose I had expected God to "strike me down" for this, but He did not. All I could feel was a quiet, stillness around me. Then, I would quickly climb down from the roof and regain my composure before entering my house.

In time, I believed that I had figured out what was going on. I came to the conclusion that God had put me into this situation temporarily. Perhaps I was supposed to be learning something important. However, I was certain that God would be sending my "real" family to come and rescue me. I prepared myself for this reunion with weekly trips to the local library. While there I would read books on exotic places, etiquette, and literature, as I knew that once my real family arrived my life would be completely different. I did not want to embarrass them, and I wanted them to be proud of me. So, I prepared and prepared. But the years passed, and my "real" family did not come. Life continued as it had been, amidst the violence, fear, and pain.

About halfway into my healing process, my memories of this time came back to me. I was sitting quietly in the meadow by our mountain cabin. Blades of fresh sweet grass swayed in the breeze, and the sound of river water trickling over stones helped to soothe me. Nakota and Cheyenne, my spirithorses, were grazing nearby and enjoying the spring sunlight on their backs. My son was searching for bugs amongst the plants and bushes. These things were helpful reminders that I was no longer a small, trapped girl living in circumstances that felt hopeless.

Suddenly, the Archangel Raphael appeared before me. He had a wonderful, comforting energy and had always humbly presented himself to me as a loving, protective older brother. Such a presentation helped to keep my fear and self-judgment at bay long enough for Heaven to help me to heal from the issue at hand. He told me that Creator had sent him to answer my question. When I did not answer him, he again encouraged me to ask my question. I did not want to look at him. I felt ungrateful even thinking about it. However, if God had taken the time to send one of His Angels, then I had to trust that there was a good reason.

Finally, through tears, I said, "I feel badly even saying these words, as I am eternally grateful. But I was just wondering ... what took you so long to come for me? I was waiting and waiting. Why didn't you come for me sooner?" This Angel gazed at me with compassion before saying, "*My sister, you always knew that your real family would come. Even when you told this to people and they laughed at you, they could not take that understanding away from you. Why do you think that the dark worked so hard to get you to a place where you could not even look at yourself in the mirror anymore?*" asked this Angel.

Oh, how I remembered hating to look into that mirror. Even as a young girl, I had been frightened to look at my reflection. I was scared that I would see a monster looking back at me. When I had to wash my face or brush my hair, I would look at one section of my face at a time. More like a puzzle with a dozen pieces than a face. I realized now that my deep fear had been that I was somehow so bad and horrible that I deserved what was happening to me. I was terrified that what my mother said to me was true, that I was "so bad I made the Angels cry." If that was the truth, I could not bear to look.

This Angel continued, "*When the people this world called your family did those things to your body when you were small, I know you remember that look in their eyes. That look was not what you believed it to be. It was not hate, but fear. For if they were doing the unspeakable to you, a little girl, and you looked at them with eyes filled with love and forgiveness, well, that is completely terrifying to the dark. For that was Heaven coming through you in spite of the darkness coming through them. We were there, my sister, and We are here now. Had you looked in the mirror without fear, you would have seen Us — the Holy Spirit — all around you. And at that point the battle would have been over. The dark would have lost,*" said the Archangel Raphael.

"When you were born, you cried and the world rejoiced. Live your life so that when you die, the world cries and you rejoice."

(White Elk — Arapaho Indian)

Chapter Seven

Forgiveness

Daughter,

That which awaits you is glorious. Responding in love again and again and arising from the ashes of that which you understood would be is the path to God, for in it lies selflessness and loving as He loves.

Do not despair and do not believe that you need to be alone or that you are ever alone. Do not judge yourself for the sins of others, for only they walk the path they walk before God. You can no more turn their eyes against their free will than We, of the Holy Spirit, can. For it is their will — a gift from God — theirs to squander or to use to elevate the world as they choose.

In giving selflessly of yourself through your life and in forgiving the many who sinned against you, you walk the path of the Father, the Son, and with Us. Far from being a reflection of a life unfulfilled, you walk in the footsteps of the only way to fulfill. The task undone is to forgive yourself, and to give your faith to Creator. In these two steps lies the final path to your healing.

The Grandmothers and the Grandfathers

Traditionally, my Plains Indian ancestors strove to master the concept that "*only Creator was perfect.*" They knew that if you could truly walk in this wisdom, then you would be able to withstand the temptation to judge yourself. They understood that if you carried the burden of self-judgment on your back, your journey would be so adversely affected by the heavy load that you would reach a point where you would no longer be able to move forward. If you could not continue to move closer to Creator, then you could not serve as a vessel for Heaven and help the world and those you loved. If you could not fully love during your time here on this earth, then you could not be "*all that Creator made you to be.*"

Culturally, this concept was so critical that many of the tribe's best artisans would create beautiful works of art and purposely leave one error in the piece that was easy for all to see. The grandmother who had long ago mastered the art of quill working would leave one section of the quillwork that was not in keeping with the rest. The man who had been making bows and arrows throughout his whole life would leave one obvious imperfection while crafting his weapons. These people did this to remind themselves, the person gifted with the work, and those who viewed the work, that only Creator was perfect. Yes, we should strive each day to be closer to Him, but we were not Him and we should, therefore, not judge ourselves as if we were.

As Heaven guided me through my healing process, it became clear to me that there was something that I was still struggling to overcome. Before Heaven came to me in a manner that allowed me to see and hear the Creator's Angels, I believed that I was a broken woman with a long list of failures and mistakes. Sure, my professional resume read well, however, if anyone knew how badly I felt about myself when I looked into the mirror they likely would have been shocked.

Not only did I judge myself for my perceived mistakes, I also blamed myself for the mistakes of others. It was a circle of self-judgment, shame, guilt, and fear. When in doubt, I blamed myself. Pretty soon self-blame was as normal for me as walking.

When something went wrong, or someone around me became upset, I would immediately search my mind to try to figure out whether or not I was responsible for it, and if so, in what way. I was merely surviving, and it was exhausting.

Although I was most certainly not a "woman fulfilled," I was grateful for my blessings. Growing up without many of the basic necessities of life ensured that I was appreciative of the food on my plate, the clothes on my back, and the fact that my children had all of their needs met. But being appreciative could not overshadow the belief I carried in my heart that I was unworthy of being truly loved. Because I felt this way, I worked very hard to "earn" the approval of those around me.

From the world's perspective, I was a success. I had been a poor, minority child who had participated in many of the programs that governments and non-profits put in place to help disadvantaged youth. I was the "poster child" for these programs, as I had "worked my way up from nothing" and achieved the "American dream." I had attended and graduated from prestigious universities, and I was an award-winning journalist. I had "married well" as my husband was a successful attorney, and I was a mother to three attractive children. So, why if the world was satisfied, did I feel so horrible inside? Why was it that I lived with loneliness and a sadness that penetrated my soul?

As the Archangel Raphael later taught me, "*God's Grace is love even when you are not worthy of it. It is love 'just because' and there is nothing that you can do to earn it, and nothing you can do to lose it. It is what We, the Grandmothers and the Grandfathers, bring down from Heaven when we come here to this earth. It is what can heal every disease known to mankind.*" However, such Grace was not anything that I understood existed for me. It took time for me to change my view of God, Heaven, and myself so as to allow such love to become a part of my daily life.

One of the reasons that I did not know such Grace in my life was because I had not forgiven others for what they had truly done to me, and I had not applied what I knew about forgiveness to myself. As the Archangel Raphael said, "*The definition of forgive is different for different people because they have different feelings as they do it. Faith and forgiveness are very similar in nature. You had faith as a child, but it was different for you than it is now. But you still needed it. Your ancestors had a saying that they strove to live by. It was 'Every breath a prayer.' Forgiveness is something that you should strive to do with every breath.*"

The Archangel Michael had taught me about forgiveness in a way that was very effective. There was a woman who had been coming to the prayer groups for some time. She practiced Buddhism in her daily life, and she was very much "ready to work" when she came to these gatherings. As they often lasted for hours, she came prepared with her seat cushion, a shawl, and her bottle of water. This woman communicated in a very direct, "no-nonsense" manner with the Angels. Her questions were to the point, and she seemed prepared to apply the answers the Angels gave her as soon as she understood them.

One day, I noticed that she appeared "out of sorts." The previous time she had come, the Archangel Michael had suggested to her that she turn her attention toward forgiving those in her life who had wronged her. This time, as she began to discuss the topic of forgiveness with the Archangel Michael, she said, "I know you are saying I need to forgive. But I don't think I can do it. Something inside of me is saying, 'no' and I don't know why. I would like some help with this."

The Archangel Michael smiled at her and said, "*Ah, my Daughter. The reason you are having trouble with this issue is that you do not understand what forgiveness truly is. By forgiving you are not saying, 'I liked what you did to me, so go ahead and do it again.' What you are saying is, 'I understand what you did to me, and I no longer hold it against you. I am giving it to God and I am allowing Him to be the judge.' We are not telling you to stand still the next time that person wants to hurt you again. On the contrary, we want you to understand it for what it is so that you can remove yourself from harm if you so choose. Once you have done that, we would ask you to understand that God is their father too, and that His system of justice is as perfect as mankind's system is imperfect.*"

At that, the woman nodded. She was serious about her spiritual growth and she was ready. She closed her eyes. As the Archangel Michael lifted his hand above her head to put in the Grace of God, she let out a roar. I was surprised at the sound that came out of this serious, little person. Her face softened. She opened her eyes and said, "Thank you. I feel much better now." With that, she arose from the chair very matter-of-factly and made her way back to her seat. So, it was as easy as that — understanding what forgiveness truly is and deciding that anything else has no place in you. Beautiful!

As a child I understood the concept of forgiving others well. In the summers, my grandmother offered to pay me a nickel for every page in the Bible that I read. I found that I actually liked sitting next to her and reading while she crocheted colorful blankets. She would turn off her little black and white television set so that the house was quiet. At times she would take out her Bible, which was a Spanish language version, flip to specific passages about forgiveness, and read them aloud to me. After a while, I did not attempt to collect the money from her anymore. She seemed to find some sense of peace during these moments, and that made me happy.

I remember liking Jesus's teachings about forgiveness. It gave me hope to see the way that Jesus "walked the walk." He taught others about kindness, forgiveness, and faith, and He was willing to do the heavy lifting himself by practicing these things in his own life. I was puzzled as to why I did not see more of this in the world around me. Were not these people reading the same sections I was reading? Did they not also want to try to honor God each day by showing kindness to others instead of "kicking people when they were down?"

I had done my best to forgive in my life before the Angels came to me in 2005. However, as I had heaped the majority of the responsibility upon my own shoulders, I really had not forgiven people for what they had truly done. I had not understood that people had actually intended to hurt me in my life. Instead, I believed that the things they had done to me were simply "accidents" or "honest mistakes" based upon some sort of miscommunication on my part. However, Heaven worked hard to help me to understand that I had wounds that were in need of healing. In order for Heaven to be able to take out the sickness, I needed to take another look at what I believed to be true, reject the illusion, and forgive.

As the Archangel Michael explained to me, "*It was not even your response to those who hurt you in your life that is at issue. As Jesus taught and as many of your ancestors taught, you turned the other cheek and you forgave them. You did not hold what they did to you against them. That is aligned with Heaven and through that the Holy Spirit could work. It was your understanding of what had happened that is at issue. By taking responsibility for that which was not your fault, your soul became injured.*"

Heaven was asking me to have the courage and faith to forgive the people in my life for things they had actually done, as opposed to forgiving them for what I had concluded had happened. My conclusions were often times based upon explanations I had accepted in order to be able to cope with what was happening to and around me. I did not want to live in a world that had evil, nor did I understand such "absence of God." So, even though evil was often "knocking at my door," I simply did not see it as what it was. If my mother was self-medicating by taking both prescription and illegal drugs, I chose to believe her when she told me that she was taking "vitamins." If my cousins were sexually molesting me, I chose to believe that what they had done to me was "no big deal." If a "friend" raped me, I chose to believe that they "hadn't meant to do it" and I did not report them to authorities.

Although I did not understand at that point how much I would have to review or how much this process would affect me physically, emotionally, and psychologically, I knew that Heaven would never lead me in the wrong direction. I also wanted to help those who had wronged me as much as possible, as I truly believed that those who caused injury to others were simply confused. If I could assist Heaven in their mission to resurrect souls, then I was willing to make the changes necessary in my life to do so.

The Grandmothers and Grandfathers had taught me that every soul here on this earth must go through the same process in order to return home to the state of being we call "Heaven." As they explained to me, "*This world is a part of Creator's kingdom. It is a part of what you call 'Heaven.' Heaven is actually a state of being created by selfless love. It is where all life began and it is where all life returns.*"

When a person "dies," the Holy Spirit refers to it as "passes from flesh" because all life is eternal and the soul simply sheds its vessel at this time. The soul continues along on its journey. When a person passes from flesh, the soul will see a light. At the end of that light stands the being known to many in this world as the Archangel Michael. Creator grants this Angel permission to appear to each soul in the manner that is most likely to teach that person about God's Grace. As the soul approaches the figure of the Archangel Michael, this Angel says, "*I would like to welcome you into the Kingdom of Heaven, but first will you agree to look at your life?*"

Although some souls agree and take his hand, many others are too terrified to face what they believe they have done in their lives. They have already "played God" and passed judgment upon themselves. They are so ashamed and so frightened to see and feel the results of their actions that they, instead, take the hand of the being known to many as "Lucifer." The dark stands to the other side of Michael. Like a hustler desperate to close the sale, the dark one lies to the soul and promises it "relief" from the pain of having to look if it will simply take his hand rather than the hand of Michael. As God has gifted each of His children with freewill, the soul who now stands before both the light and the dark, can choose which hand to take.

As an example of how this process works, the Archangel Michael told me the story of a soul that he had recently attempted to guide home to Heaven. She was a woman who was raised in the Muslim faith, and she had passed from flesh when the explosives that were tied to her body ignited. She was standing in a crowded marketplace when the bombs she carried went off. "*The world would look at this situation and condemn her. However, the fault in what occurred lies upon the shoulders of another. The leader of her husband's military faction had sexually violated her while her husband was on a mission and he knew her to be alone. After he had raped her, he told her that what happened was her fault, as she had seduced him and he could see from the look in her eyes that 'she wanted it.' Although what was done to her was not her fault, this leader threatened to expose her to the community and to her husband as an 'adulteress' and a 'whore.' This woman was told that the only way that she could redeem herself and save her family's honor was to 'die' in this manner in the name of God.*"

The Archangel Michael explained that this woman agreed to allow this man to strap explosives to her and send her into a heavily populated area because she was told that it was the only act that could possibly redeem her for what "she" had done. As she had taken responsibility for something that was not her fault and he was an authority figure in her community, she believed what he told her was her only "correct" alternative. "*When this daughter passed from flesh and saw the light, she was too frightened to look at what she believed that she had done to her husband and family that was against Creator. Rather than take my outstretched hand, she chose to take the hand of my brother,*" said this Angel, with tears in his eyes.

This Angel explained that although the dark one was using this women's self-judgment to trick her into walking away from the light, he, the Archangel Michael, was prevented from speaking about this women's life with her unless she gave her consent. "*As we have taught you, God gifted each of His children with free-will. I cannot tell my children anything about their experiences during their time here on this earth unless they grant me permission to do so,*" explained the Archangel Michael.

He asked me to please pray for this woman, as she was suffering greatly. This Angel explained that once a soul chooses "relief" rather than looking at the truth, Lucifer traps them at the point where their fear is the greatest. "*This set of events will play over and over for her until the power of selfless love penetrates the illusion. Who will pray for her, my daughter? To the world she is a monster who took her own life, as well as the lives of dozens of men, women, and children, or a 'violent martyr' for people fighting a never-ending war. Neither is true. Who will pray for the ones who in their confusion have destroyed nations, communities, and families? To Heaven, this woman is a child of Creator who the dark managed to trick and confuse. We would like her suffering to end. We would like to welcome her home,*" said the Archangel Michael, his hands folded in prayer.

I could not get this woman and her story out of my mind. That night, I went out into the cold, winter air and faced the sacred mountain that was only miles from our home. I lit a braid of sweetgrass, and I prayed very hard for this woman whose name I did not even know. I could relate to her pain, and I understood the horror that goes with taking responsibility for things that are not your fault. I knew what it felt like to be tortured in the name of God, and I knew what it felt like to be taken, used, discarded, and left to "clean up the mess" that they had left behind. Most importantly, I knew the empty, sorrowful feeling that comes from believing that you stand outside of Creator's Grace, alone in your pain.

Heaven loved this woman, and so did I. As I prayed, I asked for Creator to break through the prison walls the dark had built for her and show her the truth. I prayed for her to know unconditional love, and for her to know forgiveness. As I did this, I could see the Archangel Michael appear in the distance. He smiled and whispered, "*Heaven thanks you.*" I could see the figure of a woman walking toward him. She was hesitant, but she finally reached him. I could see that they were speaking together. Then I saw her slowly turn her head to look at me. I could see that she was frightened, but she had hope. She nodded to me in acknowledgement, and turned toward the Archangel Michael. As she put her delicate hand into His, the amount of love I could feel from Heaven at that moment took my breath away. This daughter was weeping with joy as her loved ones from Heaven descended around her. This was Creator's process in all of its glory. Despite everything that the world had done to her, this daughter was choosing truth over illusion. As a result, she was returning home to Heaven.

The Archangel Michael taught me the following: "*If a woman can truly forgive others for what they actually did to her, this act enables the Holy Spirit to reach those who are most in need. It allows Us to help them in their return home to Heaven. Remember, there are no shortcuts with God. Every soul must agree to look at their life, feel the effects of their actions and intent, and forgive in order to enter the Kingdom of Heaven. This is not cruelty, but an opportunity for each and every soul to grow closer to God by learning more about compassion, faith, and forgiveness.*"

Once I had taken Heaven's hand and truly looked at my life, felt what had been done to me, and forgiven those whose actions and intent had caused me pain, it was time for me to focus my efforts on the part of Creator's process that would prove to be the most difficult for me. There was one more burden that I had yet to hand over to Creator. This sack was worn, as I had carried it on my shoulders since I was a little girl. It was also heavy, as I had been putting things into it every year since that time. It was time for me to forgive myself, and I had no idea how to hand my self-judgment over to Creator. I was not yet living in the wisdom that my ancestors strove to incorporate into their daily lives. "*Only Creator is perfect*," I would remind myself each and every morning. Yet, I still believed I could have done "a better job" in my life in so many ways and I could not shake that feeling.

As the Archangel Raphael explained to me, "*Faith, forgiveness, and prayer are all part of the same. They are like breathing. The only way forward is to live in forgiveness, and you must extend that forgiveness to yourself if you wish to be everything Creator made you to be here on this earth. If you are trying to seek out all of the details to measure whether you will or will not forgive, well, then my sister, you do not have it. You are not always going to have executed perfect judgment or perfect morals. Therefore, being able to forgive yourself for not being as perfect as God is a very important part of His process.*"

This Angel explained to me that when a soul comes to this world, regardless of how close to God they are in Heaven, that soul does not have access to her memories or "all of herself." However, each soul is gifted with the understanding of what is "right" or "wrong." Since we come to this earth without all of our memories and without perfect understanding, and because the people who teach us how to navigate this world are also "not as perfect as God," our understanding, judgment, and choices will naturally be imperfect. "*Why would God judge His children on a scale of perfection if He did not design it as such? This experience here was designed to be a journey, my sister, and it is about learning as much about how to love and be loved as possible while you are here,"* said the Archangel Raphael. "*Not about being 'perfect.'*"

This Angel explained that it is the lack of forgiveness of the self that haunts people. Indeed, it was those moments when I was trying to still my mind before falling asleep that the self-judgment would plague me. "I could have done better," or "I would have tried harder if I had only known," or "I should not have trusted that person." The "could have," "would have," and "should have's" would run through my mind, preventing me from obtaining the real peace and joy I knew was waiting for me. I could feel that these thoughts were giving Iktomi a place inside of me. I could almost see the little spider trickster weaving his shadowy web in the corner of my bedroom. This was the only wound I had left inside of me and he was desperate for me to keep it.

With the women's groups, Heaven was regularly bringing a number of women together in prayer. At times there were over one hundred women together who were all bringing love through them and directing it to others. Despite the beauty of this, I had noticed that many of them seemed to get "stuck" in the same place. If Heaven would talk to them about their lives or a specific incident and tell them that what happened was "not their fault," I could see the doubt in their faces. If they were like me in the beginning, they liked hearing those words being said, but they could not understand how they could be true. They either remembered, "making a choice" to be there, recalled some level of participation, or they had simply accepted responsibility for the incident as soon as it had occurred.

When I prayed for answers about this, the Archangel Raphael appeared. This Angel explained the following: "*Women can remember 'knowing' that something was far from God and doing it anyway. They remember thinking that they 'liked' the sexual feeling that they experienced from an encounter. They remember 'enjoying' the feeling of the drugs in their system. Although what happened to them may not have been their fault, they do have a sense of responsibility for what came out of them in those instances. They remember these things and that the outcome was severely impoverished, so they look back and they fail to forgive themselves for not being as perfect as God. They may be culpable in certain circumstances, or they may have been in them because they believed lies about themselves. All this really means is that they became confused in the battle, and they are not less sacred because of it."*

I worked very hard to forgive myself. I no longer wanted to judge myself, as it was Creator's job. I tried different things to help me to do this. Sometimes I found beautiful stones. I would take these stones in my hand and recall something for which I judged myself. Once I had captured the feeling of shame that went along with it, I would direct that shame into the stone and throw it into the water so that Creator could wash it clean. Other times, I would burn sage or sweet grass as I remembered moments of self-loathing and ask Creator to take the feeling from me and take it up to Heaven along with the smoke. This way it could be purified and Creator could do something wonderful with the energy.

One day, Creator graced me with a Heavenly visit from an Angel who was known in this world as Whiteshield. Whiteshield was a Cheyenne warrior who served as a Peace Chief for his people in the 1800s. This was a difficult time for Indian people, as the United States government was relocating those who had survived the "Indian Wars" to areas of land called "reservations." During a time when many chiefs had decided to fight back in a worldly manner, rather than "sit back" and watch their women and children be destroyed, Whiteshield was a leader that strove to hold onto the "old ways," which meant less brawn and more prayer, faith, and forgiveness.

Whiteshield was not always popular or celebrated for this, but when I researched his life I saw Heaven through many of his actions and decisions. He also happened to be my maternal great-great-grandfather. I remember saying a prayer of gratitude the day I discovered that this was the case. I said, "Thank you God, for giving me something of beauty to carry forward." I believed in the "old ways," and I knew that through them Creator could grant great miracles.

While researching my family history, I had come across a photograph of Whiteshield that was commissioned by the U.S government. I became very emotional when I saw this black and white picture. Those who took the photograph had used a U.S. military coat and a horse blanket to cover his traditional American Indian attire. They also used a scarf to secure a large, tin cross around his neck in an attempt to hide the beaded choker he wore. He is wearing a rosary, and a St. Christopher medal dangles over his hand. Yet, despite this change in attire, they could not mask his kindness or his compassion. They could not hide the fact that he was an Indian man who loved greatly.

Creator sent this sincere Angel to help me to come full circle. He was soft-spoken and warm when he addressed me. Truthfully, I just wanted to hug him, sit next to him, and ask him to tell me stories about our people. What was it like to live without fences and without physical boundaries? What was it like to live in a time when your horses were your family and the buffalo were your brothers? What did it feel like to live in a community where the elderly were respected for their wisdom and a person's proximity to Creator was valued more than his or her possessions?

He smiled kindly at me, as he was here to discuss forgiveness. "*Creator did not make us to be 'perfect.' For, if you cannot choose, you cannot truly love. In a spiritual world, to hate is to hate your own brother, because we are all related. So, hating a part of you destroys things, not lifts them up. Nothing can be restored with hate. Compassion, love, and forgiveness — this is the path to Heaven. Forgiveness is the perfect weapon, for if there is no hate left, there is no more place for the fear to go. And then, you are truly free,"* explained Whiteshield.

As for my questions regarding what it was like for him to live the "old way" with his people. Yes, he answered them. Yet what I found the most moving was when he told me what it was like to try and love through the hate that surrounded him once his people were rounded up and forced to live like caged animals. He described what it was like as a man — a caretaker of his people's bodies, minds, and souls — to have to watch the women he loved being raped "in exchange" for food for their children. He spoke about what it was like to have to watch young girls, who had been taught the sacred nature of women, being taken by men filled with alcohol. He talked to me about what it felt like to stand by while the children were starved and beaten.

> *How do you forgive when they take everything, leave you with nothing, and treat what they have taken with contempt? For that is rape. It is rape of a woman, it is rape of a people, it is rape of Mother Earth. How do you forgive when what your ancestors have spent thousands of years honoring is bought and sold for what it can do for a moment, not what it is?*
>
> *This describes how mothers are treated. We say that Mother Earth is a woman. The woman is somehow positioned so her body can be used or leered at so that it becomes a 'thing,' a tool, rather than what it is. Women can be compelled to believe they are a thing, that different parts of their body are separate somehow from the whole to cause a reaction, to arouse the base.*
>
> *You can only forgive because such beings that do these things are so far removed from what is sacred that*

they truly cannot know what they have done. So, how do you fix the mother? All women are mothers, because that is a part of them. Creator made them and with Him everything is made again. There is no other answer, and the only path to Creator is the true strength that lies in the heart. Compassion, forgiveness, and prayer for those that believe they are so unloved that they seek to turn the sacred into something they can relate to, which is only the profane.

Whiteshield explained that once his people were removed to Oklahoma, the hunger, disease, violence, and abuse began to chip away at their hearts. He could not hunt for them as he used to, he could not physically remove them to safety, and he could not protect them with weapons of this world. However, he could turn to prayer as his father had taught him to do when he was a small child. Yet, the U.S. government had forbidden the American Indian people from openly worshiping Creator the way that their ancestors had taught them to do. Whiteshield and his people were prohibited from praying in the manner that the Cheyenne prophet, Sweet Medicine, had brought to them from Heaven.

"*They told us that we could no longer worship Creator our own way. But, my daughter, Creator is Creator. There is only one of Him and He is everywhere. A piece of Him is in every plant, animal, and person. A piece of Him is in the water that flows through our rivers and our oceans. He is in the Mother Earth that feeds us, and provides our body with everything it needs. He is love, and they could not take this wisdom away from me. So, I decided to continue praying to Creator. Even if I had to change the way my prayers looked on the outside, I understood that Creator can see in our hearts and He knows all that is true,*" said Whiteshield, who adjusted to these laws by attending and joining the Mennonite church that was established on his reservation.

Then my great, great grandfather paused. He breathed deeply, and stopped to listen to the birds. He listened to the trees as they rustled in the wind, and he told me that he "liked my spirit-horses." He said that he was grateful that Creator allowed us to have this moment and that he wanted to say something important to me before our time together in this way was finished.

"*My daughter, I know that in your life it was not the taking part that was so hard, it was the discarding of what they had taken so soon after they had taken it. For you see, it is never enough. How do you please the insatiable? You know that Creator sent Sweet Medicine to our people. He was a man who became more than 'just a man' with his faith, prayers, compassion, and forgiveness. He did not simply forgive those who had wronged him. He forgave himself for not being as perfect as Creator. There are times in this world when Creator sends souls whose purpose in coming is to show us what walking the path to Creator looks like. If we follow the footsteps of these ancestors, they will lead us back Home,*" said Whiteshield, raising his arms up to the sky.

This Angel explained that we do not honor Creator, or the memory of our ancestors who reached up to bring Heaven's love back to the people, if we simply say "*well, we are not as 'holy,' sacred,' or 'divine' as they were.*" Rather, he stated that such "holy people" become this way by applying the principles handed down by the Creator. In doing this, they provide living examples for others to follow. They show us what "walking the path of Creator" looks like so that we can mirror it and find our way home to Heaven if we so choose. "*My daughter, I would ask you to follow in these footsteps. If not for yourself, your husband, and your children, please do so for The People. Sweet Medicine taught us that the women are sacred, because through them Creator brings life into this world. So, our People say that 'the war is not over until the hearts of the women are on the ground.' If their hearts are not broken and they have their faith in Creator, then the children and the men can be all that Creator made them to be and the people are whole,"* said Whiteshield, as a single tear rolled down his face. "*We ask that you help to lift the hearts of your sisters, my daughter. We are here to tell you that the war is not over!*"

With that, my ancestor left the mountain meadow and returned to Heaven. And with him, went my fear. That day I knew that not only would my heart never touch the ground again, I was committed to helping to lift the hearts of my sisters who were also being hurt in the battle. We had a prayer group that afternoon, and I was going in armed with the strongest weapons in existence — love, faith, prayer, and forgiveness. I prayed hard as I prepared. I prayed hard as I put on my medicine dress, armbands, and my moccasins. There was a battle to win, and I was ready.

As the women and men selected their seats and prepared themselves for another "prayer marathon," I stood to give the introduction. However, this introduction was in no way "standard." In front of more than a hundred people, I gave my story to Creator. It was not "mine" anymore. It was His to do with as He wished. I thanked the people present for all of the love that they had been generating from their seats for the past year and a half. I talked about the pain, fear, abuse, rapes, and the incest. And I spoke about the way that I had judged myself for these things that were done to me. I confessed that I used to live in terror that others would discover what I believed to be the truth — that I was unworthy of Creator's love and that my essence was simply "not good enough." I cried as I spoke, and my tears served to emphasize the truth.

That day, I did not stand before these people for myself. I stood before them because I loved them, and I wanted them to know that they were not alone. I wanted them to know that

Creator loved them, and that if He could lift a woman who had experienced the things that I had experienced in my life, then there was hope for each and every one of them. Most importantly, I wanted to honor them for who and what they were, and for taking the risk to fight in this battle alongside me.

That day, my battle with the dark ended. I no longer lived in illusion. I had decided not only to forgive those who had done me harm, but to forgive myself for not having been perfect in my life. It felt wonderful, and the emptiness that I had felt throughout my whole life was completely gone. I was one with Heaven and I could feel it. I bowed my head as Mary Magdalene came forward. She asked me to sit before her. She lifted her hand above me and said, "*My daughter, it is over. Your family in Heaven is rejoicing, and we are sending her to you at this time.*" An incredible wave of energy came over me. I believe that Mary said more, but I do not remember what it was. That date was November 3, 2007.

One of the side effects of the attacks that I experienced in 2005 in New Mexico was that medical doctors told me that I could no longer bear children. The internal physical and neurological damage was so severe that the experts did not believe I could ever conceive again. However, on August 29, 2008, our daughter was born. It was as I had always imagined it would be. She was perfectly healthy, and I was able to deliver her without the use of chemicals. Looking down at her, I knew that I could teach her that which Heaven had handed down to me.

There was great peace. Instead of the insecurity and the fear, there was gratitude and joy. When I looked at her, I felt love, forever. I realized that it was critical to surround my family and myself with things that stimulated such feelings inside of us every day. For me, such a life in the year 2012 does not look much different than it would have if I were living in the year 1650. You see, every day I am learning to extend my forgiveness. I have even forgiven those people from "across the great waters" who came before me who tried to put an end to a way of life that many of my ancestors from these lands cherished. For, they were also my ancestors, and I understand that Creator loves them unconditionally. In doing this, I choose to use my free will to reverse what was put in place by those who were frightened and confused.

So, my family has grown enormously. Not only did Creator gift us with another child to caretake, He gifted us with the responsibility of caring for many of what is left of our people's sacred animals. Currently, our family includes seven bands of spirithorses, a herd of buffalo, sacred sheep from the Diné people, wolves, birds, and many other wonderful creatures. We strive each day to create a haven for these creatures, so that those who come here to pray and receive help in their lives can see the glory of Creator. The land that we chose to borrow from Mother Earth for this purpose is land that was once considered sacred to my husband's people. It had been left discarded, and was poisoned and dumped upon for years. It is now dotted with prayer circles, prayer tipis, and other places for people to pray and feel their Creator.

Our home is a place of thanksgiving and gratitude. All of the life that resides here, including the land, was once used only for the value of its particular commercial purpose and then discarded. But, with love, prayer, faith, and forgiveness, all is resurrected. As the Archangel Raphael said to me one day while I was walking amongst the horses, "*When you forgive, you are returned to your natural state. In that, all of Heaven can work through and with you. If you are angry you cannot see what Creator would have you see. When you return to your essence you can exercise that in the way you want it to be.*"

It was Heaven for me to pray with these animals. Most of them had been very ill when we found them and brought them here to live "the old way" with us. I looked at Yana Miracle, the Blackfoot curly mare whose twisted intestine was considered "too severe" for her to live. She galloped over to me. I picked a handful of pears from a nearby tree and fed them to her. After what had been done to her in her life, she was still learning to trust. I felt her joy as she bit into the sweet fruit, and I said a prayer for her.

I walked over to Nakota's pasture, the mare who "started it all" for me, and I felt her happiness as she nursed her brand new foal. The majestic grulla Choctaw stallion that she had chosen to love stood grazing nearby. He was standing guard, protecting his family of mares and foals. I recalled how sick he was when we first spotted him, dying in a barn filled with manure. He reached this state after he was taken from the wild in an attempt to protect him and his herd from being shot down by timber company helicopters. The man who loved him took us to him and asked us if we could help. This horse's body was completely broken, and his spirit was losing the fight. As this horse stood in the dark barn, we could see his silhouette. He turned his head to look at my husband and me, and we felt the Grandmothers and the Grandfathers enter us. At that moment, we knew that he was an answer to prayer. The man who loved him and had done his best to save him, helped us to load him into our horse trailer so that we could bring him home.

Over the next two weeks, I watched Nakota do for this dying stallion what she had done for me. She planted herself next to his corral and she closed her eyes. I could feel Heaven working through her to help revive his broken spirit. She would not leave his side. I had seen this amazing mare at work before, and I had complete confidence that she knew what she was doing. I brought her hay to her, and moved her water closer to where she stood. In loving completely and selflessly, this mare was bringing Heaven down for this stallion. To see him today — happy, healthy, and adored — brings us all happiness and strengthens our faith.

The Archangel Raphael continued his teaching: "*You will*

see many women suffer between the middle and the end of their healing process, much like giving birth towards the end when a new life is about to begin. It becomes difficult to carry, and more is required. Many will see their past as an impediment to their future walk, indeed, that they have to go back to go forward. They believe that they will have to do something extraordinary — usually more suffering — in order to be worthy to carry such medicine to their people, to all people. This is not true, for they are already extraordinary, they just have to understand this and be all that their Creator made them to be," explained this Angel. *"As your ancestors would have said, 'Step into these moccasins and there will be peace, but sometimes it may take time to find the moccasins that fit. Do not be afraid to try different moccasins.'"*

As this Angel spoke, I remembered the moment in my healing process when Mary Magdalene came to help me to understand that it was time for me to "step into my moccasins." I had gotten to a place in my healing process where I had done everything except learn to regard myself as a child of the Creator. I had not forgiven myself, and I did not understand that I was "enough." I knew that I could love others selflessly, but I did not understand how to be loved selflessly in return.

Mary gently explained to me that Heaven knew how much enthusiasm I had for this spiritual work, but that in order for the Holy Spirit to be able to use me fully as a vessel, it was critical that I learn to regard myself as sacred. She told me that the Creator did not give me this life simply to suffer, and that it would honor Creator if I had a full life — a whole life that was filled with the joy of understanding that there was no separation between Creator and myself. "*A life to love, and to be loved. Most of all, for you to accept love and allow yourself to feel it,*" Mary said.

I remember crying when this beautiful Angel said these things to me, as I instinctively knew how difficult these next steps would be. I did not know how to regard myself in this way or accept real love from others, but I could feel that what Mary was telling me was the truth. Creator truly was a "circle" as my ancestors taught. He was not going to leave me "out of the equation" as I was so willing to do and as I had been taught by the world to do. The Creator had already woven me into the blanket of love that He spread across the world.

After thinking about these things, I walked over to the top of the hill of our property. I could see "Medicine," the white, buffalo bull that the Creator sent as an answer to great prayer. He was running in circles around the pasture with his four "wives," as our son refers to them. As the Creator had promised He would do, He is sending His children around the world signs that He is coming back for them and that this world will once again return to Heaven. This, indeed, was Heaven for me as it was for my People so long ago. The Archangel Raphael continued to speak to me.

"*Returning to each woman's true nature is going to be different for different people. You will not have a 'one size fits all' outcome. If every woman had to gather native horses and buffalo, there would not be enough to go around. But, they can put their hands in clay, help children, care for animals, love another, stand for a community, fight for a People, or do all of the above,*" said this Angel. "*Forgiveness is what brings them back.*"

As this Angel returned to Heaven, my husband exited our home, and my children ran to me. Together, we watched the rose-colored sky as the sun began to set. Our Native horses grazed contentedly and you could feel their love for each other. The world was no longer the frightening, hopeless, and disappointing place it once was, and I no longer felt like someone who did not "belong." Life was now love, joy, and beauty. Indeed, it is forgiveness that allows for healing and resurrection. It is forgiveness that completes Creator's circle of love. The Creator has it for each and every one of us, and it is time for us to extend such forgiveness to one another and to ourselves. With it, all is washed clean.

May Creator bless you on your journey!

"My Daughter,
You will know when you have
finished the healing process,
because at the end you will find joy."
(Mary Magdalene)

My Prayer to the Creator for You

Traditionally, people of faith around the world began and ended everything of import with a prayer. These prayers served to express gratitude to the Creator, to communicate the intent of the person praying, and to provide our Creator and the ancestors in Heaven with the opportunity to intervene. Some of the most powerful prayers are those that are offered up to Heaven for a particular soul on behalf of another person who has overcome fear enough to love that soul selflessly. This is a prayer that I offer up to Heaven with great love. It is my prayer to the Creator for you, my sister.

Creator,

Thank you for granting my sister the gift of life, and for answering her prayers and the prayers of her family in Heaven.
Thank you for allowing her to come to this world to fight what is far from you with her love.
Thank you for giving her this opportunity to learn about faith, compassion, and forgiveness.
Thank you for giving her the gift of free will.

Please help her to understand her life so that she may heal and, in doing so, be given the opportunity to serve as a pure vessel for your love if she so chooses.
May she begin to see herself through Heaven's eyes.
Please help her to understand that she is truly free and whole, despite what those in this world may have done to her.
Thank you Creator, for granting her the gift of prayer, so that she may always be connected to you and to her ancestors in Heaven.
Thank you for keeping your promise to love her completely and unconditionally, and for the many signs you send her to help her to remember that you are here for her.
May she see them through the illusion of darkness that often haunts her here in this world.
Thank you, Creator, for sending your Angels to provide her with the guiding light she needs to find her way Home.

Hey-so-no-ne-hoe
(The translation of this phrase from
the Arapaho language to English is:
"*Great Spirit [God], that is the way I want it.*")

Women's Testimonies

"A Mother's Journey Home"

2008 was the year that would change my life forever...I lost a child and found God at the same time. In March, I was eight months pregnant with my third child, when my oldest, Adalin, a beautiful five and half year-old girl, was diagnosed with a very rare and terminal pelvic tumor. I had lost my mother to cancer when I was sixteen, so the information about Adalin immediately filled me with shock and fear. As a very protective mother, I thought I was supposed to do all that I could to save her. Even though I tried so hard to hide my fears and show her that I wasn't scared, my mind was crippled with thoughts of a life without her. How would I be able to survive and be there for my husband and two other children?

After losing my mother, my teenage and college years were filled with a deep longing to be loved and a yearning to be able to love back without any fear of abandonment or judgment. When doctors talked to me about my daughter and quoted medical statistics, all of these emotions from my youth came flooding back. I wanted to run away with Adalin and cradle her safely in my arms, as I did when she was a baby. Of course, I prayed to God to help her, but I felt very ignorant and unsure if my prayers would or could be heard. I didn't feel I had a strong spiritual foundation and reaching out to God in a "911 situation" didn't feel genuine. I remember as a child and an adult being so envious of my friends and relatives who spoke so confidently about their knowledge of the Bible and their special relationship with God.

In early April, we began the protocol of chemotherapy, radiation, and eventually surgery that was set up for Adalin. In the world of pediatric oncology, you learn very quickly that much of the research and medicines were originally designed for adults and that much of the road map for children is over uncharted terrain. The unknown was both surprisingly terrifying and speckled with glimpses of hope. Maybe Adalin could beat the statistical odds. During this time I knew that I had to role up my sleeves and start building a relationship with God. I thought it was something that I needed to do for Adalin and my family and NOT really for myself.

In September, when it came time for surgery, we were told by many doctors the only way to give her the best chance of total cure was a hemipelvectomy (a rare and high level pelvic amputation). At five-years-old she would be the youngest to ever have this surgery performed in the United States. After that phone call I remember the world beginning to spin, and when I walked outside I dropped to my knees and prayed for God to give us other options. The silence and helpless feeling that came over me was suffocating, however, I continued to PRAY. Something inside me began to stir that I couldn't explain.

The very next week St. Jude Children's Hospital in Memphis, Tennessee called and said they felt they could perform a surgery that could remove the tumor and save her leg. As we headed to St. Judes, the unknown fears began to dissipate and when I prayed an excitement grew that I couldn't explain. I remember dropping to my knees and pleading with God to bring healing to my child and also to fill me with His grace and peace so that I could be all that Adalin and my family needed. Little did I know that our lives would soon be bonded forever with Medicine Road, her loving husband, and their family.

On the eve of my daughter's surgery, my life long protective brother called and said there was an amazing couple we had to meet. He said that miraculous healing had occurred on many occasions when this couple prayed with and for people. I was speechless when he told me that Medicine Road's husband would be passing through Memphis on the day of Adalin's surgery and wanted to meet us. I spoke with him on the phone that night, and he told me about their journey and how the Angels come to them and taught them how to bring Heaven here on earth. As we spoke, that same unexplained excitement began to stir in my soul.

The moment we met him I felt my "mother bear" guard go down. What transpired next in Adalin's recovery room was a true gift from GOD. He and Adalin spoke immediately like old friends and the LOVE in the room was mesmerizing. Even though she was heavily medicated, as a family we prayed over her and we felt waves of heat, chills, and most of all LOVE radiate from her and through all of us! When we finished we all had tears streaming down our faces. When we asked Adalin what she felt, she softly said, LOVE! Over the next few hours this man we had only just met taught us — and especially Adalin — how to keep Heaven close to her at all times. He showed my husband and me how to bring Heaven to her and our entire family through prayer. As we said our goodbyes, Medicine Road's husband said he couldn't wait for us to meet the "A-Team" (Medicine Road and their children).

When I got the chance to meet Medicine Road, I truly understood the meaning of grace. Her loving spirit radiates from her soul. To hear the compassion in her voice or observe the love and tenderness she has when she is with her family and pets, one would never imagine she has walked such a long and difficult road in life. When you are near her, you truly feel the warmth and protectiveness of the Angels all around you.

After this, my daily prayers felt natural and productive. I

personally craved the opportunity to grow in my connection to Heaven. I wasn't just praying in dire despair for Adalin. My longing for spiritual education was being transformed with the first hand knowledge of how to connect in loving prayer to our Creator. I remember Medicine Road and her husband telling me that the Angels said my daughter had come to this world as a gift and that her purpose was to bring others closer to God. I know they were talking about my husband and me for sure. Though it was a beautiful message, I was also nervous that when her "job" was done, she would leave me. Would I be able to thank God for this gift and let her go at the same time?

God would give us more time than medical professionals predicted, and periodically she would be "miraculously healed." Over the next three years, Adalin experienced God-given time periods of being cured, and then she would relapse, only to be treated with chemo treatments and more surgeries. During this time my excitement about our new connection boiled over to any and everyone I could talk to. Most of the time, I truly felt God's peace and grace and felt like I could function with a purpose.

Adalin, throughout this entire journey, was very inspiring. She faced new challenges with calmness and maturity beyond her years, even when she was in excruciating pain. Trying to be diligent, I often asked her if she was praying and staying connected. Like preparing for a test, in good times and in tough times, I wanted to make sure she was doing her homework. One day when I was really upset about her declining health, she calmly said, "Mommy, I am already connected and I will be ok." We are very grateful that Medicine Road and her family have been by our side every step of the way.

In October of 2012, my daughter turned nine-years-old and spent the last three weeks of her life in the hospital. There were many times I would watch her sleep and notice she was having a conversation that was not meant for me or others in this world. I felt the Angels all around us. The nights before she died, my husband and I had the chills from head to toe. We were totally at peace to say good-bye to our daughter and give her back to God.

As the days, weeks, and months have passed, I can honestly say my faith is strengthened daily. I am grateful to God and my daughter for taking my hand and bringing me home. In only nine years, my daughter was able to touch the lives of thousands of people with her love, faith, strength of character, and her story. While I miss her with every breath I take, I am also determined to do my part to keep Heaven close and complete the "job" God has intended for me. I now understand what it is like to love completely and to be loved completely, and I work hard each day to make sure that my husband and my children feel this love from me. When a parent aches at the loss of a child, I now know that these children are the greatest gifts we can receive, and when it is time, with great love we can give back to our Creator.

Tammy Farnum

"The World Had no Place of Value for Me"

God came for me at a time in my life when I believed that there was nothing good for me and no place for me in this world. If it were not for God, His Angels, and Medicine Road, I know that I would not be alive today. Actually, there were many, many days that I wished my life to be over. If I had passed from flesh during those times, I most certainly would have been in hell.

I've done so many things in my life that I am not proud of, including hurting others and hurting myself. The truth is that I didn't understand that I am lovable. I had been in my body for 36 years, and not once had I understood that I had value. Not the kind of value that leads to a happy, healthy, fulfilled life. I did not understand that I am beautiful. I did not understand that

I am sacred. I did not understand that God loves me. I did not understand that God always loved me, and that He always will.

If it were not for Medicine Road and the knowledge she has shared in this book, I would have no hope and no example of how to live. I would not know how to pick up the pieces of my brokenness and hold my head up with pride and joy.

I am African American. I am Native American. I am Irish. Sadly, I can't tell you anything more about my ethnicity. I was a product of rape, and I didn't know my biological father. I was 3-years-old the first time the man who I was told to call "Dad" threw me down, molested me, and raped me. That is the man who taught me about what this world had to offer me. He pushed his beliefs upon me, along with his version of who and what he had decided I would be.

"Dad," taught me that love was rape, violence, and slavery. I had felt so completely destroyed and damaged for as long as I could remember that I did not believe that I could ever be whole. "You are a whore," he would tell me, as he hit me, held me down, pulled my hair, and raped me. I used to scream back at him that I would "never be a whore," even though I did not understand what that word meant at the time.

At the age of 36, within the first few months of meeting Medicine Road and her family, the Archangel Michael came to speak with me. I was thinking of running again, as had become normal for me. This Angel explained to me that I was very, very sick. I could not grasp what He could be talking about. It never occurred to me that I was mentally and physically ill, and I did not know that I had an incurable disease. At the time, my body was lean, muscular, and appeared to be in great condition.

In my household as a child, the abuse that my siblings, my mother, and I, suffered was extreme. Over time, the hypnosis, brainwashing, and torture took its toll on my soul. As a result, my body and mind became very sick. I had no self-esteem, and the people I was surrounded by were as far from God as my parents had been. I had been conditioned as a child to believe that such bad treatment was "love." One thing that confused me is that I could never feel my body. I could not feel when others touched me. I could not feel any sensations of pleasure, and all pain was dulled. I was numb.

From a very young age I can remember my "dad" laughing and joking with his friends that he had gotten a "five finger discount" on the lumber he had gotten from his work. At one point he had stolen so much lumber from work that he made a wooden shed behind the trailer we lived in. When I got a little older and finally understood what a "five finger discount" meant, I remember being disgusted by him and his stealing. I knew the difference between right and wrong, and I knew stealing was wrong. We did not have money when I was a little kid. My "dad" hunted illegally so we could have meat, and I remember eating dog food on the porch after school because I had not eaten all day and my siblings and I were locked out of the house until our parents got home. (This was before the school systems in our area gave free lunch to those in need.)

I remember the first time that I stole. It was at a local grocery store and my mother would leave us to run the isles as she shopped. I stole candy. When my mother found me and caught me eating the candy, she took me back inside the store and made me give back the remains of the candy and apologize. I was humiliated, and I was furious with her! I didn't understand why it was "ok" for my "dad" to steal, but not for me. I believed that she was a hypocrite. There was so much in our household that was wrong, yet she turned her back to it. I hated her for humiliating me, and I hated how my parents always made me feel small. No matter what I did. No matter how hard I tried to "be good" and make them happy, they were never happy with me. Truthfully, I was angry with my mother for allowing so many bad things to happen to me and for never standing up for me. I was angry because she turned a blind eye to other members in my household doing things that were far from God.

So, I decided right there at the store I stole my candy from, that I'd "get good" at stealing. I decided that I would be so good at it, that I would never get caught again. It was my silent middle finger in the air to her. It filled a need in me. I was always so happy when I had stolen and gotten away with it, and happy with what I had stolen. It was an addiction, and an impulse that I did not control. It put happiness in my life when there wasn't any. Keeping what I had stolen from my family's eyes was an adrenaline rush. At first, I stole food. As I grew older, I started stealing clothes. I stole clothes because I didn't have any. Every piece of clothing I'd ever owned was a hand-me-down from my older siblings or from Goodwill. I stole clothes to feel good about myself, to fit in, and to be liked. I stole for the same reasons I stole as a child. I stole to feel that I had some power, because I believed that I had none.

In my household, we were taught to "do as I say, not as I do." My siblings often did things that were far from God and they would tell my parents that I had done it. I was always in trouble. Soon I decided that if I was going to get hit for something I hadn't done, then I should start doing "bad" things, that way I'd at least have the satisfaction of doing it. That way at least I would "deserve" the beating. I started to swear, even thought I felt badly when I did it. At first, it made me cry to say those words, but then I continued to do it in hopes of appearing "tough." I thought it would protect me from future attacks.

I remember my mother's reaction to my swearing. She was horrified, and she was disappointed in me. I felt ashamed, but then angry again. Her reaction was just one more charade to cover the truth of what truly went on in our house. For during the days when my father was not home, she would scream at us, beat us, and swear herself. My swearing became one more middle finger in the air to her. I wanted her to know that I did not respect her, and that I thought she was a hypocrite. I wanted her to know that she was a bad example to us, because she swore at us just like my "dad" did. As I got older, my "dad" took pride in teaching me bad words in Spanish. Those happen to be the only "good" memories I have with him.

I've only just begun to understand some of the perceptions that my siblings and I developed from our childhoods. After my mother finally got the courage to leave my "dad" and leave the state, I could not understand why my siblings sided with him. It did not make sense to me. Despite everything, I loved my mother, and I felt bad that her life was so hard. I mean surely my brother and sisters must have remembered the beatings, the nights he put a gun to our mother's head while rip-roaring drunk and threaten to kill us all ... didn't they? Could they not remember the hell we survived? But, I finally "get it." I finally understand that my siblings were angry with my mother for turning a blind eye to the abuse, rather than protecting her own children. And I finally "get it" when I think of the hell my parents lived through as children to make them believe that violence, rape, and slavery were "normal." And because of this, and because I love them still, I pray for them.

After leaving my home, what I had been taught about myself and about the treatment I could expect from the world, continued. For years, I would meet people who would drug me and use me in much the same way as my parents had. But I could only take this for so long before I "broke" even further, as I had in the grocery store or when I "made the decision" to swear even though I hated the way the words felt in my mind and coming out of my mouth. I simply broke ... and the "real me" went away. I embraced the dark and sad world of "stripping" and allowed others to convince me that it was a "career." They told me that glamorous women around the world did this, and that these women had exciting lives. The truth is, I believed that if I willingly made the decision to take my clothes off, then at least

I had "made the choice" and "had the power." In doing this, I worked hard to push away the memories of my "dad" making my sister and I put on little sexual "shows" for him. I willed myself not to feel, just as I had done when I was small.

Little did I know that within those clubs I would become truly powerless. I was being drugged, hypnotized, beaten, and sold. My soul, body, and mind were dying. I will tell you that I NEVER dreamed of becoming a stripper. Little girls just do not have those ideas in their minds. The world has to work very hard to put such ideas into them. On top of the drugs that were being given to me without my knowledge, I used drugs to get through the day and the long, never-ending nights.

One night I was scheduled to work at a newly opened club that was located in a different city. This city has a reputation for being very dangerous, so I was worried. However, there was another dancer who I had become friends with, and she invited me to stay at the home she rented in that city. She seemed nice, and I trusted her. So, I went. It was our "night off" and this woman invited some of her "friends" to meet us at a local bar. When the bar closed, she invited these people back to her place. As I had nowhere else to go, I did not say anything when she announced that we were "having visitors" that night.

When these four men arrived, they and this woman went into a different room for a little bit. When they returned, they surrounded me and began undressing me from every direction. They proceeded to do whatever they wanted to me, and I can remember hoping that they would be "finished" soon. I did not believe that there was anything that I could do to make them stop. After they were done using me, the men threw money on the fireplace mantle. They laughed at me as they walked out. As they left, they called me a "whore." By this point, I knew what this word meant.

Because I was so terrified, I was furious. I screamed at this woman, and I did not know what to do about what had happened. From that moment on, I believed that what my "dad" had told me all of those years ago was true. "You are a whore," he had said, over and over. That day, I believed that I was such a person. The world had finally turned me into something that I fought my whole life not to become. On this day, I believed that no man would or could ever love me.

At this point, I knew that no matter how many times I moved, and no matter where I went, I would always end up in the same bad situations surrounded by people who enjoyed hurting me. I had always believed in God. However, for the first time since I was a child I began to pray to him aloud. I begged Him to help me. I told Him that if He would help me just enough, that I would dedicate what was left of my life to helping others like me who believed that they had nothing to live for.

And this is when my life changed. God sent His Angels, and He sent people who truly wanted to help me. He sent people who did not judge me. He sent people whose love, faith, and prayers could bring Heaven here. Because of these things I could begin to heal. I began to get enough memories to fill in the missing pieces of my life. These memories began to help me to understand the terror I had survived. It has been years since the Angels first came to me. Since that time, I have tried to help my mother and my youngest sister. And although I became scared and gave up on myself and on my ability to be a vessel for God during their visits with me, I know that God will give me another opportunity to try and help them. It was easy at that time for my mother to convince me that I was "small" again, and now I understand that that is simply not true. They are as terrified as I used to be, and they do not want to look at their lives and feel the consequences of their behavior and the behavior of others. I pray for them, and it hurts me that they are still hurting.

Although I am not completely healed yet, I will tell you that I cry most days simply because I am so happy. I find pleasure in the most simple of things ... time with my sons, being able to give a smile to another who is suffering, helping others, saying my prayers, and being able to feel Heaven around me. Oh, and my "incurable disease," well, God took it — it is not longer a part of my life, and I no longer have to live with it in any way. When I think of how my life used to be, and how terrible it was to be immersed in a life filled with drugs, stripping, stealing, and so much pain, I shudder and thank God that I am now free. Sure, I still struggle each day not to have fear, but I know that I will keep healing until all that is left is ... me. Beautiful, as God made me. Sacred, as God made me. God, His Angels, and Medicine Road gently guide me, and remind me that, "*everything is possible with God*."

And by the way, I will make good on the promise that I made to God. I will do everything I can to stand for the women like me who the world felt righteous in destroying. You know, I finally understand that what was done to me was not my fault, and it was not their fault. The world had to work very hard to tear us down. Every day I pray for those who are still trapped — both the women who were taught that they are slaves and the people who abuse them. Because of this, I learn more about how to love and how to be loved each day. Thank you for listening to my story. It is my prayer that it can help others.

Running Water

"God Remembered Who I Was"

I could stare for hours at my own reflection.
Who was the girl that was staring back?
I had no recollection.

I had forgotten what it had meant to "feel,"
and had lost all of the parts of me that made up
who I am,

I was in a condition that only God could
completely heal.

God remembered who I was,
He reminded me of all that I had forgotten,
Most importantly that I was loved, no matter what any
person says or does.

He glued me back together, Piece by piece,
And told me that I would be part of Heaven forever.

God renewed who I am today,
He reminded me that I had purpose,
And he wanted me to be here on Earth to stay.

I had worn myself down over the years,
God told me that I didn't deserve that,
And He was always there to wipe away my tears.

I am now stronger,
and I wear my battle scars with pride,
For I am ashamed of them no longer.

So now, every night, to God I pray,
And thank for Him all that I went through,
I wouldn't have it any other way.

Our God, I am undeserving of.
I will forever embrace and rejoice,
His everlasting love.

(The poem above was written by Leah, 14-years-old, who struggled with an eating disorder. With God's love and guidance she overcame it and now helps others.)

"I prayed and they came, I asked for guidance and it was given…"

For Christmas 2010 my mother gave me a painting of the Archangel Michael, which she painted herself. I hung it in my room above the area that I spent time praying. My mother gave this to me after an attempted break into my home by a man I knew from a family connection and from the local gym. He was a mechanic, and I needed someone to fix a vehicle of mine. But I didn't have much money to pay a mechanic. I was friendly to him, as I am to all people with whom I come in contact. It's who I am. I attract people who are hurting and in need of help. I befriended him, and before I knew it he was "coming on to me." I made it clear to him that we were only friends, or so I thought I had made it clear to him.

One night while asleep in my bed I woke up from a deep sleep. I felt like I was being pulled up out of bed to sit straight up. I knew something was wrong. I looked to my bedroom window, and then heard it crack. I saw the light from a flashlight looking through my window. I set off my home alarm system and called the police. I knew at that moment that it was the guy from the gym. It was a "gut feeling" I had, which I now know to be the Angels. Later that day, and over the course of the next several weeks, the evidence pointed to him. I took him to court and was able to get a restraining order for fifty years. Not even fifty years could be long enough. What was he going to do to me when he got into my house? How did he know which was my bedroom window?" He must have been watching my house for some time. Many thoughts raced through my head. All this happened a year after the suicide death of my husband of 8 months.

That was not the only time the Angel's saved my life. After leaving my children's father I feared I would find someone worse.

Well, I did. My boyfriend of five years was also very abusive. Along with the fear and physical beatings, he attempted to kill me by drowning me in my bathtub. I heard a voice in my head telling me to not fight it, to relax. When I did, he let go. I left him after a dream. In that dream an Angel asked me as I looked in a mirror, "Are you ready to go home, my dear (to Heaven)?" I thought about it and said, "No, I have more to do here."

So, I ended that relationship only to get married to a high school boyfriend who wanted to change EVERYTHING about me. When I wouldn't change he threatened suicide. We divorced, and two days later I was at my Grandmother's house and something told me, "Don't go home" so I didn't. He kept calling me and I didn't answer. Later I found out he was waiting for me at my house, got tired of waiting and left. When I finally went home I answered his call. He shot himself while talking to me on the phone. I know now, that those "voices in my head," those "gut feelings," were the Angels warning me and protecting me. I just never realized it before.

What I thought was being nice to people, turned into me being a "victim," which is a roll I knew how to play well. The painting of Archangel Michael's arrival into my life was not a coincidence. I then began to pray to God to send the Archangel Michael for protection and guidance. Something I hadn't done since I was a little girl. Raised Catholic, and disgusted by the politics and corruption of the Church, I denounced everything "Catholic" but always kept my connection with Creator. Within two months of my prayers to Creator asking Him to send the Archangel Michael, I was lead to Medicine Road, the Archangel Michael, and the Archangel Raphael.

Even though my healing had begun before this time, Medicine Road and the Angels provided me with clear guidance, acceptance, and unconditional love. These are things that I always felt in my heart, but the world tried very hard to make sure that I would forget them. I became pregnant at 16, so that

I would have someone to love me. I grew up without a "father" and for most of my life without a "mother." My grandmother and many family members raised me. I never really "belonged." At 16 I searched for that feeling of "belonging," took matters into my own hands, and had my first son. His father, who was three years older than me, was extremely abusive to me. I had nowhere and no one to turn to, as my family had abandoned me when I became pregnant and made it very clear to me that "if I was old enough to get pregnant, I was old enough to be on my own."

I had two more children with this man, and for ten years he taught me that I was worthless and that love did not exist. He told me he loved me one moment, and the next moment he would hurt me. He would force me to have sex with him while I cried. He would see my tears, and continue on with his "business." I would think that if he knew how much it hurt me he would stop, but he didn't. I could feel my soul's detachment from my body, and I lost my will to live. A smile was something that my face had not felt for many years. I would wonder what a smile would feel like, what joy would feel like. They both seemed as far away as the stars.

When Medicine Road and the Angels came into my life, with their guidance I began to pray for my eyes to be opened so that I could see things as they truly are. I began to pray for my freewill to be returned to me, among many other prayers. I can now see things as they really are, and how the dark worked through these men and my family to try to bring me down. I have learned so much about forgiveness and unconditional love. I have learned to recognize a "bear" and love and pray for them from afar. I am healing day by day with the help of the Angels. I feel like an onion being peeled one layer at a time, healing one layer and then the next.

It is not always easy, the feelings that come up, or the situations that help me to grow, but I can now honor them for what they are, bless them, learn from them, and continue forward. The hardest part was learning to forgive myself, and to realize that I really didn't have a choice in the situation. What happened to me through men wasn't really my "fault," yet I had been taught it was for so long. I am learning to look in the mirror and see myself and know that I am worthy. Medicine Road told me that, "If you learn to regard yourself as a child of Creator, then you are not prideful. You are honoring your Father in Heaven. If you understand that you are a part of Creator, then He can work through you fully to help others."

She told me this when I was struggling with the idea of believing I was worthy. I felt that feeling worthy meant I was feeling prideful. When she explained this to me, I then understood that if I wanted to continue to help others I would need to overcome the feelings of unworthiness that I have carried. I have come to a place where joy and smiling are a part of each and every day. I have learned to forgive all those in my life, including myself. I now have people in my life who love me unconditionally the way I love them. The Angels are always with me. I feel them with me, in me, and around me. I am now able to recognize when the dark is using someone else to try to bring me down, so I pray for them. I pray in gratitude every day for all the wonderful blessings that I have been given, through prayer, intent, and faith.

I pray for you my sisters for your healing. I pray for my daughter that she will not have to suffer the way I did. I pray for all of God's children every day to be returned to the light. Thank you Medicine Road for helping me through my healing and loving me unconditionally. My sisters, if you pray they will also come to help you. I learned that all you have to do is ask.

White Bear Woman

"The Gentle Whisper of God"

> The LORD said, "Go out and stand on the mountain in the presence of the LORD, for the LORD is about to pass by." Then a great and powerful wind tore the mountains apart and shattered the rocks before the LORD, but the LORD was not in the wind. After the wind there was an earthquake, but the LORD was not in the earthquake. [12] After the earthquake came a fire, but the LORD was not in the fire. And after the fire came a gentle whisper. [13] When Elijah heard it, he pulled his cloak over his face and went out and stood at the mouth of the cave. Then a voice said to him, "What are you doing here, Elijah?"
>
> (1 Kings 19:11-13)

I often worry that my life has been too easy, too perfect. I have never known the intense pain that divorce, rape, or abuse can bring. I was raised by loving parents in a Christian home. I grew up in the church. I professed my faith in Jesus at 11. When the church doors were open, I was there. I studied religion in college. I was always doing a Bible study, listening to Christian music, surrounded by Christian friends. I had Bible verses taped around my room, my bathroom, and on the dash of my car. I worked on church staffs, Christian summer camps, and led Bible studies for young girls. I mentored teenage moms, worked in soup kitchens, helped with vacation Bible schools. I could speak the "church lingo." I knew how to be perfect, look perfect, and say the perfect things. However, I knew that there had to be something more. I knew that God was real, I never doubted that, yet I felt that the church had boxed God in. I concluded that the church must be keeping something from me. That there had to be "more" to God than I knew.

The truth is most modern day churches have forgotten what God feels like, so they go to great lengths to convince themselves He is there and only there. The truth is instead of going out of their cave to seek Him, like Elijah did, they often hide. The gentle whisper of God terrifies the church. Let me be clear, God uses the church and faithful followers in the community. I have seen, felt, and experienced Him there in a very real and powerful way. However, the church cannot contain our Creator.

I am a seeker. I know the heart-wrenching cries to God well. I know them not because of my personal pain or despair. I know them because I feel trapped in a world that yearns so deeply to be rescued. I felt God calling me to seek Him ... that He would come to me. Reveal Himself to me. But the world is hard, and because I was searching so deeply for something real, I would be easily discouraged. I could feel God so clearly at times; it was often unbearable for me when I couldn't feel Him. I was prone to depression. The medical community told me that it was genetic, just take these pills, you'll be fine. So I did. For 10 years I took them. For 10 years, I felt nothing.

While I was pregnant with my 3rd child, I lost my grandfather whom I loved dearly and had been a huge part of my life. Two weeks before I received the news that one of my mentors while I was a college youth counselor was charged with molesting nine teenage boys. Forty-four days later, I lost one of my dearest friends in a tragic boating accident. I was devastated, confused, and heartbroken, but most of all, I was mad at God. Around this time, I was at church one Sunday and I heard someone talking about a Native American prayer circle and I remember thinking that it sounded interesting, but I was so mad at God I quickly dismissed it. However, nearly a year later, "something" reminded me about it and so I asked a friend who had gone and she introduced me to Medicine Road.

When I first met Medicine Road, and listened to her story of redemption and healing from God, I was dumbfounded. I couldn't wrap my mind around everything I was hearing, but while I sat and listened to her, I could feel a peaceful presence in the room. I can still remember how I felt that day while sitting in her kitchen. I can still recall that peace. I had spent 32 years in the church and not once had I felt the peace that I felt that day. As I told her my story and why I was mad at God, she listened to me and then gently suggested that I might want to pray about coming off my medication. What? Why would I do that? I am depressed! It's genetic. I was born defective. I will be medicated forever. It's just the way it is.

After that day, I prayed fervently for Truth to be revealed to me from God. I wanted to know, I was fearless with my questions. I needed answers. I ached for purpose. Over the next few months I talked many times with Medicine Road, asked her many questions and wrestled with this view of Heaven that was being described to me. I would go from a conversation with her, compare it with Scripture, than pray about it all. I was trying to process this new information as fast as I could. The teachings of the church were so engrained in my mind, but so were all the holes that the church couldn't explain and I was told to "just accept" and "not question." But the more I learned about the way God really worked and how the Angels were here to help us on our journey, those "holes" that the church couldn't answer began to be filled. God was being faithful and answering my prayers. He was showing me His Truth. Through it all, I remember that I would feel a gentle stirring in my soul that seemed to be whispering to me Colossians 3:10 "Put on your new nature, and be renewed as you learn to know your Creator and become like Him." Because of His faithfulness, I decided to take a leap of faith. I decided to quit my medication.

I weaned myself off of my medicine over the course of a month. I told people close to me of what I was doing, so that they would be aware of any rash changes in my personality and for the safety of my children. And I prayed. I prayed more than ever before. When I began to feel again, I began to understand things differently. I began to understand why I was so prone to depression. It was because not only could I feel what was going on in my life... I can feel the pain of others. The Angels began to explain to me that it was my gift and it was from God and it was good. If I can pray selflessly for another, I can help them. This is not a mental disease. It was a blessing. The world says my ability to feel is abnormal and needs to be corrected. Heaven says that my ability to feel is beautiful and needs to be celebrated.

Over the last year, Heaven has given me the great honor of introducing other women to Medicine Road. I have often awakened in the middle of the night in a cold sweat with a woman's name on my mind and not known why, only to contact them and find out that they had been praying at that exact same moment for God to help them. I have had women drive by my house and stop just because they felt like they were "suppose to talk to me" and when I looked at their eyes, I could feel their pain and I would know, the Angels had sent them. I was to tell them my story. Strangers in the grocery store, fellow moms on school field trips, there was no rhyme or reason to how our paths crossed. But one thing was always the same ... I could feel their pain and I knew. Their Creator was reaching out to them and He was answering their prayers for help. He was healing these women from the scars of abuse, neglect, rape, divorce, eating disorders, and self-judgment. Each time, I knew that I was witnessing something unbelievably sacred and I would literally tremble and weep at the awesomeness of it all. He was answering my prayers just by allowing me to be a small part of their healing process. My whole life I have searched for God, pleaded for purpose. God heard my cries. He hears yours too.

Emily Rhodes

Wakan Tanka, Tunkasila, Unsi Maka, pilamaya ye. Ahé'hee' Diyin Diné'e, biyazhi nishlí.

I begin with a prayer of gratitude in Lak ól'iyapi (Lakota language) and Diné Bizaad (Navajo language), to The Great Sacred (Creator), Grandmother Earth (Creation), and Our spiritual allies, the Holy People (or Angels). There are so many ways to call a rose but it always smells the same... All of these aspects of "Heaven" saved me in my darkest moment and taught me the exquisite art of self-liberation. It brings a smile to my face to think of what these forces have done just for me and what they will do just for you. My entire being is filled with complete joy and gratitude. Now I live to pass on this gift of compassion to everyone I meet. Now I know this is why I came to Earth in the first place.

On February 27, 2010 I shattered the right side of my pelvis and sacral-iliac joint and fractured three vertebrae in an 8.8 magnitude earthquake in Chile. I jumped from a third story balcony attempting to escape a crumbling apartment building and upon impact I had dismantled my hip muscles and bones. Thereafter, I fell into the deepest and darkest depression I have ever known. Later, the Archangel Raphael would tell me things I could scarcely believe. "Sometimes when you hit the ground it's hard... And sometimes, it's not," he said as he smiled. I know now that the laws of physics can be bent and broken to save a dying soul. It was so strange that my feet, ankles, and knees were unscathed by the impact. Pelvic experts could not explain the fracture and told me it was an impossible injury. Interestingly, Raphael also said, "But some injuries happen for a reason."

It may sound odd when I say this, but shattering my pelvis and my spine was the greatest thing that ever happened to me. It brought me into the darkest place I have ever known, but I emerged with plenty of extremely powerful tools I could use to help others. It taught me the beauty, sanctity, and fragility of this body that holds me. Before the accident I would cut and burn myself just to feel my mortality. I would ingest mass amounts of drugs, alcohol, and junk food because I didn't think I mattered. But standing on the edge of "death" helps us to see just how beautiful this body is and how important it is to preserve it, especially if we came here to bring about The Restoration. And thirdly, the accident brought me closer to Wakan Tanka, the Great Sacred, Creator and Creation. Sometimes you have got to hit rock bottom before you have the humility and clarity to seek the Creator. When you do, you wonder why you had waited so long. Sometimes, if you are asleep at the wheel, the only thing that will wake you up is a massive bump in the road. And wow, was I asleep...

Today I can run several miles without pain and my faith in the Creator and *in myself* is unwavering. The Archangel Michael would later tell me: "You wanted to help this world in selfless compassion. You knew it wasn't going to be easy. But you came anyway. You had to go through the battle in order to help others who are in the battle." In other words, how can you help someone with a problem when you have never experienced that problem for yourself? How can We teach a child how to confront a bully at school if We have never overcome a bully Ourselves? I came to this world to confront the darkness, surmount it, and once I had found a way to untangle myself from its wicked knot, teach others to do the same. I came here to liberate us from Ourselves. And so did you. This is the type of compassion We hold within us. This is the type of sacrifice Our souls are willing to make in order to create The Restoration of Heaven on Earth: We will come to a world full of dark intention and the thick illusion of pain and suffering in hopes that we could rise above it and heal it from within. We would dive into the heart of darkness as warriors of light to illuminate the Grace of God.

I have shattered the illusion for myself, as Medicine Road has done for herself, and as you will do for yourself. Soon, We will remember together that there is nothing to fear, nothing to rebel against and no reason to suffer any more. There is only the need to celebrate Our beauty and Our victory over the darkness within us. I capitalize "We" and "Our" in the manner that the bible capitalizes the word "God" in honor of Our sanctity and Our beauty. We are born beautiful for a joyful life. We are astounding in body and in soul. The name my people give to themselves is Diyin Nohookáá Dine'é, The Holy Earth Surface Walkers. We acknowledged our own divinity every step of the way. There was a time when We as human beings understood the magnitude of Our beauty and holiness. It is time that We understand this again.

You hold in your hand the greatest teaching a human being can know: that you are deeply loved by the ancestors and by the benevolent, nourishing energy of Creator, that the darkness is a sick friend who will be healed in time and that *you* are a part of this healing. All along they were waiting for me to realize the beauty I held within me, the potential I had to liberate my people. All We are waiting for is for you to realize that it is safe to shine. It is safe to sit up straight and express your brilliance for the world.

Every human being on Earth is endowed with special gifts. This is your medicine. This is the unique way that you restore health, the way you restore Heaven. It is easy to detect because it is what you are good at. It is what makes you feel alive. It is what you could spend hours doing and love it. It is probably something the darkness has worked quite hard to muffle, medicate, suppress, and ridicule you for. God knows we can't have medicine women and medicine men being what they are! It might create a heavenly Earth! Or perhaps darkness has convinced you that this will make you rich and famous. It will give you all the things you ever dreamed of.

I will be so bold as to say that your gifts were never meant to do these things. They were meant to heal your people. Now you know, it is safe to be *all that you are*. It is not only okay to do this; it is imperative that you do. We need you to understand your potential to heal yourself and the world. This fearless generosity, brazen expression will empower others to do the same. After all, revolutions are best carried out with the help of friends. The Restoration will be as simple as the choosing of love over hatred, choosing faith over fear. And The Restoration will begin within. May you always understand who and what you are. As our ancestors would say:

Mitakue Oyasin
(To All My Relations).

Hózhónáházdlíí',
Hózh□́náházdlíí',
Hózh□́náházdlíí',
Hózh□́náházdlíí'.
(Beauty is Restored Again).

Asdzá Niłch□i Diyin Bik'idéez'íí (She Carries the Wind)

"Walking the Trail of the Spirit"

When I was a little girl, the most happy and important thing I could do was to get outside to play. I played outside until it was too dark to see every opportunity I got. I have always felt the nearness of something bigger than myself. I have always heard my heart. I didn't remember this until I was given the opportunity to look at my life through the eyes of Creator a few years ago. I didn't remember the innocence of my spirit nor the pure love that lived inside of me ... until I was asked to look at my life.

I am 55 years in this body on Earth. Lots of experiences stacked up over these years. So many of the things that happened to me were the result of pain ... my own and others. I didn't always see it this way. I thought I was responsible for myself and many adults and their choices. But I didn't remember things correctly.

I am the only child of my parents and one of several grandchildren. My parents were teens when I was born. So, from the beginning of my experience here with them in my family, I was the center intersection for the feelings of my parents. Lots of secrets. Subjects no one talked about. Certain feelings were not allowed nor tolerated. Trust outside the household frowned upon.

My parents both attended a strict religious school. Their parents were hard working people and also came from very strict religious teachings. Lots of fear and rules in their church. Good people, but with only a little joy from my perspective.

My mom is the most excellent person I know. She has quietly and purposefully gone through her life making a difference by using the tender love and encouragement of her heart. She is my hero.

The challenge and turmoil of my arrival was covered with judgment and harsh words and treatment from her church and school. Tender hearts were wounded. This happened to my mother and her parents. My mother took the brunt of the judgment from the people in her school and church. My mother and her family have given me an amazing example of forgiveness. Judgment comes through fear. I pray for freedom of both.

I am thankful to my sweet mother for keeping my life. I thank my father for giving me his name. They had a very difficult start, middle, and finish to their relationship. I wish to honor them. I simply appreciate that they did what they knew to do.

I felt love from all of my grandparents and have many very happy thoughts of them always. I appreciate their care and laughter with me.

I haven't needed much in the way of human companionship. I am a fairly self-contained person. This was a good way to survive. Learn how to cover all bases and be prepared for any/all situations at a moment's notice. Oh yes, and prepare for the other shoe to drop heavily from nowhere with no warning and be able to handle the disaster it will leave. All can be lost in a moment. Some of the tools I learned ... not great ones, but the continual exhaustion and fear took its toll on me.

It is easy to get caught in the trick of feeling responsible for the fearful choices of other people. If you believe you are not wanted or loved or that you have messed up so much you are useless ... you are being tricked. It's not true. It wasn't your fault. The scariest and meanest joke of all is when religion backs up the trick in the name of God. Courage and forgiveness are the two tools to help when you need freedom.

I learned to be deathly afraid of God from the moment I could learn. I was placed in church and expected to live teachings of fear in God. I had no hope. I went to sleep at night praying that God would come in judgment in between my sleepy-eyed prayers for forgiveness and my first waking moment for forgiveness for SOMETHING. I was not sure what was so bad or wrong, but that's what I was taught. Then I pled not to dream anything that would be offensive to a very mighty and furious God ... No peace. No rest. No hope. No chance. Exhaustion.

When I was given the invitation by Heaven to look at my life through the eyes of the Creator, I was sure that the view could only be the long list of my wrongs and sins. I had very little reason to think that my life was anything other than I saw in my own eyes. I didn't know how God truly saw me.

The words I heard from Heaven matched up instantly with a small memory. I remembered playing outside until dark catching fire flies. I got a flash of that little girl and the truth of how loved I was by God ... I remembered being spunky. Tirelessly playing. A kid with sparkly eyes, curly hair, dirty little hands from making mud pies ... I remembered knowing the hearts of animals ... I remembered flying as high as the rope swing could reach ... bicycle wrecks, horses, kittens, ice-cream licked from a freezer on the porch ... a bird dog ... walking in my grandfathers' footsteps in the summer vegetable garden, picking my mother's tulips.

I also got a memory flash of people yelling ... and fights, severe whippings, bruises, many tears, dark things from older men, my father leaving my life completely, the broken heart of my mother, the "no place to fit" ever again ... alcohol and pills ... the poor choices of relationships with people, marriages and divorces, always the church/God fear creeping around, dreams abandoned. No peace. No rest. No hope. Exhausted.

I needed help. Help came.

My heritage is Welsh, as well as Native American. In learning about my people, I have learned that the Spiritual Life is lived quietly and peacefully each day with joy and thanksgiving. I learned that being open to hearing what God says is not meant to cause fear. The messages for us come.

Heaven has a very personal touch when God extends the invitation to take a look at life. So, I got a visit from a stranger who told me what Angels have told people for zillions of years. It was not a new message:

> "FEAR NOT. GOD HAS SOME PLANS FOR YOU. THE PLANS ARE GOOD ... FULL OF HOPE. YOUR PRAYERS HAVE BEEN ANSWERED ... THE PLANS ARE A LITTLE UNUSUAL, BUT DON'T WORRY BECAUSE GOD IS WITH YOU ALWAYS. YOU ARE LOVED. ALL IS WELL."

From Heaven the courage came to look at both sides of my life. The pain I had caused was a trail of destruction. The pain I had suffered left me with wounds I thought were too big to cross. I asked and I believed that God would help me to look at both so that I could heal. So, I prayed. No fancy words or promises ... just asked for help.

Things changed. My heart began to heal ... really heal.

I was convinced that there was no hope, no peace, no rest. So I slowly self-destructed into a place that feels too deep to ever leave. I was there. I was shown the pain of the people who hurt me, and I saw the pain of the people I had hurt. Not a simple look, but a real look complete with matching feelings of the damage on both sides. I was shown how to forgive and be forgiven.

I got a glimpse ... a very rapid glimpse that changed me. That glimpse let me know that the trick was over.

I simply felt the long ago presence of my Creator ... the kind of, "Oh, yes, I remember this from a long time ago" ... No herald trumpets. No flapping wings. No hocus pocus voo doo.

What happened to me was familiar. Calm. Sobering. Peace-filled. Love. "Finally." My place to fit. Wanted. Invited. Welcomed. Accepted. Known. My heart finally in true rhythm. I felt the arms of Heaven.

Each person has a framework of truths, which give roots for growth. My framework has been a mixture of many cultures and beliefs. I asked God to help me without any concept of God to go by ... only my heart.

You can ask for whatever you need to help you look at your life. You can forgive. You can be forgiven. You can heal and be useful to God and your fellow travelers. You will be amazed before you are halfway through. You will know that you have always been totally loved. Nothing has ever changed that. No conditions. No strings. Just loved.

I met Medicine Road as part of the journey. She is living the love of Creator to all. It is my honor to walk in friendship with her. I appreciate the freedom she has given me to believe as I see fit. I appreciate walking the trail of the Spirit.

Lynn McLean

"The Way to Have Love in One's Life is to be Loving"

(The following two paragraphs are part of a note I sent to Medicine Road)

I have just finished reading your amazing book. It has taken many, many hours as every few pages my eyes are so full of tears I can't see the words. I send you a deeply heartfelt thank you for this very moving, truth-filled, wise and compassionate book. What a generous gift it is for us all, especially our sisters. And what a richly profound account of some native history.

Most native history is written by Anglos from the head, and allows the non-native reader to respond from the head with distance. You have written from the heart rendering the terms "they" and "them" meaningless, returning us to the true reality of "we" and "us" and "our."

****

I consider myself a member of the human family residing on planet earth. I prefer not being defined beyond that. Although I have delved into several religions and respect and am inspired by their core revelations and teachings, I have no affiliations. Religions always become institutions, and institutions are administered by egos whose agendas are rarely those of spirit.

Medicine Road speaks of a Plains tradition of receiving 4 different names denoting the different stages through out one's lifetime. Up until now, I have received three names. Looking back on them, they have marked a road for me to travel. I will tell about them to introduce myself.

I was born in 1936 in Nebraska, to a dysfunctional, frightened, and joyless family. The pregnancy had intensified my mother's ill health, putting her out of commission for an extended time and totally disrupting the day-to-day life of every one in the family. I was unwanted, unwelcome and unloved.

My father was born in tsarist Russia and orphaned. He had early childhood memories of the sound of hoof beats overhead. The villagers would kindly hide him in a cellar when the Cossacks came looking for Jews and Gypsies to kill. We had a vague awareness of what was happening to Jews in Europe and my father was afraid. My family was defined as Jewish but we did not practice.

In those early decades of the last century in Middle America people were anti-Semetic, anti-Negro, anti anybody different from themselves. What people thought about you was all-important. Addictions and abuses and emotional difficulties were shameful secrets. All therapies were viewed with total suspicion, so no help was available. Nice women weren't sexual. Children born outside of traditional marriage were 'bastards.' Any exploration off the beaten track was referred to as 'that's different' and 'different' was not a good thing. As I grew up it felt terribly stifling.

My grandmother was an angry, unhappy, mean spirited person. My father supported her and had made her a private apartment inside our house. In the sixteen years we lived together she never spoke to him. From the time I was three or four she would point a finger in my face and rant, "You nearly killed your mother when you were born and you've been trying to finish her off ever since."

Whatever I did, someone would let me know that it was wrong. I knew there had to be some other way to live. In those days middle class women were wives and mothers. We didn't know any one with a career or a different life. In my late teens not having any other resource I got married to run away from home. Not knowing better I married someone who was just like my mother. The marriage was a train wreck, and I had failed at the only thing I was supposed to do in life. Suicide seemed like the best course. Fortunately a dear friend redirected me and I began to look for some other way to live.

At the end of World War II there was a charity called "Care Package," comparable to the currant "Save The Children." A high school friend commented that I would be a perfect poster face for Care Package solicitation. That is one sad view of the story. Another preferable version would be how fortunate I am to have not been accepted in my birth family. This rejection required me to find another path in life. This alternate path has been filled with wise mentors and their generous teachings, good friends, and lovely light and love.

I knew that I was ill equipped to survive and in desperation became a Zen student and practiced for nine years. Zen emerged from Buddhism in medieval Japan in response to a need of the samurai warriors whose lives were constantly at risk.

I had two teachers. The young one trained me in survival, in discipline, in how to stay the course, how to move into and through pain. And in practical matters like being on time, and how to efficiently clean a temple, My older teacher, Nakagawa Soen Roshi, was a remarkable man, he became my spiritual father, kind and loving grandmother, and introduced me to joy, delight, and gratefulness. Was he an incarnate Angel? Certainly he was a blessing and I was able to begin a new life.

Marsha Louise was the first name I was given to honor my deceased grandfather Morris. I didn't like it and was looking for alternatives in a name book when I discovered that both names referred to warriors Marsha to Mars, the god of war and

Louise to a Celtic female warrior. My mother, a sad frightened, unrealized woman, unaware, had set me on the necessary road.

Soen Roshi gave me the name "Koshu," master hand. It was a play on my last name and because I cooked for retreats and made pottery and flower arrangements for the zendo. Koshu came from a verse about a master swordsman who no longer needed a sword. In traditional martial art schools, once one has mastered the physical and become invincible, the final mastery is in not needing to fight.

Manjusri, the bodhisattva of transcendental wisdom, carries a very sharp sword. He doesn't harm creatures, but when it comes to delusions he is uncompromising. Could this be how Archangel Michael is described in Asia?

Soen Roshi was no longer available on this plane, and being only half-baked I looked for another teacher. Feeling like a fish that had been hooked and reeled in I spent two and a half years in India at the Rajneesh ashram. Just being in India is an incredible expansive eye opener.

Rajneesh, was for me, a great benefactor and thief. There is Zen wisdom that the best teachers steal your delusions and give you back, make known to you, your true self.

I don't suppose the Angels wish to be called thieves but this seems like a fair description of our interactions!

Rajnessh gave me the name Ma Deva Amrita. Amrit is the elixir of immortality.

This elixir comes from distilling a great ocean involving the mountain at the center of the world and an enormous snake. A less poetic version of this distillation is to totally clean out the closet of one's ego. For the samurai it was "to die before you die."

****

A friend invited me to come with her to a "healing circle." I am open to investigation but always come with skepticism. About half a dubious hour into the circle I sensed a beautiful sparkling light flowing among us. Suddenly I was amazed to realize that out of nowhere and not having thought of her in decades, I had just forgiven my grandmother.

I was irresistibly drawn to the circle and began attending twice a week. I had recently quit my job at a local yarn store. The formal job description was to mind the store, sell yarn, and teach knitting. My private job description was to encourage folks to trust their own creativity and to leave the store feeling more alive than when they came in. Jobless, I suddenly was living a hermit's life and missed the chance to come into contact with many beings. The healing circle was a perfect community opportunity.

One day I asked Archangel Michael how I could best be used. Soon after, I had a stroke that paralyzed my left side and then, a broken leg requiring that I spend the next year and a half in hospitals, and assisted living facilities. When I next spoke with Michael he said I had been helpful to many? ! ?

Over the last several years, in the circle, I have witnessed many people being healed of a wide range of diseases, addictions, destructive relationships, negative self-judgments, and self blame.

It is impossible to comprehend, and heart numbing to witness the countless women and children, both male and female, who have been badly abused and raped. We the human family must come together to heal those who have been injured and to heal the epidemic that perpetuates this terrible injury generation after generation.

I have been privileged to sit next to Archangel Michael for countless hours, being a witness, hearing his counsel, and feeling the energy. These hours have been a rich education that I will do my best to share.

I don't believe that we are children that the Angels have come to rescue. We do behave as children, but it feels like they have come to encourage and assist us in maturing, and healing ourselves. They constantly remind us that we have free will. So we get to choose. There is a Sufi saying, "Allah will take care, but you must tether your own camel."

The Angels work ceaselessly to assist us in clarifying our spirits. We are all "works in progress." Although the Angels are anciently older and wiser than we, because we have free will they can only counsel and encourage us and demonstrate by example. Doing the work is entirely up to each one of us.

We are sentient beings. The dictionary definition: having the ability to feel and perceive. This is an incredible gift. It allows us to not only perceive creation but to also participate in creation as co-creators. Many folks complain that they feel too much, that feeling is too painful. Our culture with its numbing drugs and chemicals does not encourage us to honor authentic feeling. If Medicine Road had deadened her feeling as prescribed she would not have healed and would not be here with us today.

Medicine Road, and her loving partner, who stood by in support without judgment, and who now lends his body to the Angels, have been through enormous suffering and desperation. Their willingness to feel and face the suffering and desperation is what cultivated them, dug them so deeply, and opened them so widely. For me, they are an outrageous (as in amazing, and rarely met with) model of generosity and compassion.

The Angels are constantly demonstrating for us. They are not storage containers. They are creators, and transformers. The beings, who come to sit before Michael are rarely joyful. Mostly what they hold is fear, pain, and sorrow. I feel it all — well, I feel a share of it, and am able to stay hour after hour because I am not storing or incorporating the pain. A compost pile is capable of transforming garbage into rich fertile soil with endless nurturing possibilities. I have become a dedicated composter. Love is the catalyst that transforms and grounds fear, pain, and sorrow. Our universe is abundantly rich in love. It is our birthright, our very being.

Our stories are just that, stories. Every story can be viewed from different perspectives, and spun into many different versions.

The love of my life abruptly and unkindly departed, and for ten years I carried a story that my heart was broken. Eventually, it became clear that the story kept me connected to him so that I didn't have to totally face the loss. My mentor for this healing was Eckhart Tolle and his book The Power of Now. Eckhart counseled: look at the situation straight on, feel it, just as it is, don't fix anything. In looking straight on, it was obvious that certainly my heart ached, but remained whole and unbroken. In being willing to look and truly feel, I tasted unconditional love, and my heart emerged as an expansive possibility. The simple and painful act of just looking and feeling became a transformative miracle!

No one is an isolated island. Each of us has a sphere of influence. Some spheres are large and some smaller, but absolutely every one of us affects other beings. Michael repeatedly confirms that there is no need to physically touch. Whether we are near or far doesn't matter. We each have a wide range of possible vibrations, ranging from fear, mistrust, disrespect, hatred, and violence to the flip side, trust, care, respect, compassion, and love. We are all consciously or unconsciously perpetually emanating. The Christ, the Angels, all the profound teachers in human history have urged that we become conscious and loving. Michael invites us to be conscious in an ever-expanding sphere.

It has taken more than half my lifetime to wake up to the truth: "The way to have love in one's life is to be loving."

Marsha Feinhandler

"Amazing Grace"

For more years than I care to remember, grief and guilt have kept me from feeling God. In spite of this, throughout my life, God has always been near. From Sunday school age to adulthood, most of my life I thought I knew God, or at least had some notion of what I believed. I recall that about junior high school age, I actually said out loud, "Does God really exist? If so how can it be that so many are dying in VietNam? How can so many people in the world be suffering? " I promptly received a slap across my face, the very last one my mother ever gave me.

Even if it was rhetorical, and I don't think it was, it was a silly question. The question pre-supposes that terrible things in the world are God's doing, or at least His fault for not preventing or undoing them. In my late twenties, I recall flying, night after night, throughout the universe, light as a feather, propelled by Heavenly Spirit, high above the planet, weaving among the stars, waking up as I re-entered my body. I recall that as many older people I knew began to pass away, I would see them in my dreams, saying goodbye, reassuring me that they were OK, and leaving instructions for their families and friends. I would awaken to learn that the person in my dream had actually died in the night, or days before I was told.

I also recall feeling I was an outsider in my family. Yet, just when everything seemed the most disconnected, there was always someone to remind me I was loved. I recall being in a life threatening situation where facing an unexpected violent death seemed too incredible to accept. Rather than panic and fear, I was flooded with a feeling of love and peace, and I was left knowing that day was not my day to die.

So God has always been present in my life. And I have known it. I recall feeling God inside of me and in my life. But knowing this did not stop me from making decisions that moved me, at times, away from God. Now I understand it is one thing to do things — to act far from God — it is quite another to be far from God. Not to feel God. Not to feel His love. Not to be able feel much of anything. To be in bondage, with a weight so heavy not even my slave ancestors could bear it. Not to be able to love others, to truly love with the depth of love I was brought here to give. It is a difference I never want to know again, ever. That is what being healed means to me. That is what God has taught me through His Angels to understand. To be "of God" is a simple choice, moment to moment. To be far from God is also a choice. If ever there were a verse meant for me, my own personal mantra, it is "Amazing Grace, how sweet the sound, that saved a wretch like me. I once was lost, but now I'm found, was blind, but now I see."

I lived for some time doing things that were far from God because I believed I had to in order to love others and give them what they so clearly wanted from me. Even though my intent was not "bad," the way people taught me to "love" them kept me farther from God than I wanted to be. Looking back, I can see that some hurts In my life were caused by others, but most hurts were self-inflicted, a result of my own will. Because I did not believe I was worthy and I judged myself, I did not have the family I always dreamed of having. I did not marry the "man of my dreams," and I did not have biological children. The peak of this painful time was, ironically, when I could not feel hurt, happiness, and most importantly, God. I was not sure I even still had a soul that was my own. It was a period during which almost all of my immediate family, and immediate family circle, died. My remaining siblings and I went on living very separate lives. The only feeling I allowed myself was to feel alone in the universe. But even in my "unfeeling" state, I knew that what I believed about my isolation was not true. Friends tried to reach out to me, and I began to feel a tug at my heart.

I finally began to pray, to seek God. I would cry until

emotionally spent. I would cry because I had sought God again, and now I could grieve, and release the hurt. I could substitute sadness for the love I felt for those I lost. It was the beginning of my healing. During this time I travelled to visit friends who also were on their personal journey to God. My friends explained that they had something fantastic to share.

On the first evening with my friends, the Archangel Raphael visited with me. I was awestruck. I believed in Angels but as far I knew, I had never met one. I was humbled and timid in his presence. Admittedly, I was also frightened. Not so much of the Angel because he was quiet, peaceful, and gentle. I was frightened, of course, believing that facing my sins was about to be a "here and now experience," not some future event in the afterlife. And I believed I had a lot of sins to account for. To my surprise, I was put somewhat at ease. This Angel shared with me my Native American name, "White Dove," meaning, "pure heart."

Although I was frightened of Heaven's judgment that day, I have come to understand that this Angel was telling me that God knows my heart, as He knows your heart. And if you believe that there are wrongdoings in your past, when you ask God for forgiveness, He will always forgive. It is when I remember these things, and this beautiful name that Heaven gave to me, that I work very hard to be close to God in my actions, intent, and thoughts. It is harder than I ever imagined to live up to such a blessed name as White Dove. So, often I still have moments when I grumble at work, or snap a laser tongue at a friend, or ignore the homeless person, or envy someone else's' prosperity, or their happy family. It is a daily effort not to be "far from God" in some aspect. But my spiritual name is a constant reminder for me to try.

My healing, though still in progress as I have so much to learn, nonetheless continues. I am a work in progress. Several Angels began to teach me how to look at my life more for what it is than what I was afraid it was. White Earth touched me and gave me a gentle understanding of how I came to make choices outside of God's will for me. I began facing so many of my own acts that were wrong. The more I faced in my life, the more I remembered how far from God I have acted throughout my life- — how far from God I was. The pain of those wrong doings became overwhelming. But I was feeling again, even if it was pain. I prayed to God to forgive me, to increase my faith, and to stay with me.

My prayers for myself are to be as my spiritual name signifies — that my heart may really become pure; and to love others as God has loved me. I learned most importantly from Archangel Michael that, "*Not to forgive yourself when God has not only forgiven your sins, but He has forgotten them, is to dishonor God.*" We are souls who God allows to come to earth and in agreement with Him, to do such as is His will for us. Our daily road map is to follow the path of the Christ Jesus when he was on earth, as best we can, and to love as God has loved us. We all have our own pathway to do so. To stay stuck in grief and guilt kept me from feeling God, His love for me, and sharing that love with all I can.

Now prayer is a constant in my life. I pray for others and the world. We have been told that miracles are God showing us His presence. Visiting with Angels is a great miracle in my life and each encounter is an amazing blessing. The more I pray, the more God reaches out to me. The Archangel Michael shared with me once that my family make-up was not as I had grown up to believe. It explained my feelings of being an "outsider." As shocking as the news was, it made sense and that knowledge was an incredible gift. I was able to understand that I was chosen to live in my family, regardless of my origin. My parents' love and sacrifices were much more of a special gift, rather than a duty, than I could have ever imagined. And God has even answered my prayers for a family, as He is sending me those who need to be loved as only a mother can love them. As I look around me, my family grows.

I am an African-American woman who outwardly reflects all of the multi-ethnicity my heritage contains. My ancestors come from Africa, Asia, America, and Europe. It used to frustrate me that I was not immediately identifiable to those outside my family and circle as belonging to one ethnicity, as I was often shunned by one or another. During my life, I have travelled so many places in the world and been asked if I am Asian, Native American, South American, Maltese, Hawaiian, and more. I have never felt particularly attached to any one place I have visited. Recently, I recalled my flights throughout the universe, and realized that I think of myself, especially since I no longer have an earthly father or mother, as a child of the universe, a child of God the Father. While ethnic, cultural awareness, and family ties matter, "belonging" no longer matters. I accept my heritage as God's gift to allow me to move with such ease among so many to share His love, and live a life of truly ... Amazing Grace.

White Dove

"A Sister's Love"

I live in the mountains of northern New Mexico. Next door to me is a spiritual center that I help take care of, the house of my teacher, the mystic and painter, Herman Rednick, where the Angels meet with us. I came here from the east, forty years ago, seeking, and I found through Herman a genuine path--of love and the Christ within the heart. Just visible from his house is the golden crown of our stupa, a sacred Tibetan Buddhist monument representing the other path followed here, of the compassion and wisdom of the Buddha. I practice them both, East and West, and am blessed with the Grace of the Angels, which clears the way within and without to walk my walk. The heaven-on-earth walk.

I'm a poet and writing teacher to young people.

I raised my family here, in the house my husband built—two boys grown now and settled in the Northwest.

My first family raised my siblings and me in upstate New York. Our parents loved each other and us, though as the oldest, I had left for college while the younger ones still had their struggles. My parents were serious about Jesus' message to "love your neighbor as yourself," and worked within the Protestant church and in impassioned new kinds of forms to bring alive the immediacy the early Christians must have felt trying to really live Christ's teachings. But I had to find my own way, outside of anything established. My family blessed me on that journey.

Andrew, my middle brother, had a troubled time in the same setting that supported me—in a way, each child in the same house has a different family. And he was so smart and impulsive and angry, no one knew what he needed. He found relief in alcohol early, and it didn't disintegrate him until later.

I always thought of him as my twin. I knew we were identical inside, specifically identical. But from that beginning place, our roads unrolled, and on mine, everything was given, and on his, everything was taken away.

Carl Jung says, "Neurosis is always a substitute for legitimate suffering." I thought about this with Andrew. How the only real healing of what I saw behind his eyes, would have to address the first rupture after the first wholeness. And so it did.

****

My brother came across the country to live with me when his life hit bottom. I don't know what inner demons contended in him, but I know the alcohol he was so vulnerable to, made them worse.

From childhood, I knew his sensitivity and pure heart. But they had no place that anyone valued in his fast-paced professional life of competition, brilliance, and material gain. I had seen him hit the pinnacle of worldly success, and now, ten years later, the void of self-destruction and near-despair. And between who he really was and what he had become in his own mind, lay an abyss. Unspoken wounds filled it, and their poisons of shame, helplessness, and depression. A sister's love and the mountains and stars had done all they could, but it wasn't enough.

When I asked him if he would come with me to the Angels' healing circle, he was afraid of what a true eye would see in him. His voice shook as he told me this later. And his bravery in taking that risk still astonishes me. When he did sit before Archangel Michael, undefended and revealed, the Angel spoke of nothing but my brother's love. This, and this alone. His heart. His dedication to his wife. His goodness. Later, Angel Raphael thanked me for bringing him to Them. It must have been just in time.

The hardness, the sickness, the bitter armor fell away. A complete physical healing would take more time, but the inner healing poured in with power. The Angels are always kind, unbelievably kind, but to my brother they were an elixir of tenderness. They must have known.

A few months later my brother was dead, suddenly, of a massive brain hemorrhage. But he passed out of flesh a healed man.

In the hospital, just before the machines were unplugged, I stood with his wife while she spoke her love and her last goodbye into his ear. And then in the silence, something happened beyond the world. My little brother, brain dead in the ICU, slowly, slowly raised his arms from his sides and curved them above his heart like an embrace. It was a kind of miracle, this last message that shouldn't have been possible. But the real miracle had already happened, hadn't it, sweetheart? And since that is possible, so is everything else.

Gabrielle Liana Herbertson

"The Creator is Here for Us"

This book is an answer to women's prayers. Medicine Road uses her own life and healing experiences to selflessly help her sisters. Her book shines a light on false beliefs that make us sick and keep us from being who we truly are. I shed many tears reading this book — tears where I felt Creator's presence and love coming through the words, tears of sadness, and tears because I could relate to many of the feelings described. Reading about her experiences and the experiences of the other women detailed in these pages helped me to think about what happened to me in my own life. The tears I shed led me closer toward my own healing. This book gives tools to help us to understand what we confront in this world, how we can change and, ultimately, how we can help others.

Medicine Road asked me to share something about my life with you. It is important that all women know that God/Creator is here for them. I grew up in a small German town in the 1960s and was raised Roman Catholic. Strict rules governing what was acceptable behavior and unacceptable behavior were applied. Strong, overpowering authority figures were to be obeyed without question and corporal punishment was the norm.

As a child and a young woman, I felt that I had to live within a very small frame of what was acceptable behavior in society's eyes, and if someone stepped out of that frame, she/he was punished. It was suffocating. The world had built a box for me (and everyone else) that was just too small. There was a lot of judgment, and always someone telling me what to do and how to be. Over time, I started to believe that I was not worthy, and that I was not good enough the way I was. I felt that I could never do anything right. I believed these lies and put myself in a narrow prison. The bars of my cell were self-judgment and low self-esteem.

These false beliefs led to a life that was more about existing and surviving than living. Deep down I felt that there was something else, and I knew that there was something missing. I was searching for this "something" my whole life, but I was stuck. Because of what I believed about myself, I ended up in relationships that were not healthy. I wanted to be loved and to truly love another, but because I did not know that I was worthy and I was used to having to make myself "small," I was simply used by others. Because my personal boundaries had been violated at a very young age, I did not believe that I could say "no" to these men. I believed I had to obey, even when it was against my will or better judgment.

But even through this, I held onto the feeling that there was "more" and I was searching for something deeper, and I did not even know at the time what exactly I was looking for. I did not take drugs and I did not drink alcohol. These things did not interest me, but finding what I felt to be missing did interest me. When I was old enough, I left the Catholic Church and started to seek elsewhere. I studied with a Native American shaman, looked into Buddhism, consulted New Age healers, read about Indian gurus .... Even though I would think that I had found something in the beginning, it never lasted for long. I realized that even though the frames were different, there was still someone who would tell me what to do, how to be, what to wear, and how to behave.

Most importantly, I could clearly see the abuse of power that is so often a part of the lives of the people "in charge." The egos, the power trips, the money ... I was repulsed and angered by the notion of giving another human power over me in order to find Spirit — and to pay for it. I started to rebel. This just did not feel right! I felt that I needed to find what I was looking for inside. So I started to take the spiritual truths that I learned with a grain of salt, and I used only what I believed to be true. Even though I was in that tight prison, a part of me was strong and I wanted OUT! I decided to follow my heart. I believed in God — not in a God as the church pictured Him — but a loving God. I believed in Angels, and in a Higher Power.

But through all my life I followed "my gut"; when I felt that something was the right thing to do, I would do it. Often times, my friends and family were not supportive of my decisions. I packed my bags and moved to the United States in the 1990s. I quit jobs when I felt they were not right for me. I left bad relationships and tried to learn from my mistakes. I would try to "make it better" next time. However, over time I became discouraged and decided that relationships were not for me and that I would be happier living alone. I would have a good life by trying to help others, and "give up" my attempt to find true love with the partner that I had always been seeking.

Then, in 2007, I heard about a prayer circle that meets in Taos, New Mexico every few months. I heard about this couple that would gather with others in order to "bring Heaven down." This was Medicine Road and her husband. Because of what had happened to them and how they responded, they were able to serve as vessels for God, The Creator and they would help others to learn how to do this so that they, too, would understand that Creator was always with them. At times, the Holy Spirit and individual Angels would enter them and speak with people on a personal level. People would receive direct help from Heaven in this way. The healings were powerful and lives were being changed.

These people refused to take any money, gifts, or donations. I did not have to "sign up" or join anything, and they did not want anything from me in return. We gathered to sit and pray for others, and our love helped to "bring Heaven here." I knew that this was right. I had no idea what to expect when I went there for the first time. Archangel Michael and later Mary Magdalene talked to me, and I felt so much love and understanding that I cried for hours. These tears helped to release the deep-seated pain that I had carried with me all my life. It was selfless love that I was experiencing. Heaven was here to help me to understand that I was perfect the way I am! There was no judgment, just love, understanding, and healing.

My life has changed drastically since that day — all in very good and beautiful ways. In order to heal, I had to begin to look at my life. Not to suffer or beat myself up, but to gain understanding, forgive those who hurt me, and learn to have compassion for others and for myself. I have grown more into the person I truly am. Change is not easy, and it takes time and dedication. Even with all the ups and downs I can truly tell you that it is so worth it! I found my soul mate in the process. He is a man who is also willing to "do the work" — to grow, change, and reach his true potential and the reason we came to this earth. As Archangel Raphael put it one day: "*We come here to learn how to love!*"

Ute Bonn

"Hallelujah! Praise be to God, the Creator"

(Rather than a full story, Susan Esther shared a few vignettes from her life and her experience of reading this book. She concluded with a statement regarding her work with the Sacred Healing Circle...)

Baruch atah Adonai elohaynu melech
ha-olam she-hechiyanu v'ki-yimanu v'higi-yanu lazman hazeh

A prayer in the Hebrew tradition that my mother recited on special occasions, when there was a cause for celebration:

Blessed art Thou, oh Lord our God, King of the Universe who has granted us life, sustained us and enabled us to reach this moment.

Tears stream down my eyes. Tears are streaming down my eyes as I remember the words to this prayer...because I did not know whether I would have the strength, the stamina and the sheer will to survive. I did not believe that I had the courage it would take to continue to live. But I have survived to celebrate this day. Hallelujah! Praise be to God, the Creator.

****

Medicine Road requested more than a month ago that I share my story. Like a starving child, I immediately opened the book, reading, seeking any morsel that might offer deeper understanding and insight. But little did I know the emotional toll that would be asked—by the second half I was breaking down into sobs and releasing powerful, raw feelings at frequent intervals—the pure, naked feelings of an infant or very young child who has not yet a context of words or language as a container.* My guess is that, consequently, my earliest memories remained frozen in some central core of Self, impervious to any attempts to unearth....so it is still very difficult to share my beginnings; yet those pieces that have come into my consciousness are telling...

*Much of the abuse I was subject to started when I was still pre-verbal.

****

I was born of Jewish blood. My father's name was Sholom, a Hebrew greeting for "hello"...."goodbye," but its literal meaning is PEACE. As in "peace be with you." But there was anything but peace in our home. It was, in so many ways, like a war zone.

My birth occurred in May of 1947, just a few years following the World War. Still, a peace treaty cannot erase in a second the raging anti-Semitism that had been so prevalent. My grandparents, immigrants, lived in a small New England town and my grandfather was targeted by a Dark element for attack. My guess: it was this stress that caused his death (attributed to asthma) several years before I was born.

My father, too, was prey to the dark energy of Iktomi. After his father died, he dropped out of high school to work, to help his family to survive. With time, Iktomi twisted his mind; he turned from a tall, slim, bespectacled, idealistic young man (who wrote a stirring poem about the Holocaust)—the man my mother married—to one who became bitter, prejudiced, abusive, authoritarian. Fear was the food my siblings and I were raised upon. And, indeed, his increasing anger, self-loathing, and blame were projected onto me, the eldest daughter. "It's all Susan's fault,"--his booming voice pointing a finger towards me—became a constancy in my life. I was to be the scapegoat.

****

At some point (exactly when, I am not sure, but certainly well before adolescence), I took what was most precious and most alive...Was it my faith? My belief in God's goodness and grace? The sanctity of my soul? My life force? I don't know... But in a desperate attempt to survive, I buried it deep, very deep inside. I encased it in a container of steel, and then placed that within a box made of iron, put both in a concrete enclosure and covered it with brick*...so that NO ONE, NO ONE, NO ONE could violate, contaminate, much less find, my core essence. The only problem thereby was that in so doing, I hid it from myself—it was totally inaccessible. And as time passed, as time went by, I eventually forgot its very existence.

*The image, this scenario, became a vivid and recurring symbol in my life.

****

The Sacred Healing Circle (I understand it to be called the Prayer Circle, as well) has become the very depth and breadth of my existence. I live and breathe it in every moment and it has brought me the meaning I have been seeking my entire life. I now understand that the earlier experiences I suffered through—as a child, a youth, a young woman, mid-age—and the heightened challenges I continue to face are all necessary... They are preparing me for the further work I am to do, what I am to complete, before I die. There is nothing I believe on earth that can bring greater satisfaction than this: to be aligned with the purpose of one's soul, the very reason for taking birth.

There is a way in which I never stop working. I live in a small town in New Mexico and wherever I go, at every turn, I never know whom I might next meet. Or, perhaps, closer to the truth, whom the Creator might place in my path. I live a simple life; for some time I have sensed that my circumstances (little money, no car, frequent moving about—for several years I was homeless--) may have been my soul's choice as the means to fulfill a mission. The assignment: reach as many people as possible—as many races, diverse ages, social strata, ethnicities, religious/spiritual persuasions, idiosyncratic orientations, as you can. So I have the opportunity, at almost any moment, to open the door (perhaps in answer to a prayer) to the Healing Circle and, what's more, to God. To <u>feeling</u> God. What could be more critical? Sometimes I smile when I am hitchhiking and it takes me a long while to catch a ride—my guess...the Angels have not quite arranged the connection as yet—and I ask God, "OK, whom do you want me to meet?" It has occurred to me, especially after reading Medicine Road's book, that I am not unlike the Cheyenne of her ancestry in this work.

It was maybe four years ago that Archangel Michael said to me, "You know you are working with us, don't you?" I shrugged my shoulders, said a meager "Yes"...I assumed he was referring to the calling list (I am the person who notifies others of the next date, time, and location of the healing circles.) When Marcia left, moved to another state, I offered to take over the original phone list she had started. In point of fact, my personal list had already exceeded her own...But I still laugh when I remember that time...little did I know the extent of what Michael had in mind when he made that statement!

There are now a few others who help to call to tell particulars of the next Circle (date, place, etc.). I am still reluctant to move to an email system for this reason especially: the Angels are so personal, so intimate with each of us, that I wish to maintain that sentiment. And there are people who have the need to ask a question or share their experience of the Angels. Regardless, I am awed that so many people continue to come simply by word of mouth or invitation of their friends, names which never appear on any list. I am very persistent, reluctant to remove anyone, even if a person has not come in quite some time. There is a chance, always the chance, that someone may return...which does, indeed, happen, and is not so uncommon.

I am near fanatical in my devotion. And I DO NOT GIVE UP. But it is not easy work. There are a few whom I have encouraged for literally years and continue to alert, even though they have never come...at least, not yet...But I continue. For it is my greatest joy to see one whom I have invited appear for the very first time, to know that I have been an instrument for the work of the Divine. And a greater blessing yet to watch the changes that occur with that individual if they choose to continue, by their free will, with this work. My greatest pain is to watch a woman, young adult or youth, whom Mary Magdalen comes forth to greet. For then I know there has been yet one more abuse, violation of a female. It strengthens my resolve; I vow to redouble my efforts.

My words would not be complete without offering a note of eternal gratitude to Medicine Road, her husband and family...I am immediately reminded of the truism that, "One person (or, in this case, one woman) CAN make a difference." Medicine Road, initially, reached out to just ONE other woman who was hurting. Each of us has this ability. ONE to ONE, ONE by ONE, working together, we can accomplish this mission --of anchoring Heaven here upon our beloved planet, Earth.

So I say again, Medicine Road, (on behalf of every woman)--for all that you do to contribute to "Heaven Descending," may God bless you. WE LOVE YOU! God, indeed, has touched each one of us through you and your work.

Susan Esther Braune

Bibliography

Websites:
Members.tripod.com/~Glove_r/Sweet.html (Sweet Medicine)
www.legendsofamerica.com/NA-BlackKettle.html (Black Kettle)

Books:

At the Side of Torture Survivors: Treating a Terrible Assault on Human Dignity, Edited by: Sepp Graessner, M.D., Norbert Gurris, and Christian Pross, M.D., Johns Hopkins University Press, Baltimore 2001.

Greene, Jerome A. and Scott, Douglas D., *Finding Sand Creek: History, Archeology, and the 1864 Massacre Site*, University f Oklahoma Press: Norman, 2004

Grinnell, George Bird, *The Cheyenne Indians: History and Society, Volume I*, University of Nebraska Press, Lincoln and London, 1972.

Groth, A. Nicholas. *Men who Rape: The Psychology of the Offender*. New York: Plenum Press, 1979.

Marshall III, Joseph M., *The Day the World Ended at Little Bighorn: A Lakota History*, 2007 Penguin Group USA New York

Matsakis, Aphrodite Ph.D, *Trust After Trauma: A Guide to Relationships for Survivors and Those Who Love Them*, New Harbinger Publications, California 1998.

Ofer, Dalia and Weitzman, Lenore J., *Women in the Holocaust*, Yale University Press, New Haven and London, 1998.

Powell, Peter J., *Sweet Medicine Volume One*, University of Oklahoma Press, Norman 1969.

Magazines:
The Economist, *Gambling on Nation-Building*. April 7, 2012.

Documentaries:
"The Great Indian Wars, 1540 — 1890" Disc I

Notes

1. There were seven bands of the Lakota people, two bands of the Nakota people and four bands of the Dakota people. "The Lakota, Dakota, and Nakota alliance reached up to twenty-five thousand people in the mid-1800s ..." (Marshall III, The Day the World Ended at Little Bighorn, 19)
2. "American-Indian women are four times as likely to be raped and ten times as likely to be murdered as white American women." (The Economist, *Gambling on Nation-Building*, 35.)
3. In helping women and children to heal, I have found that the path walked by Jesus of Nazareth and the teachings, understanding, and traditions of my Native American ancestors, as handed down and practiced before the Europeans crossed the "great water," provide a clear path to Heaven. This does not mean that other cultures or religions are not close to God, or that all Christian denominations and Native American belief systems "had it right." What it means is that Jesus Christ, the being, and many of the people native to the Americas at a particular time in history, strove each day to walk the path of God and bring Heaven here. They understood that a part of the Creator was in every living creature, whether it was a person, animal, plant, or even a drop of water. Creator never left them because they were always with Him. Therefore, it was imperative that all life be respected. Everything "of Him" was sacred. They believed that Heaven and Earth become one through faith, prayer, and the selfless love of others. Heaven was and is here. Creator sends his Angels before Him. They are here now. The world can be as it was for First Century Christians, my Native American ancestors, and other tribes around the world who understood these truths. The presence of God and His Holy Spirit is as real and tangible today as it was then. We only have to create the conditions and walk the road to Heaven without fear.

It is the understanding and application of this approach that will return this world to Heaven.

4. In the Plains Indian cultures, each person traditionally receives a series of names during their time here in flesh. An elder bestows these names upon a person. Such elders receive these names from the Holy Spirit during prayer. The first name is given to a person when they are born, the second is given during adolescence, a third name may be given when a person has "earned" it by their actions, responses, and the way in which they conduct themselves, and the fourth one may be given to a person in old age before they pass from flesh. "Sweet Flower" is my first name. "Sweet Bear Flower" is my second name, and "Medicine Road" is my third name.

5. "Jesus said and did some things that were remembered and passed down orally. People did not repeat everything he said and did, but only what was particularly memorable or distinctive, especially what was of use in the early churches for preaching, teaching, ritual practices, and other aspects of community life. His parables and his sayings (called aphorisms) were often so striking, so pithy and memorable, that they were repeated again and again." (King, *The Gospel of Mary of Magdala*, 93-94.)

6. There is no record of any ancient Native American tribe from North America having had a formal, written language. This is not because they "were not smart enough" to develop such a system of communication, but because they believed that such a system did not allow the person on the receiving end to feel God as well as oral communication and/or the use of symbols. Life here on Earth was about helping one another to return to our essence, which is what is "of God."

7. During the period that the Bible was actually written, the word that we see in the Bible today as "miracle" was actually "sign" or evidence of "power." According to Archangel Michael, this distinction is important. A "miracle" is something that is out of the ordinary, while a "sign" or evidence of God's "power" is something from God and Heaven directly given to remind us of who we are and why we came.

8. (All Bible references from the New Testament are taken from *The Disciples New Testament: The Galilean Edition* as translated by Victor N. Alexander. It is a direct translation into English from the Ancient Aramaic New Testament. Aramaic was the language spoken by Jesus and the apostles, and it was the language in which

the Biblical scribes originally wrote. This allows for less error on the part of translators over time.)

In the Biblical passage John 8:31-33 Jesus taught people the power of "truth."

And Jesus said to those Jews who believed in him, "If you are loyal to my manifestation, you are truly my disciples. ***You shall know the Truth and the Truth shall set you free."*** *They said to him, "We are the offspring of Abraham, and we never perform work for any human being. How can you say that we shall be free?" Jesus told them, "Amen, amen, I am telling you, that whoever commits sin is the slave of sin. And the slave is forever unable to hold on to his home, but the Son establishes you till eternity. For thus the Son shall make you free, that truly you shall be the Sons of the Free."* [My emphasis added.]

9. Jesus taught this lesson more than 2,000 years ago. In Mark 10:27 Jesus explains this concept to his disciples. "*Jesus gazed at them and told them, 'This cannot be, according to human beings, except according to God, for everything is possible according to God.'*"
10. According to Federal authorities, this couple and others with whom they worked had been targeting families in the United States for years. They have also operated in New York, Chicago, San Diego, Miami, and the Caribbean, among other places. Their "scam" involved surreptitiously drugging men, women, and children. While these "victims" were under the influence of drugs, they were raped, tortured and otherwise humiliated. All of this was recorded. These recordings were then copied onto DVDs and sold around the world.
11. Since mankind has inhabited this earth, people have either "climbed" or gone "into" Mother Earth in an attempt to feel God's Grace and communicate with the Holy Spirit. Some cultures traditionally climbed mountains or built mounds in an attempt to get closer to Heaven, while others constructed holes in Mother earth or utilized caves in an attempt to be surrounded by what is "of God" during prayer.
12. Although I am Native American by blood (100 percent on my mother's side and an unknown percentage on my father's side), I did not grow up celebrating the traditions of my ancestors. Because of the stigma and persecution associated with being Native American, which still exists in the United States today, my mother told my brothers and I that we were "mostly Dutch and English"

and that our dark skin and ethnic features were a result of some "Spanish blood from the *conquistadors.*" Although my maternal grandmother shared stories about her childhood in the jungles of Southern Mexico and we witnessed her using Mayan healing techniques, my mother clung to her claim that our bloodlines were European. The Holy Spirit and individual Angels of the Lord understood this and were gracious enough to serve as my spiritual teachers. Black Kettle lovingly and patiently taught me many of the ceremonial traditions observed by my people, as well as the purpose behind them. For example, Black Kettle showed me how to open my prayers to Creator in the traditional manner by placing blades of sweet grass or sage into the eyes and nose of a buffalo skull and offering it to the Grandmothers and Grandfathers whose love and prayers "hold" the four directions of this world.

13. When Heaven first began sending my Ancestors to teach me the "old ways," I did not understand the significance of working with animal skins. As I do not like to kill anything and I love animals, I was not comfortable using their hides during prayer. However, once Heaven explained the significance to me, I began to use them frequently. The Holy Spirit explained that as with human beings, there are certain animals that come to this earth specifically to help and to serve. Although their body may pass, the soul of that animal can still be "called upon" through prayer to help others. When using an animal skin in ceremony or prayer, the hide/skin is representative of the true essence of the animal. It is that "essence" which "comes" to help to lift the person in need, or the person praying, closer to the Creator.

14. The concept of the Holy Spirit using people as vessels and speaking through them is one that is present in many religious. There are many references to this in the Bible. In Mark 13:11 Jesus sits on the Mount of Olives with some of his apostles and says: "*When they come near to you then, to deliver you, do not go forth at a loss as to what you will say, and do not rehearse, except say that which will be given to you in that hour, that is what you are to say. For it will not be you who speaks, except the Holy Spirit.*" This concept is referenced again in Luke 1:67-68: "*And the Holy Spirit filled Zechariah, and he prophesied and said, 'Blessed is the Lord God of Israel, who consecrates [Binds with] him and makes him a savior.*'" There are also many references of Jesus being filled with the Holy Spirit, such as in Luke 4:1: "*Jesus, then, as he was filled*

with the Holy Spirit left the Jordan River and the Spirit fetched him to the wilderness."

15. "Judith L. Herman writes that 'a definitive dissolution of trauma is just as impossible as a total cure. The victim is going to feel the aftereffects of the traumatic event for a lifetime.'" (Herman 1994, 303) (Karcher, *At the Side of Torture Survivors*, 76)
16. The drugs this group used on me included high doses of an anesthetic that creates memory loss. In my case, much of my memory loss was temporary. Over a two-year period I was able to recount under oath for Federal Authorities most of what occurred.
17. According to the Holy Spirit, there are two kinds of Angels that work here on earth and in Heaven. One is a Healing Angel and one is an Archangel. Only an Archangel can go into hell after a soul who is suffering and help set them free. I thank God that the Archangel Michael came for me, and that I could continue to serve Our Father in Heaven in this manner.
18. Once a person in flesh becomes a vessel for the Holy Spirit, an Angel such as the Archangel Michael can continue to work with that soul to do God's work long after that soul has passed from flesh. My people have known this for thousands of years. In the beginning, Bear Feathers and Archangel Michael would come together to surround me with Heaven so that I could sleep.
19. At the time that this occurred, my children and I did not understand that Bear Feathers and the Archangel Michael were filling us with the Grace of God. All we understood was that an Angel entered my husband's body and lifted a hand toward us. As energy emanated from the hand, our fear and pain would subside enough that we could fall asleep. The children began to refer to this as "zapping," since it reminded them of something that might occur in a movie. This is but one of the ways that I experience Angels, the Holy Spirit, and the Grace of God. However, initially it was very important, as it was so "tangible" and the energy that emanated from the vessel was so "undeniable."
20. The definition for "pacifism" in the Merriam-Webster.com dictionary is: "1. opposition to war or violence as a means of settling disputes; specifically [the] refusal to bear arms on moral or religious grounds. 2: an attitude or policy of nonresistance."
21. The following is from a personal narrative by Liza Chapnik: "In October 1942, Gestapo men came to our apartment to search for Grisha [her brother] and me. Grisha had already escaped to

Bialystok, and I was in my shelter on the roof. When they didn't find us, they took my father. They warned him that if he didn't tell them where his son and daughter were, they would hang him. Our neighbor and relatives told me that my father was smiling as he left home. Maybe he went fearlessly, erect, and behaved with dignity because he was religious and for him it was 'kiddush hashem' — sanctification in the name of God." (Ofer, *Women in the Holocaust*, 114)

22. According to the Holy Spirit, there is no beginning and no end to life once God creates it. Our time here on this earth is an experience that we pray to God to have so that we can grow closer to Him by learning love, compassion, and forgiveness. Since we are immortal beings who live forever, there is no "death" as we have come to believe in this world. Those souls who are here in a body are referred to as those "in flesh" and the transition a soul undergoes when their body "dies" is referred to as "passing from flesh."

23. Luke 23:34 states: "*However, Jesus said, 'Father, forgive them, for they know not what they do.' And they divided his garments and cast lots over them.*"

24. According to some historians, "It is said that no tribe suffered more during the Indian Wars than the Cheyenne." (The Great Indian Wars, 1540 — 1890, Disc I) Although only God can measure the suffering of His children, the Holy Spirit has confirmed that the Cheyenne suffered greatly during this time in history. Overall, their faith in Creator and their commitment to serving Heaven was very strong. Many anthropologists and other tribes of the time considered them to be among the "most spiritual" of the Plains Indians. "... of all the plains tribes, the Cheyennes most completely centered their lives upon the sacred ceremonies." (Powell, *Sweet Medicine*, xxv) Those within the U.S. government and military who were in a position of power understood that they could not "break" the Cheyenne as easily as they could other tribes, therefore, they were afraid of them and targeted them.

25. Not all Cheyenne chiefs were willing to "make peace" with the United States at this time in history. Many were tired of "negotiating" treaties with the "white man" only to find that they had been tricked and lied to. They were tired of watching their people die. Black Kettle firmly believed that peace, Creator's way, was the only way. He suffered ridicule from other Cheyenne leaders for this stance both before and after the massacre.

26. The Holy Spirit taught me that there was spiritual significance to the soldiers' decision to mutilate the bodies. The Plains Indians believed that their bodies had to be "whole" in order for them to ascend to Heaven. In mutilating the already dead bodies of these men, women, and children, they were attempting to spiritually "trap" them in this world and prevent their return home to Heaven.
27. (Greene and Scott, *The Sand Creek Massacre*, 14-21)
28. When Europeans came to the Americas and began trying to understand the "religion" of the Native Americans, they observed this way of life and mistakenly concluded that Native Americans were pagans and worshipped many gods. The truth is that the majority of Native American tribes at this time were monotheistic. They believed in one God, the Creator of all life, whose essence was in everything that had life. By showing respect to every living creature, they were showing respect to God the Father.
29. In Luke 6:27-28 Jesus clearly teaches His followers to "love their enemies" rather than the Old Testament view of an "eye for an eye": "*But to you who listen, I say, Love your enemies and do good to those who hate you. And bless those who curse you and pray for those who exploit you.*"
30. Although today many websites and books refer to *Iktomi* as a "Lakota Indian cultural hero," the Ancestors have explained to me that the cultural perspective regarding *Iktomi* has been altered over time.
31. I prayed very hard to God to help me help those who Lucifer has tricked into fighting for him. I also prayed very hard for God to help Lucifer. The Holy Spirit shared part of his story with me so that I could help others "*see Lucifer as he really is, not as he pretends to be.*" The story of Lucifer's fall is as follows: "*Lucifer had a soul mate and they loved each other greatly. This soul mate loved God and wanted to be as close to God as possible. 'She' (there is no gender in Heaven nor marriage as we understand it here) worked very hard to grow in love and compassion so 'she' could grow closer to God. Lucifer did not want to make the changes in his life necessary to 'keep up with her.' Rather than look at his own behavior, Lucifer blamed God for 'stealing' his soul mate from him.*"
32. One of Lucifer's tricks has been to confuse those who have translated the Bible into different languages or edited various versions of

it. As most people know, changing even a single word in a sentence can completely alter its message. In Matthew 18:8, Jesus is quoted as having said the following: "*If then your hand or foot lead you to commit an atrocity, cut it off and cast it away from you. For you are better off entering everlasting life a cripple, rather than whole, such that with two hands and two feet you should fall into the everlasting fire.*" When you look at the footnote Mr. Alexander inserted for this section in his Biblical translation directly from Ancient Aramaic to English, "into the everlasting fire" is literally translated as, "*by the fire that to the [end of the] universe.*" As recorded in Matthew 25:46, Jesus said: "*and they will go these to eternal torment and the saintly to eternal life.*" Again Mr. Alexander in the footnote indicated that the word "eternal" means "to the universe." According to the Holy Spirit, "to the universe" means the following: "*Upon Jesus's return to this world, God has ordained a different frame for this world. Both those in spirit and in flesh who can understand this frame will become one with God, Heaven and the Holy Spirit. However, there will be some souls who cannot understand this frame at that moment because the world, as they understood it, no longer exists. It is these souls who will be 'cast into the universe.' From that point, because of this disconnect, it will be more difficult for them to find their way back home to Heaven. However, the journey is never impossible.*"

33. My husband knew that I had grown up hungry and very poor. He worked very hard to provide our family with "everything money could buy" in an attempt to be a "good" husband to me and a "good" father to our children. The stress of keeping such a rigorous pace, combined with the affects of having lived a difficult life, had adverse effects on his health. I was determined to provide a healthy life for my husband and children. In order to do so I chose an environment I believed would be conducive to a more "simple" lifestyle so he did not feel the need to work so hard.

34. "The purpose behind these torture methods injurious to the sense of honor is not confession; rather its aim is the dissolution of personal identity. The greater the horrors portrayed, and the more fragile the remnants of identity, the greater the likelihood that the victim will lack credibility." (Graessner, *At the Side of Torture Survivors*, 166)

35. Creator sent other Angels to teach me about the role that chemicals have played in the destruction of American Indian people and other cultures. One of these Angels was "Little Wolf," a

Cheyenne Chief and Spiritual Leader in the 1800s. This Angel explained that opiates were regularly combined with alcohol (known as Laudanum), and given to the American Indians. Under the influence of such a concoction, Little Wolf became enraged and murdered another Cheyenne who was acting inappropriately toward the women in his family. As a result, Little Wolf placed himself in voluntary exile as punishment for his actions. This Angel explained to me that chemicals are still being used on our people today to destroy their bodies, minds, and souls by tricking them into doing things that are counter to their nature. He explained that traditionally the people did not use chemicals, which allowed them to keep a strong connection to Creator.

36. "Maheo" is the word for "God" in the Cheyenne language.
37. My mother in flesh was a victim of rape, incest, physical, and psychological abuse. By the time God sent my brothers and me to her she was what Bear Feathers describes as a "bear." She routinely sexually, physically, and psychologically abused my brothers and myself, as well as allowing others in her family to do the same.
38. A tipi (also spelled *tepee*) is a conical tent originally made from wooden poles and animal skins. The Plains Indians lived in such structures. A "medicine tipi" was used for prayer and healing. Traditionally, medicine tipis were white and decorated with symbols and designs that had spiritual significance for the medicine person who prayed and served Creator in the tipi.
39. One woman who experienced incest at the hands of her mother described her feelings as follows: "It's so much more complicated for me to deal with my mother's abuse of me. After all, she was my *mom*; I expected more from her — like nurturing. My father, well, hell, I can accept distance, even face abuse. But *she* was the one I turned to ... she's *like* me. We are both *women*. How could she do this to me?" (Blume, *Secret Survivors*, 31)
40. The Holy Spirit ministered to each of my brothers. I am grateful for the fact that each of them now understands — to varying degrees — that God is "real" and He is there for them.
41. "Many professionals who work with adult incest survivors believe that the child's emotional, cognitive, and other age-related development is arrested at the time the incest begins... More than their growth being totally, universally retarded, I have found that there are gaps and distortions in individual areas, related to specific tasks." (Blume, Secret Survivors, 11-12).

42. As a slave, my grandmother lived with the reality that her body was not her own. As a young woman she was married to a man who used to "beat her with sticks and logs" when she was pregnant. Upon his death, my grandmother was left with three children. As widows in Mexico did not have rights to property at that time, her husband's blood relatives claimed the family home, furniture, and livestock. At times she was forced into prostitution in order to provide food and shelter for her children.
43. "Amnesia, or 'blocking,' is the most common feature of Post-Incest Syndrome. It can take many forms, affecting memory, feelings, or perceptions. It can result from efforts the victim makes to separate from what is happening to her at the time of the abuse, or from techniques she resorts to after the abuse. It is achieved through dissociation." (Blume, Secret Survivors, 81)
44. White Earth brought with her countless Angels, who she referred to as "Corn Maidens." These Angels had each experienced life here in this world as a woman. The air was so thick with these beings that I could barely see my husband's body standing before me. White Earth explained that these Angels were entering my body and "repairing" cells that had been damaged as a result of the abuse I suffered around my mother's inability to be a mother to me, and the psychological, spiritual, and physical damage that occurs when the person who hurts a child is one they have been biologically "wired" to love. I remember being shocked that I could feel the Angels "working" inside of me. My head ached and felt hot, and my limbs were heavy and tingling.
45. According to an account called *The Life and Death of Sweet Medicine* as recorded by Richard Erdoes and told by members of the Strange Owl Family on the Lame Deer Indian Reservation in Montana in 1967, the young woman "told her parents that no man had touched her, and they believed her. But others would not be likely to, and the girl hid her condition. When she felt the birth pangs coming on, she went out into the prairie far from the camp and built herself a brush shelter. Doing everything herself, she gave birth to a baby boy. She dried the baby, wrapped him in soft moss, and left him there in the wickiup, for in her village a baby without a father would be scorned and treated badly. Praying that someone would find him, she went sadly home to her parents."
46. The translation of the original names of most Native American tribes was "the people."

47. "The Cheyenne young women and girls always wore the protective rope, and most of them still do. This is a small rope or line, which passes about the waist, is knotted in front, passes down and backward between the thighs, and each branch is wound around the thigh down nearly to the knee... It is worn always at night and during the day when women go abroad. It is a complete protection to the woman wearing it and is assumed by girls as soon as the period of puberty is reached. All men, young and old, respect this rope, and anyone violating it would certainly be killed by the male relations of the girl." (Grinnell, *The Cheyenne Indians*, 131)

48. Grinnell was introduced to the Cheyenne in 1890 and visited with them every year until this book was published in 1923. (Grinnell, *The Cheyenne Indians*, 156)

49. This gift of free will extends to souls in Heaven, as well as those experiencing other worlds created by God.

50. In 2006 my husband drove me across many states to seek help from a counselor who was considered by his peers to be an expert in helping very traumatized people to recover. If it had not been for Archangel Michael's teachings prior to the appointment, I would have left this man's office believing I was a "victim" who on some level "wanted" to be abused and, therefore, was "highly likely to be victimized again." The above quote that a person "cannot be hypnotized to do anything he or she does not want to do" was a phrase I heard from him. Had this counselor understood the level to which the above mentioned tools and techniques are used against women by those who wish to take their free will away, our session with him would have been more beneficial.

51. When I was seventeen-years-old I was raped by a twenty seven-year-old man who was a "friend of the family." Sadly, once this occurred, I believed that I could no longer become a nun because I was not "pure" enough to serve God in such a manner. Although I knew with certainty that I had not given my consent to this person, Iktomi's trick occurred when I told my aunt about this incident the following day. Although this act was considered statutory rape in California — and as a high school teacher my aunt was considered a "mandatory reporter" of such a crime — she was adamant that I not report the incident. She told me that I was "lucky" that such a "nice, white man" wanted to "love" me. She encouraged me to "continue dating" him and often invited him over to her home for dinner. As I trusted my aunt and I wanted to "be a good woman," I did as she told me to. However, I focused my intent and prayers

on selecting a university located far from California to escape this man and my family, and to surround myself with people who were living their lives closer to God.

52. I enjoyed being present when my grandmother used her Mayan healing techniques on those who came to her for help, however, I did not understand why she "snapped" and became mean and violent other times. I wanted to help people heal. However, since I did not understand the discrepancy in my grandmother's behavior, I decided to focus my efforts on pursuing a medical degree. I felt this would be a socially accepted and effective way to help heal those in need.

53. The man I call my father married my mother when she was two months pregnant with me. He understood that I was not biologically "his," but believed that God had sent me to him just as much as he had sent me to my mother. He was a Dutch-Indonesian man who spent the first five years of his life as a prisoner of war in a Japanese concentration camp. Although he had side effects from this, such as bursts of anger, high blood pressure, and trouble concentrating, it was clear to me that he loved us and tried hard. My mother divorced him when I was four-years-old and the court system gave her primary custody of us. At this time in my life, the only "safe place" I had known was taken away. Throughout this time, my dad took us to his Christian church on the weekends. He taught us that God was "real" and loved us. For this I am eternally grateful.

54. I am thankful to those who came forward with the "missing pieces" I needed to understand more about this man and what he had been doing to me during this time. Although he came from a "good family" and had graduated from a "good school," he was both a drug addict and a drug dealer. Soon after we met he gave me a pill known as the "date rape" drug without my knowledge. He and his friend proceeded to rape me. Although it had not occurred to me at the time that this man was not the biological father, it is likely that my son was the product of this incident.

55. There are certain things that make feeling God and Heaven difficult. Fear and having drugs in your system are two of the biggest blocks to feeling God's Grace and the Holy Spirit. This includes prescription medication and alcohol. If either of these is an issue with you or those you love, be specific with your prayers. If you do not feel God's Grace right away, this does not mean He is not there. Ask Him to help you so that you can feel Him in your life.

56. My mother and grandmother had taught me when I was small that the world would treat me better if I presented as a person of European decent. Sadly, my mother understood all too well what this country has done to the Native women. In order to protect me from this, my birth certificate lists that I am "Caucasian" and that I have "green eyes." She was also relieved when the sun lightened my dark hair in the summer. When I got older, I started to lighten my hair chemically in order to make the women in my family happy.

57. "One of the key issues in working with victims of power rapes is their anger at themselves and self-blame for being victimized and not being able to escape the assault. It is important to help them realize that no strategy would necessarily have been more effective than the one they tried. What deters one assailant only encourages another, but frequently the victim feels that is she had said or done something different, she could have discouraged the assault. And it is this feeling of not having achieved her primary goal — that of escaping the offender — that affects the victim and retards her recovery from the trauma of sexual assault." (Groth, *Men who Rape: The Psychology of the Offender*, 44.)

58. The following is a more detailed list from the Holy Spirit detailing the reasons many women who are not "homosexual" find themselves in relationships or encounters with other women:

    1.) The woman has never had a positive or loving experience with a man;
    2.) The woman is literally not understanding how the female body is supposed to work;
    3.) The woman is frightened of being "raped," which to her means being out of control, physically feeling threatened, and the act of penetration. As another female's sexual organs cannot penetrate, this is interpreted as being a solution to avoiding rape in the future;
    4.) The woman is so used to being an object and so used to sex being "violence" that whether the act is committed by a woman or a man no longer matters to her;
    5.) The woman wants to love and be loved yet she has not grown up with healthy boundaries or any boundaries. Therefore, being told "this is love" she tries to accommodate that interpretation of "love";
    6.) The woman is so terrified of becoming pregnant, particularly after a rape that resulted in a pregnancy and particularly after an

aborted pregnancy, that she "chooses" women over men in order to prevent such a situation from reoccurring;
7.) The woman can be susceptible to a female sexual predator due to prior experiences and feel "compelled" to comply through fear, just as in the case of such an experience with a male;
8.) A man with whom she is intimate can "make her" have a sexual experience with another woman and in doing so is then using such woman as a proxy to rape her;
9.) Under the influence of trauma and/or chemicals, the woman can be told by her abuser that she is "gay" or that she "acts like a man," etc. which has the effect of hypnosis;
10.) After being abused, the woman can seek to abuse herself more to fit the self-image she has accepted for herself.